Lorna Jowett is a reader in Television
She is co-author of *TV Horror: Inve*
(I.B.Tauris, 2013).

Kevin Lee Robinson lectures on scriptwriting and video production and is
Creative Director for a media production company.

David Simmons is Senior Lecturer in Screen Studies and English at the University
of Northampton, and has published extensively on American popular fiction and
screen media.

'With detailed analysis and thoughtful case studies, the authors in this engaging volume approach one of the most salient – and yet overlooked – modes of television content: time travel. Each chapter deepens and extends temporal exploration of such varied shows as *Star Trek, Quantum Leap, Timeslip, Sapphire & Steel, Torchwood*, and *Life on Mars*, among many others. It's about time we had a volume that's all about time.'

Paul Booth, Associate Professor of Media and Cinema Studies, DePaul University, author of *Time on TV*: *Temporal Displacement and Mashup Television* (2012)

'This volume feels like the beginning of an important and emerging area of TV Studies. It examines a range of frequently-overlooked examples of telefantasy and provides innovative readings of how these shows engage with discourses of genre, memory and affect. During a period when television's narrative representations of temporality are becoming increasingly complex and viewers' access to television history are being reconfigured, *Time on TV*'s contributions to examining these issues are incredibly timely and welcome.'

Ross P. Garner, Lecturer in Media and Cultural Studies, Cardiff University

Edited by Lorna Jowett, Kevin Lee Robinson
and David Simmons

TIME
ON TV

Narrative Time, Time Travel
and Time Travellers
in Popular Television Culture

BLOOMSBURY ACADEMIC
LONDON • NEW YORK • OXFORD • NEW DELHI • SYDNEY

BLOOMSBURY ACADEMIC
Bloomsbury Publishing Plc
50 Bedford Square, London, WC1B 3DP, UK
1385 Broadway, New York, NY 10018, USA
29 Earlsfort Terrace, Dublin 2, Ireland

BLOOMSBURY, BLOOMSBURY ACADEMIC and the Diana logo are
trademarks of Bloomsbury Publishing Plc

First published in Great Britain 2016 by I.B. Tauris & Co. Ltd
Paperback edition first published 2021 by Bloomsbury Academic

ISBN: HB: 978-1-7845-3013-6
PB: 978-1-3502-4235-7
ePDF: 978-1-8386-0972-6
eBook: 978-1-8386-0971-9

Series: Investigating Cult TV Series

To find out more about our authors and books visit
www.bloomsbury.com and sign up for our newsletters.

Contents

Contributors

Nicola Allen is Senior Lecturer in English Literature at The University of Wolverhampton. She has published a monograph, entitled: *Marginality in the Contemporary British Novel* (2008), as well as several chapters and articles on twentieth-century and contemporary British and American fiction. She also has a jointly edited collection entitled *Reassessing the Twentieth-Century Canon: From Joseph Conrad to Zadie Smith* (2014).

Stan Beeler is Professor of English at the University of Northern British Columbia, Canada. His areas of interest include Film and Television Studies, Popular Culture, and Comparative Literature. His publications include *Reading Stargate SG-1* (with Lisa Dickson), *Investigating Charmed: The Magic Power of TV* (with Karin Beeler), and *Dance Drugs and Escape: the Club Scene in Literature, Film and Television Since the Late 1980s*. He is currently working on a book on film for children.

Pete Boss has alternated between careers in teaching and music for the last 25 years. He is an independent film studies teacher who lectures regularly on undergraduate and postgraduate programmes at Oxford Brookes University and the University of Buckingham. Pete has also taught Open Access courses for many years as an associate tutor for Oxford University's Department for Continuing Education in which he has explored the work of many key film directors and genres as well as subjects such as cinema and the Cold War, or film and terrorism. While having taught on many aspects of mainstream and world cinema, Pete's research interests have focused consistently on issues of popular genre with publications on science-fiction and body horror. Present research interests include post 9/11 film and television drama, postwar American Circus films and narrative space in contemporary combat films. As a blues musician Pete has recorded with his own band and with well-known artists such as the late Wild Child Butler and Dana Gillespie.

Lincoln Geraghty is Reader in Popular Media Cultures in the School of Creative Arts, Film and Media and Director of the Centre for Cultural and Creative Research at the University of Portsmouth. He serves as editorial advisor for *The Journal of Popular Culture, Reconstruction, Atlantis, Journal of Fandom Studies* and *Journal of Popular Television* with interests in science-fiction film and television, fandom, merchandising and collecting in popular culture. He is author of *Living with Star Trek: American Culture and the Star Trek Universe* (I.B.Tauris, 2007) and *American Science Fiction Film and Television* (Berg, 2009). He has edited *The Influence of Star Trek on Television, Film and Culture, Channeling the Future: Essays on Science Fiction and Fantasy Television, The Smallville Chronicles: Critical Essays on the Television Series* and, with Mark Jancovich, *The Shifting Definitions of Genre: Essays on Labeling Film, Television Shows and Media*. He is currently serving as Editor of the *Directory of World Cinema: American Hollywood*, an online and print publication and his most recent book, entitled *Cult Collectors: Nostalgia, Fandom and Collecting Popular Culture*, was published in 2014.

David Hipple's initial degree in English, was followed by an MA in Education. His second was in Science Fiction Studies at the University of Reading, where he then gained his PhD researching the commercial, cultural and critical heritage of science-fiction film and television. For some reason he is presently completing another first degree, in Philosophy and Psychology. David has delivered numerous conference papers, has published work on *Stargate SG-1, Star Trek* and the TV series *Heroes*, is currently developing two books on criticism of fantastic texts across media, and supports research publications at Middlesex University. He is the proprietor of *www.counterfactuality.com*, a haven for academic material on fantastic narratives and associated critical work.

John Jeffrey has been a lecturer in English, Film and Media for over 25 years and holds a BA in English from the University of Nottingham, a PGCE from the University of Hull and an MA in Film and Television Studies from the University of Warwick. He has been an examiner in A level English Literature and Media Studies course leader for the Higher National Diploma in Media and DeMontfort University's B.A. Film, Photography and Video programmes at OCVC. His areas of special interest include narrative structure and aesthetics in US science-fiction cinema in particular, the representation and signification of the alien environment, British science-fiction television from the 1960s to the present day, adaptations of classic British and European tales of the uncanny and the cinema of the Weimar Republic. John is currently a teacher at Banbury and Bicester College.

Lorna Jowett is a reader in Television Studies at the University of Northampton, where she teaches some of her favourite things, including television, horror, and science-fiction, sometimes all at once. She is the co-author with Stacey Abbott of *TV Horror: Investigating the Dark Side of the Small Screen* (I.B.Tauris, 2013), author of *Sex and the Slayer: A Gender Studies Primer for the Buffy Fan*, and is on the editorial board of *Slayage: The Journal of the Whedon Studies Association* and *Intensities: The Journal of Cult Media*. She has published many articles on television, film and popular culture, and is particularly interested in genre and representation. She is currently working on a book about gender in the new *Doctor Who* universe.

Gwyneth Peaty is an honorary research fellow at the University of Western Australia, where she recently completed a PhD exploring representations of the grotesque in popular culture. She currently teaches in the Department of Internet Studies at Curtin University. Her wider research interests include gender, monstrosity, the Gothic, and depictions of extraordinary bodies in popular media. Previous publications include: 'Infected with Life: Neo-supernaturalism and the Gothic Zombie' in *Gothic Science Fiction: 1980–2010*; '"Hatched from the Veins in Your Arms": Movement, Ontology and First-Person Gameplay in BioShock' in *Guns, Grenades and Grunts: The First Person Shooter*; and 'Zombie Time: Temporality and Living Death' in *"We're All Infected": Essays on AMC's The Walking Dead and the Fate of the Human*.

Kevin Lee Robinson lectures in scriptwriting and media production and is a verifier of national standards in media education. He is also Creative Director and in-house writer for a media production company where he is responsible for video creation and producing a range of fantasy fiction audio plays.

David Simmons is Senior Lecturer in Screen Studies and English at the University of Northampton. David is on the editorial board of *The Journal of Popular Culture, Americana: The Journal of American Popular Culture* and the advisory board of *Revenant: Critical and Creative Studies of the Supernatural*. He has published extensively in the twin fields of American popular fiction and screen media, including topics as varied as Hammer and science-fiction, the work of Chuck Palahniuk, and *South Park* and merchandising; as well as writing *The Anti-Hero in the American Novel* (2008) and editing *Heroes: Truth, Justice and Quality TV* (2011) and *New Critical Essays on H.P. Lovecraft* (2013) amongst others. David has a developing interest in convergent media and is currently writing on the subject of H.P. Lovecraft and comics.

Acknowledgements

This book was dreamed up some time ago and there are many people to thank for getting it into print. The editors would like to thank Anna Coatman and everyone at I.B.Tauris for their support and for their feedback. We would also like to thank all our contributors for their hard work, especially those who agreed to come on board further down the line.

1

Timey Wimey Stuff: Introduction to *Time on TV*

Lorna Jowett, Kevin Robinson and David Simmons

'The representation of time within individual television texts relates to larger concerns in the media environment'

(Booth, 2012: 5)

If someone travelled back in time and, say, killed Hitler, would this change the past? Would it wipe out our present? Countless TV episodes and series have taken this science fictional 'what if...?' question as their focus, presenting complex concepts about time and how it works to wide audiences. Moreover, in the twenty-first century, time seems to be increasingly malleable in relation to TV: television drama now operates as anything from a weekly episode taking up a one-hour slot, to a webisode five minutes long; cult audiences often 'binge' on DVD box sets, watching episodes in rapid succession rather than waiting a week for the next instalment. It seems therefore not just appropriate but imperative to examine the nature of time on television, and especially its contribution to cult genres like science-fiction, fantasy and horror.

Time as a television concept has been an under-discussed area, at least until very recently. While there have been numerous publications on television shows which have utilized notions of time, little has been written which considers the concept in the wider arena. For example *Doctor Who* is much discussed as a television product and a cultural phenomenon but little is written about its presentation of time specifically. Similarly, although screen and narrative time have been explored in film studies, there has been comparatively little said of these in the context of television time, particularly when presented as, for example, flashback or alternative perspectives on the nature of time. When we proposed this collection on time in

1

television, there were no other existing publications. There are now at least two. Paul Booth's *Time on TV: Temporal Displacement and Mashup Television* (2012), as the title suggests, examines how representations of time on television have been affected by and seek to negotiate broader technological and social changes that affect our understanding of time. Digital culture, he argues, as well as a range of social networking and online communications have introduced new forms of media and new aesthetics, while also 'remaining tethered to *old* processes and uses' (Booth 2012: 8, original emphasis). While Booth analyses certain conventions (such as temporal displacement via flashback or flashforward) in particular television texts, he does so in order to form an argument about digital culture and social change. The other recent book dealing with TV time is *Time and Television Narrative: Exploring Temporality in Twenty-First Century Programming*, edited by Melissa Ames (2013), and is a wide-ranging collection with sections on industry, the cultural moment, narrative structure, genres, formats and audiences.

Our project here is somewhat different, though clearly it overlaps with both of these books. Popular television, and particularly those productions notionally categorized as cult TV, is replete with examples of time as a concept, a narrative component, a telefantasy trope and a televisual construct. These essays explore aspects of time as presented in a range of television texts, from classic to contemporary. Addressing children's drama, cult horror and science-fiction, to name a few, this collection explores the narrative and cultural significance of time on television via the presentation of a series of case studies, held together by an emphasis on telefantasy. While Ames' collection restricts itself to twenty-first century television, in order to make a case about shifts in television production, structures and consumption, chapters in this book cover a number of contemporary and classic productions, demonstrating how time has always been an important aspect of television drama. Chapters examine particular aspects of how we experience time from the affective (nostalgia, memory), to the chronologic (apocalypse, immortality) to the structural (flashbacks, reboots). Our contributors approach the topic from a variety of perspectives and disciplines, applying psychoanalytic theory or philosophy, examining form and structure, or situating the TV shows within the contexts of industry, production and authorship, thus offering a variety of perspectives on associated television cultures and narratives. The aim is to provide the student reader with a source of varied discussion in support of key concepts within television studies and also the wider study of genre, while for the casual reader the essays provide accessible explorations of familiar shows and concepts.

Underpinning the analysis offered by the various contributors to this book is awareness of certain key elements in television drama. In the rest of this introduction, we sketch in what we see as the three most important contexts that inform the chapters that follow: the conventions that have arisen and developed in television to represent time; industry developments that affect how time is negotiated in television drama; and how nostalgia has become a significant element of both content and consumption in terms of television.

Conventions of Time on TV

Television has an established set of conventions for representing and dealing with time. Some are derived from storytelling in general, others from other visual media like cinema. Thus audiences are familiar with how montages, ellipses, flashback and even flashforward operate. Viewers can, for example, tell when what we see is intended as a memory (a flashback) from a different time frame than the present because of certain cues, visual, aural or structural. The nature of television also means that backstory has enhanced importance, often taking on more significance than it might have in, say, a 90-minute movie. Character development in television frequently relies on what we know about a character's history, their past experiences and relationships, and their origins (see Gwyneth Peaty's examination of *Once Upon a Time* 2011–, for instance). With a long running television drama, audiences might even have years of televized narrative to draw on when responding to characters and plotlines viewed at a given moment (as with any soap opera, or with a long-running science-fiction series such as *Star Trek* which first aired in 1966 and finished with prequel series *Star Trek: Enterprise* in 2005). Thus while some types of TV have each episode reset to default for the start of the next instalment, in others, history or series-memory might form part of complex narrative arcs that develop serially. Many drama series that draw on that memory include 'previously on' segments at the beginning of an episode, to remind viewers of significant events from earlier in the year, or even longer ago. Such reminders can also select and highlight particular memories, perhaps even reordering or revaluing a particular instance in terms of its relative significance.

All of these conventions contribute to the complex narratives and spectacular narrative aesthetic now common in 'quality' TV drama. Viewers of such series take pleasure in working out – or simply keeping up with – the narrative twists and turns of any given show. As Booth notes, 'temporally complex television "plays" with narrative, forcing the audience to reconstruct the plot from fragments of story scattered around the discourse' (2012, 33). Approaching narrative complexity from a different angle, Matt Hills observes how official and unofficial episode guides indicate the complexity of narrative structures and the many strategies available for reordering and apprehending these narratives. We can thus see, he argues, such guides as tools 'to manage seriality' in a complex serial narrative 'and make its repetitions and differences, its temporal unfoldings, more orderly and immediately present to fans as "archived" knowledge' (2005: 192). As Hills points out, this can also be an effective commercial strategy for DVD sales, with 'collections' of episodes organized around particular themes or characters (like the Barnabas Collins collection of *Dark Shadows* 1966–1971 episodes).

In addition, some TV shows engage with epic timescale (miniseries such as *Roots* 1977) that can span generations and take in several different time periods. Such timescales offer the pleasures of period drama as well as of epic narrative: costume, sets and character reflect the given period and establish atmosphere. Vampire television uses its vampire characters as a means of doing this, either more or less frequently as the style of the series and perhaps the budget allows (see Lorna Jowett's chapter). Series engaging with the fantastic might even use the concept of time travel as a means of moving into such a period setting. This can also extend to tackling the cultural attitudes and expectations of a different period, as Nicola Allen demonstrates in her evaluation of *Life on Mars* (2006–2007) and *Ashes to Ashes* (2008–2010). Other dramas might dip into different periods on an episodic basis, such as *Quantum Leap* (1989–1993), a series mentioned by several of our contributors.

The continuing and the domestic nature of television also mean that it can offer more sense of 'real time'. TV productions of all kinds align themselves with the season, offering special holiday episodes which are frequently notable 'events' in the calendar of television, attracting large audiences: the *Doctor Who* Christmas specials, for instance. Television drama, like other forms of TV, can also readily respond to or reference current events as well as history. Science-fiction series *Fringe* (2008–2013) includes several parallel worlds or timelines and in one of these New York City retains its Twin Towers. In another sense, time passing in the real world can be mirrored by familiar characters growing up as the TV show they inhabit unfolds over the years, or, at the very least, by reflecting the same sense of ageing or time passing as the target audience experience. Booth suggests that the gradual evolution of complex narrative in the televisual representation of time is a reflection of our own fragmented post-modern experience of both fractured and reconstituted narratives (2012: 25).

TV has been traditionally identified as a medium that offers sameness and stability, familiarity and reassurance. Many of the series discussed here, however, address notions of change. Time travel shows such as *Quantum Leap* (1963–1989) or *Doctor Who* (2005–) often engage with paradoxes and returns, with characters debating whether history, or the future, can be altered. Character development is frequently related to this notion too, and several of the series discussed in this volume debate individual as well as historical change and redemption. This is related to the requirements of long-form narrative on television which aims to balance familiarity (with a particular structure, premise, situation, setting and cast of characters) and novelty (new locations, changes to the cast, developing plotlines and character arcs, 'bubble' episodes). Some of these changes can be caused by external factors such as regular actors leaving to pursue new opportunities, the shooting location shifting from one city or country to another, or a change in showrunners or writing personnel. In such cases, change is inevitable, though some productions seek to revitalise ideas even when a series is successful. Any long-running series is likely to attract both praise and criticism for attempting to innovate on a winning formula, with some viewers wishing it had stayed the same, or others complaining it has lost its spark.

The way we consume TV has also changed in relation to time. Raymond Williams' popular and influential concept of television as one constant 'flow' has been developed and critiqued. Advances in technology and shifts in the industry of television mean that TV is no longer as ephemeral or as embedded in flow as it once might have been. Recording technologies leading to archived viewing have changed viewing habits, and audiences no longer rely on reruns for repeat viewing of favourite series or episodes. While watching weekly broadcast episodes forced viewers to wait for the next instalment, sales of boxsets allow us to binge through a series as quickly as we like. In this case, we might choose to fastforward through the 'previously on' segment that precedes an episode, as it may only be minutes since we finished watching the preceding one. Such relatively new viewing strategies also circumvent the suspense inherent in cliffhanger endings. This structural strategy is common to many types of television from episode to episode, as frequently seen in soap opera. Ever since the massive success of the 'Who shot J.R.?' season finale of primetime soap *Dallas* (1978–1991), serial drama has also adopted cliffhangers as a season to season structure – leaving viewers with an unresolved problem or crisis to chew over until the series returns in the following year.

On the other hand, faithful viewers and fans may choose to watch their favourite show as appointment viewing, in order to be as up to date as possible and to join in with the often instantaneous discussion of a new episode as soon as it concludes. Some may even try to get ahead by seeking out 'spoilers' and information about what's coming up next. Jonathan Gray describes how fans of *Lost* (2004–2010) could actively seek out, or stumble across, a whole range of spoilers from 'leaked plot points, leaked clues, leaked photos of filming, casting information, and plenty of "foilers" (fake spoilers) too' (2010, 147). Such practice demonstrates not only how certain types of TV drama deliberately aim for temporal complexity within their narratives, but also how viewers can actively engage with such complexity both within the world of a show, and outside of it.

Industry

As we finalized the content for the book, probably the most important example of the time travel narrative on television was celebrating its fiftieth anniversary. The term 'celebrating' is used in its loosest sense here, though. *Doctor Who* was more than celebrated. It was canonized, lionized and idolized as one of the biggest achievements of not only telefantasy but also the television industry in general. There were numerous shows and events celebrating what is undoubtedly a landmark and possibly an unrepeatable success for a 'genre' show. There can be little doubt that *Doctor Who* is a unique and mercurial series that has managed to stay a viable product in some form for half a century while weaving its own mythology into British popular culture. In addition, it has become internationally successful as both current popular television broadcasting and as part of the science-fiction landscape.

In terms of academia it is perhaps fair to say that, along with shows such as *Star Trek* (1966–2005) and *The Prisoner* (1967–68), *Doctor Who* has become one of the most written about and studied shows in television history and, in the months preceding and following its golden anniversary, a plethora of studies, guides and other publications were filling the shelves. These included everything from weighty academic tomes through to children's colouring books that helped perpetuate and expand the Whoniverse and *Who* studies.

The fiftieth anniversary of *Doctor Who* was celebrated by the television industry and, of course, specifically by the BBC and its allies with the same canon of supporting shows as you would expect to see surrounding a royal event. This is hardly surprising as, in telefantasy terms at least, *Doctor Who* has legitimate claim to the crown. The pomp and ceremony surrounding the landmark episode has ranged from party celebrations resplendent with celebrities and ex-cast members, through to light-hearted and serious documentaries about aspects of the show, and even independent productions featuring previous doctors attempting to crash the fiftieth anniversary special (*The Five-ish Doctors Reboot*). The loudest industry shout of celebration came in the BBC Two dramatization *An Adventure in Space and Time* which explored the events surrounding the creation of the show. The attachment of writer Mark Gatiss and actors such as Brian Cox and David Bradley to the drama suggest the BBC anticipated high audience numbers and good critical response for the production. Indeed, it was well-received at a critical level. *Daily Telegraph* critic Michael Hogan gave a report similar to most other critical sources, stating that 'A warm glow radiated from the screen and bathed the viewer in TV magic.' Critical and audience figures aside (it played to a very respectable 2.71 million viewers, making it a top five show for BBC Two) *An Adventure in Space and Time* is in itself a remarkable television event. The presentation was part docudrama, part historical record, and part stand-alone character drama. Interestingly, the narrative referenced the current incarnation of the show with a ghostly appearance by incumbent doctor Matt Smith acknowledging the ailing Hartnell, and by echoing the departing lines of David Tennant's tenth doctor, 'I don't want to go'.

With audio productions, books, stage plays, and a plethora of toys and merchandise, it would seem the Doctor is as much a survivor of the countless changes and pressures of the media industries as he is of repeated assaults by Daleks, Cybermen, Weeping Angels and every rubber-clad or computer generated monster he has faced. As in his on-screen adventures, the Doctor is aided and abetted in his production adventures by his trusted companions of loyal audience, commercial viability and critical success. Indeed, *Doctor Who*'s production stands as a metaphor for the industry surrounding it.

Television narrative's presentation of time, time travelling and telefantasy in general is subject to the same industrial pressures as on any show. Success is at the mercy not only of the whims of the audience in terms of viewing figures, but also of international television topography, of the technological requirements of series and episodes themselves, and of the need for 'event' television.

The hugely successful ABC show *Lost* (2004–2010) is perhaps the most prominent example of this recent desire to market serial television drama as 'event' TV. Helmed by showrunners Damon Lindelof and J.J. Abrams, at this point already on his way to becoming a recognized author brand, *Lost* was deliberately sold as something distinct from, and superior to, 'run of the mill' everyday television. The TV network Channel 4, who bought the rights to air the first season of the show in the UK, took the unusual step of spending £1 million on marketing, including a series of cinema and billboard advertisements. Advertising for the show, which emphasized a sense of *Lost* as a widescreen, high definition, movie style experience (what Matt Hills has since termed 'Telefantasy Art TV' (73) sought to foreground the show's high production values (a possible $10 million for the pilot alone) and its' bringing together of film and televisual technology and personnel.

As Roberta Pearson suggests in *Quality TV*, *Lost*'s success is perhaps most apparent in the imitators it spawned, many of which attempted to combine *Lost*'s film-like aesthetic with its science-fiction tinged approach to time as a concept. *Heroes* (2006–2010), for example, contained a character (Hiro Nakamura) with the ability to manipulate, and therefore travel through time, while the ultimately unsuccessful *Flash-Forward* incorporated the idea of time-manipulation into its very title. The proliferation of these glossy, high concept dramas also speaks to the fragmentation of the TV marketplace and the desire to target a young, hip audience of 18–35 year olds, deemed attractive to advertisers for their perceived disposable incomes. Crucial to capturing this demographic has been the progressive utilization of technology in the 'post-TV' or TV3 landscape, which, if done well, encourages audience participation and engagement. Pearson has discussed *Lost* as being at the forefront of industry innovations, observing that it was one of the first shows to be available to download on the initial wave of ipods that possessed the ability to play video. More importantly, Pearson has noted *Lost*'s crucial role as part of the vanguard of trans-media storytelling, documenting the creative team's apposite use of puzzles within both the actual continually deferred narrative of the broadcast show (the island is essentially a puzzle that needs to be solved) and in a host of surrounding hyperdiegetic (often online) material.

While this combination of technological advance and high production values ensured a production success for the show, it also reflected another industrial factor. During the latter part of the twentieth century science-fiction had matured and gained a gravitas and respect. Seminal shows such as *Babylon 5* (1994–1998) and *Star Trek: The Next Generation* (1987–1998) had trailblazed the popular culture revival by merging cult and mainstream audiences via the use of complex characters and continuing narratives. With *Babylon 5*, in particular, creator J. M. Straczynski bucked the monster of the week science-fiction imperative and produced an emotionally-charged hybrid of science-fiction and international politics. These shows were ripples in the pond of telefantasy which, by 2004, had created an environment in which the reinvented *Battlestar Galactica* could tell weekly tales from a long term story arc. Gritty, and often an assault on the emotions of the viewer, *BSG* was bleak, dirty and brutal. Science-fiction was no longer the camp space opera or the back room viewing of an elite fanbase; it was popular, quality television and it had high viewing figures. The relaunched *Doctor Who* was scheduled as primetime Saturday night viewing because by 2005 the television landscape had been prepared for the return of the Doctor: providing, as always, that people would watch. People did watch and continue to do so because, just two years after the relaunch, the *Doctor Who* Christmas episode gathered an astonishing 13.3 million viewers.

Of course it is a rather glib generalization to say that the television industry is solely based on viewing figures. This is particularly true with a broadcaster such as the BBC where the need to innovate is enshrined in the charter. However, from the industry point of view it is probably fair to say that ratings are indeed the primary yardstick of success, but that a show also needs critical and commercial success to maintain its viability. As Catherine Johnson notes the US television environment had been primed during the 1990s to accept distinctive series signatures (121). A good example of the industrial context of production in action is *Doctor Who* spin off *Torchwood* (2006–2011). While it is clear that the show would be an unlikely success without the fan base provided by the parent production of *Doctor Who* the series also uses a very clear U.S. television format. The 'monster of the week' format is familiar territory and the one hour run time, often action based plots and secret investigative team tropes are all familiar. That said *Torchwood* adopts a melange of genres and a focus on the central character of Jack Harkness (see later chapters for discussions of this) that are quite distinctive. This is never more apparent than in the third season *Torchwood: Children of Earth* (2009) which adopted an 'event' approach to the initial broadcast. Shown over five consecutive nights the show required a commitment from the viewer reminiscent of the mini-series and the legacy of 1950s event science-fiction such as *Quatermass and the Pit* (1958). Where the previous seasons of *Torchwood* were broadcast to contextually good ratings on the digital channel BBC 3, season three was given BBC 1 airtime suggesting a ratings confidence in the production. The critical and fan base appreciation for the season was over all generally very good and the show gathered public and industry recognition in the form of Bafta Wales, SFX and Saturn award nominations and wins.

Torchwood would seem to offer an excellent case study in television industry influenced productions. Conceived from a high profile show it adopts a series of television industrial and narrative contexts and develops them into a successful stand alone television series.

TV shows such as *Torchwood*, *Lost*, *Battlestar Galactica* and *Doctor Who*, then, are as much a lens through which we can examine the industrial landscape surrounding these shows as they are primetime, high budget, and quality television productions. To the television industry examples such as *Doctor Who* are perfect in that they appeal to a range of key demographics, functioning as both a family adventure show and a nostalgic chance to hide behind the sofa with their children, much as they did when they were children themselves.

Nostalgia

Another way in which concepts of time and memory have come to play a significant part in the contemporary television landscape is through the use of nostalgia. Remembering an, albeit often fabricated, sense of ourselves via the medium of television has become a common practice, and evidence of Jonathan Bignell's suggestion in *Introduction to Television Studies* (2004) that we now live in an era in which 'The sense of the individual subject having a continuity of identity across decades and a life [. . . has become . . .] more difficult to sustain' (165). What nostalgia creates is a space in which viewers can reminiscence and recollect a 'lost' sense of themselves from the past; in the process often establishing imagined communities of taste and experience that are comforting, even if highly subjective constructions. This practice is perhaps made most explicit in the popularity of non-fictional programmes such as *I Love the Eighties*, and *100 Greatest Toys*, which position the past as a reassuring haven away from the troublesome burdens of the contemporary every day, making popular culture a common thread that unites us all. Yet TV's implicit use of nostalgia permeates many different types of programming, from soap operas (where *Coronation Street* 1960– recalls a bygone version of working class northern life) to sitcoms (*Dad's Army* 1968–1977 and its sense of Britain's wartime efforts), through to reality TV (examples such as *Strictly Come Dancing* 2004– trade on longstanding stereotypes of early twentieth-century Britishness). An interesting trend in recent years has been the increase in historical recreation as an element of 'factual' television shows, including *That'll Teach 'em* (2003–), *Wartime Kitchen and Garden* (2003–), and *Benefits Britain 1949* (2013). Such shows are noticeable for the way in which they both foreground the 'constructed-ness' of the past; reminding the viewer that they are watching experts re-enacting roles, while simultaneously asking the audience to recognise the accuracy and verisimilitude of their respective 'created' televisual version of history. It would appear that TV's ability to create the past has become increasingly post-modern and self-reflexive in the TV2 and TV3 eras, to the extent that the hyper-reality of historical depictions on TV is no longer considered to be problematic for audiences.

Indeed, in the field of telefantasy, there have been a number of prominent examples that have relied on nostalgia. The time travel component of long running shows such as *Red Dwarf* (1988–), *Star Trek*, and *Doctor Who* (amongst many others) have seen the central characters or crew frequently transported back to both recognisable points in history, and to points in the diegetic history of the show. The appeal of this latter approach seem to rest on the potential for intradiegetic play, (not entirely dissimilar to the trend for the sitcom flashback episode) where the show's creators draw attention to the usual conventions in use by breaking them or by offering an alternative take, mediated through a different setting in time. While this device can prove fruitful, see the use in *Sliders* (1995–2000) of alternative histories, it can also be potentially risky. When the makers of *Star Trek: Enterprise*; a series that was itself arguably based on the nostalgic appeal of seeing the 'early' days of the Federation, decided to 'retcon' the failing show by intradiegetically repositioning the episodes leading up to the final episode, 'These Are the Voyages...' (4:22), as a holodeck simulation in the *Star Trek: The Next Generation* timeline, the result was a vehement fan backlash. Many invested viewers decried the finale for its inauthenticity and lack of cohesion, with some going so far as to claim that it ruined the host show completely. Indeed, this response was not one of pleasurable nostalgia – of seeing characters (and actors) from *The Next Generation* on screen once again – but rather a feeling of betrayal, in which the events of *Enterprise* were seen as de-authenticated by the repositioning of the world as a kind of historical simulation. This fervent response amongst many fans suggests intradiegetic allusion works best when subservient to the host show's narrative, acting as a temporary break from normal continuity, rather than changing such continuity in any significant manner. While these shows utilise the appeal of nostalgia on an occasional episodic basis there are also instances where nostalgia becomes the main focus of the narrative.

Quantum Leap and, to a lesser extent, its progeny such as *Journeyman* (2007), exemplifies this trend. In the show, Dr Sam Beckett finds himself travelling back through the period of his own lifetime, tasked with a very loosely explained need to 'change history for the better' by temporarily inhabiting the bodies of others. Upon solving each 'case' Sam would then jump into another body, and time period, and the process would begin anew. This basic structure allowed the show's makers to depict Sam in a number of key moments throughout US history (something Donald Bellisario termed 'kisses with history'), including the Civil Rights movement, the shooting of JFK and the conflict in Vietnam. Interestingly, Sam's mission to 'put right what once went wrong' saw the character actively engaged with the historicising process, with the protagonist frequently asked to re-evaluate the historical 'truths' that he encountered on his many jumps due to the 'personal' stories he would inevitably become embroiled in. These jumps, therefore, often entailed a revision of the nostalgic view of a particular historical period, with the show arguably offering a more nuanced depiction of the 1950s

('The Color of Truth', 'Rebel Without A Clue'), 1960s ('Nuclear Family', 'Black and White on Fire') and 1970s ('Dr Ruth') than that found in previous nostalgia based shows such as *Happy Days* (1974–1984).

Special mention must be made here of BBC One sitcom *Goodnight Sweetheart* (1993–1999), in which TV repairman Gary Sparrow finds he is able to travel back and forth between London's East End of the 1990s and that of the 1940s. Sparrow, who is married in the present, attempts to woo pub landlady, Phoebe, in the 1940s, by telling her he is a spy and a songwriter (passing off a host of contemporary songs as his own). As well as offering a nascent (and somewhat under-developed) exploration of the crisis of masculinity that would come to define much 'quality' US TV, the show is also notable for its linkage of emasculation with Gary's nostalgic views of the past. Gary is depicted as initially sharing some perceived viewer's peculiarly rose-tinted view of the World War II era. In 'Rites of Passage' (1:1), caught at his wife's party, techno music blasting on the stereo, Garry and his new friend Ron sit around lamenting their present-day emasculation and nostalgically reminiscing about the more satisfying lives of their fathers and grandfathers: 'What we men lack in society today is a rite of passage. Our fathers, they did national service, their fathers fought in the war, experiences that marked their shift into manhood.' Indeed, as if to suggest Gary's concerns with authenticity, upon entering the time portal for the first time and finding himself in the 1940s, Gary is convinced that he has entered a theme park simulation of World War II Britain, not World War II era Britain itself. As the show progresses, however, Gary's rose-tinted view of 1940s Britain is challenged as he (re)learns about the era and its people, often exposing the workaday 'truth' of his discoveries to others back in the present: 'Don't you have a go at Vera. You might see her as some old dear who just bashes out endless renditions of "The White Cliffs of Dover", but in my other life she's a major babe' ('And Mother Came Too' 4:4). Much of Gary's desire for the 1940s seems to be based upon his more satisfying relationship with Phoebe, a character who embodies stereotypical ideas of femininity that his wife in the present rejects (Yvonne is career driven and bossy). Ultimately torn between the past and the present, *Goodnight Sweetheart* finally opts to trap Gary in the 1940s, suggesting that the show's makers believed viewers wished for Gary to enjoy the simplicity of life with Phoebe, and more clearly delineated gender roles, than suffer the problematic complexities of contemporary heterosexual romance.

In many ways, *Goodnight Sweetheart*'s nascent, self-reflexive engagement with ideas of history, memory and nostalgia is built upon in *Life on Mars* and *Ashes to Ashes*. Both shows allow for a more straightforward, surface level engagement with the nostalgia offered through the period setting of the central text, as Paul Booth suggests:

> for many viewers of these shows . . . part of the joy of the show lies in the nostalgic
> trip to the past: I'm enthralled not just in the period costumes or typical (lack

of) technology, but also in the stylistics (the credit sequence to Ashes to Ashes, for example, recalls many an 80s action/adventure program from my childhood, complete with electric guitar riffs and videographic titles). (88)

Yet, nostalgia also forms an integral part of the diegetic world of each show, with the central 'time travelling' characters in both examples aware, to varying degrees, of their own temporal displacement. In *Life on Mars* and *Ashes to Ashes* Sam Tyler and Alex Drake go through a similar procedure to the viewer, gradually recognizing the reconstructed and 'artificial' nature of the historical period/s they find themselves in. Though it is significant that, in spite of this realization, both characters find some solace in the past, even if it is an artificial, media-influenced construct. Indeed, Sam chooses to remain behind in the 'past' in the final episode of *Life on Mars* in what is a fairly explicit acknowledgement of the strong pull that the nostalgic, coma-induced version of the 1970s has over him. Matt Hills has suggested that, while initially depicted as uncanny and invasive, *Life on Mars* ultimately shows TV as a conduit for the messages that Sam needs in order to attain 'a state of happiness, belonging, and sheer aliveness' (114).

Whether ultimately supportive of a version of the past mediated through the prism of TV or not, both *Life on Mars* and *Ashes to Ashes* appear to encourage a decidedly more complex interrogation of nostalgia as an ontological concept, and the role that television (and the media more generally) has played in constructing a version of history for viewers, than shows such as *Happy Days* or *Goodnight Sweetheart*. Part of the reason for this more nuanced engagement may be due to both *Life on Mars* and *Ashes to Ashes'* desire to be seen as 'quality' TV; meaning that they consciously foreground modes of viewing as a means of aligning themselves, in the minds of viewers, with other 'quality' shows that similarly invite critical discussion around complex thematic concerns. While nostalgia itself might be thought of as a rather simplistic way of appealing to viewers, as a device for engaging with abstract theoretical issues it continues to play a significant part in a host of critically successful shows (*Deadwood* 2004–2006, *Breaking Bad* 2008–2013) that, as Robin Nelson proposes, centralize 'complex seeing' (20).

The overtly fantastical and science-fiction elements of these shows also throw up an interesting, often commented upon incongruity, which is that science-fiction, a genre ostensibly concerned with the future of humankind, is more frequently occupied with a nostalgic view of mankind's past; as Adam Roberts suggests 'The truth is that most SF texts are more interested in the way things have been' (26). Whether the examples outlined above can be considered truly radical, or indeed truly science-fiction, given their predilection for the past, is perhaps debatable. It often appears as though science-fiction on television, at least in a US-centric reading of the genre, is concerned with 'looking back rather than forward' (94). Given this status it is surprising that very few shows, as of the time of writing, have successfully embraced the kind of retro-futurism of J.J. Abrams' rebooted

Star Trek films. This may be due to the lack of a consistent visual aesthetic in television science-fiction, from which retro-futurist examples might oscillate, or a result of the previous budgetary constraints that so governed what might be achieved, visually, in the field.

Reading Time on TV

The original essays that follow are written by established TV scholars as well as emerging researchers and are arranged under two main headings: Structuring Time and Affective Time.

The essays in the first section primarily address conventions for representing time, especially in terms of time travel or other manipulations of time. Thus Lincoln Geraghty analyses patterns of narrative history in the various incarnations of *Star Trek* and how the series, despite being futuristic science-fiction, often returns to history in structuring its stories and developing its own long-running narratives. Both Stan Beeler in his chapter on *Eureka* and John Jeffrey in an examination of the *Primeval* anomaly investigate representations of time as flow, yet Beeler focuses on the radically disruptive effect time travel has on *Eureka*'s own narrative and genre structures, while Jeffrey highlights the aesthetic choices made in designing and vizualizing time portals for mainstream television. Production elements are also a feature of Pete Boss's chapter on *Timeslip*, in which he delineates the industrial and historical contexts affecting the representation of science in a neglected children's series. This section concludes with Kevin Lee Robinson's investigation of how screenwriters can develop highly individual approaches to representing time, as exemplified here by the work of P. J. Hammond. Robinson's chapter incorporates new insights from Hammond himself, following a recent interview.

The emotional or affective aspects of television time are the focus of the second section, which opens with an examination of contemporary fairytale drama *Once Upon a Time*, a series that, as Gwyneth Peaty argues, consistently foregrounds the personal temporal experience of its characters, most of whom are 'timeless' fairytale characters transplanted into modern-day North America. Nicola Allen's analysis of time travel police procedurals *Life on Mars* and *Ashes to Ashes* also deals with characterization in relation to temporal displacement, focusing on the gap between past and present that is mined by both series, and how this affects viewer engagement as well as character development. Staying with the crime genre, David Hipple's essay on *Crime Traveller* also considers characterization, in this case how its protagonists seek to derail the operation of linear time, but situated more broadly in a discussion of the market for genre television and the continuing popularity of time travel. A different genre is explored in Lorna Jowett's analysis of vampire television from *Dark Shadows* to *The Vampire Diaries*, which demonstrates how the vampire's undead nature is used to extend and develop existing conventions for representing time, often featuring as personal history. The section concludes with a detailed examination of nostalgia which, as David Simmons argues, can be a key factor in the immediate appeal and ongoing popularity of a time travel series like *Quantum Leap*.

Taken as a whole, the essays in this collection make a strong case for the significance of time as a structuring element, a representational strategy, a means of aesthetic distinctiveness, and as an informing context for a wide range of telefantasy series. While the TV shows examined in this introduction suggest that time has always played a role in television across a range of genres and formats, a focus on time has perhaps been most obvious in the fantasy genres that the chapters in this collection analyse The current popularity of such genres, however hybridized, in the expanded, post-digital television landscape indicates that time will continue to feature in TV drama for the foreseeable future.

Part I

Structuring Time

2

'Time is a Companion . . . Who Goes with Us on the Journey': *Star Trek*, Time Travel and Patterns of Narrative History

Lincoln Geraghty

This chapter examines *Star Trek*'s use of time in its various guises and, through specific case studies of time travel and historical episodes, argues that despite the series' reputation for depicting the future it is very much a science-fiction series that looks to times past for inspiration, storylines and meaning. All of the *Star Trek* television series to date[1] offer viewers multiple visions of dystopic or utopic futures, with time travel and alternate timelines often used as plot devices to highlight the contrast between what might have been and what is yet to come. Moreover, it is the very nature of the franchise's seriality which allows for an emphasis on history and the importance of time in making sense of the past, present and future. With the use of individual episodes, two-parters, and story arcs across series, *Star Trek* has constructed a meta-narrative that not only grounds the franchise in historical reality but uses historical time periods, events and personalities, alongside traditional time travel, to provide recognisable cultural touch points for viewers.

Star Trek's use of time travel and patterns of real and alternate history can be broken down into three distinct modes. In the first, one-off episodic time travel stories use the timelines of history as a chalk board for learning lessons from our past. These episodes often suggest that, by engaging with the past, we can better understand our world today. In the second type of episode, where the fictional narrative over a two- or three-part story becomes an extension of contemporary history (seen in the Eugenics Wars storyline from the original series, for example) audiences are shown how humanity has progressed in order to achieve its utopia – these episodes, in turn, establish alternate worlds through which the series uses history as an allegory for our present. The third mode, the story arc, relies on the cycles of history to maintain its narrative. In this last mode the televisual flow dictates the historical contexts of the series, so over the span of 22–24 episodes in a season the show is able to draw out the vagaries of time as each episode creates a context for the next – an epic narrative discourse builds, spanning time and space. This is best seen in the *Deep Space Nine* Dominion War story arc that fed both the audiences' expectations of what a *Star Trek* story should and could be, and also provided a stable and continuous narrative world through which the regular *DS9* characters, familiar plots, and personal histories could develop.[2] This particular use of time and history follows the format of traditional science-fiction television, but also borrows generic elements from soap opera and melodrama to help maintain its fictional world.

Episodic Time

Star Trek's representation of a reality through its fictitious future time has not only been entrenched as a possible outcome for society; it has become reality for some people who want to believe that it is true, or, as David Gerrold (1996: 228) suggests, 'it represents a future we would like to make real'. Its connections to history only add legitimacy to its figuration of the future; they have both become inseparable from each other, making *Star Trek* a signifier of both the future and the past. The show acts as a certified history of the real past and a proper history of the soon-to-be-real future.

In its episodic format *Star Trek* uses history in three ways to comment on contemporary society. It recounts famous events to help frame its episodic storylines. For example, in the *Voyager* two-part episode 'The Killing Game' (4.18,19) the crew are held hostage in a holodeck recreation of World War II occupied France. Being completely immersed in their respective roles as French Resistance fighters, soldiers and villagers, the crew have to combat the aggressive Hirogen who have taken on the role of the Nazis. *Star Trek* also changes narrative history altogether and sets up an alternative historical reality grounded in its perception of the future. Each episode brings yet another small detail that will potentially help fill in the gaps in *Star Trek's* future history. For instance, the *Voyager* episode 'One Small Step . . .' (6.8) recounted the mission of the first manned space flight to Mars in 2032; the film *Star Trek: First Contact* (1996) revealed how humans achieved warp flight and encountered the Vulcans in 2063; and, most significantly, *Enterprise* was set in 2151 between *First Contact* and the voyages of Captain Kirk, allowing viewers to see how the Federation was born and how humans became the technologically advanced species synonymous with *Star Trek's* view of humanity. *Star Trek* also relocates historical events and contemporary issues into a science-fiction format so that its stories are understood by the audience as fictitious, but the social messages conveyed can be digested without resentment. For example, the ongoing conflict between the Klingons and the Federation in the original series reflected North America's Cold War with the Soviets and the fiftieth anniversary of the dropping of the atomic bomb on Hiroshima provided the occasion for *Voyager's* allegorical treatment of its consequences in the episode 'Jetrel' (1.15). All three plot devices serve to ingrain *Star Trek* as a culturally aware television series that uses historical time and narrative to dramatize its stories and bring about a new social awareness. However, while *Star Trek* is in tune with the North American zeitgeist, it also relies upon multiple histories for its critical, but ultimately utopian, look to a possible future.

Steve Anderson observed that *Star Trek* used narrative plot devices such as 'encountering worlds that have developed like Earth' (2000: 20) in order to try and change the show's fictional history for the better since, in reality, Earth's history was neither so neat nor progressive as society would wish. This not only establishes the series as a morally correct and consummate disseminator of history to the public, but it also promotes it as a benchmark for what North Americans should strive to achieve in their short lives. The need to 'learn from the mistakes of the past' has been an integral part of coming to grips with issues such as 'who we were', 'what we have now become', and 'where we will end up in the future'. As Anderson asserts, 'in various corners of the galaxy, Captain Kirk succeeds in reforming a 1920s-style Chicago crime syndicate, ousting a corrupt Roman proconsul, dethroning a despotic Greek emperor, and overthrowing a proto-Nazi regime' (2000: 20), all in the name of doing what is right. What history lesson could be better than having the chance to relive entire eras and being able to take part in the actual events knowing you had the opportunity to change things for the better? On a narrative level, the television time travelling series *Quantum Leap* (1989–1993) shared many of these qualities with *Star Trek*; both involved a determined sense of duty 'to put right what once went wrong' and 'change history for the better' as *Quantum Leap's* opening credits stirringly eulogized [see David Simmons' essay in this collection]. Nevertheless, its attempts at showing how history could be changed for the better were channelled through the very idealistic and strong-headed Sam Beckett, who would be willing to change history to facilitate his return to his own time, so long as Al or Ziggy would allow it. This is the exact opposite to what the characters can do in any of the *Star Trek* series since they are supposedly governed by a strict policy of non-interference: the Temporal Prime Directive. This directive does not allow for history to be changed (what happened in the past is quite literally history); rather, it enables the narrative of the time travelling episodes to posit questions such as 'what can be learned from the lessons of history?' and 'how can we not repeat the same mistakes?' In this sense *Star Trek* acts as a moral guide to humanity's progress in life, making obvious what needs to be done, but not providing its audience with all of the answers.

This use of history is particularly pertinent to the original series where the ethos of the show was very much a reaction to the cultural and social upheavals occurring at the time. Many episodes dealt with topical and historically significant problems such as racism ('Let That Be Your Last Battlefield' 3.15) and youth disenfranchisement ('The Way to Eden' 3.20) or the political ramifications of the Vietnam War ('The City on the Edge of Forever' 1.28 and 'A Private Little War' 2.19). *Star Trek*'s interaction with historical events in such episodes typically emphasized the choice between right and wrong and how those choices affected both the crew – usually Kirk, Spock and McCoy – and the innocent inhabitants of an alien planet. Being set in the future disconnected the series from reality and signified that humanity had progressed from the current turmoil of the Sixties. For those viewers who were daunted by the prospect of an escalation of the war in Vietnam or the threat of nuclear fallout, *Star Trek* prophesied that humans would survive the twentieth century but, at the same time, stressed that dramatic change was needed to bring about the utopian future portrayed on screen.

However, contrary to the view that *Star Trek* used history to teach America about right and wrong, Jay Goulding contends that famous episodes such as 'Tomorrow is Yesterday' (1.19) and 'The City on the Edge of Forever' established *Star Trek* as a purveyor of 'a false sense of power'. To tell the audience that we might be able to put things right and change the future 'generates a static vision where democracy triumphs over all time dimensions', making *Star Trek* just as oppressive and imperialistic as the North American society it was trying to critique in the turbulent Sixties (1985: 40). Goulding recognizes that the dichotomy which characterizes *Star Trek*'s use of historically motivated stories comes from its attempts to correct North American history for the better and sanctify whatever mistakes may have happened in the past in the name of democracy: 'It promises an omniscience and omnipotence which is an horrific concept, but necessary for the mythology which prides itself on the craft of changing what has happened' (40). To some extent Goulding is right about *Star Trek*'s need to sanitize history but what he does not recognize is that *Star Trek* only allowed for the possibility of change through the interventions of Kirk and his crew rather than changing history itself. The narrative of the series offered those alien worlds the chance to redeem their own mistakes since the *Enterprise* would always leave orbit and let the inhabitants choose to take action, giving them a chance to change history for themselves. In 'The Omega Glory' (2.23) Kirk teaches a tribe of Yang warriors, who had misinterpreted the preamble to the Constitution as an order to exclude their Kohm enemies, that the words 'must apply to everyone or they mean nothing'. Spock declares Kirk's idealistic and interfering action as a breach of the Prime Directive but Kirk replies: 'We merely showed them the meaning of what they were fighting for ... I suggest we leave them to discover their history, and their liberty'. This sequence embodies the series' optimism in view of the fact that the future was not set in stone, it was up to the aliens – and likewise us – to take control of destiny.

It is interesting to note that this episode was to be originally aired as the second pilot after 'The Cage' (1.1) yet it did not receive the go-ahead by television executives. However, after deciding that they wanted an episode to symbolize *Star Trek*'s explorative origins rather than its moralistic overtones, the producers replaced 'The Omega Glory' with 'Where No Man Has Gone Before' (1.3). This decision epitomises the interplay at the heart of the show's ethos: it represents both typical science-fiction action adventure and serious socio-political commentary.

Learning Earth History

Star Trek's pilgrimages into US and world histories do not just depict the past but also give the audience a definitive guide to the history of the future. All incarnations of the series are set in our future, with *Enterprise* in the twenty-second century and the three spin-offs set in and after the twenty-third century, with *Voyager* finishing late in the twenty-fourth century. The gaps between real time and series time, and between the original series and later incarnations, have been filled by the writers and producers with many historic events: World War III, the discovery of alien life, scientific advancement in space travel, the founding of the United Federation of Planets (to name but a few). This evolution is further highlighted by early publications such as *The Star Trek Encyclopaedia: A Reference Guide to the Future* (1997) and *Star Trek Chronology: A History of the Future* (1993), both updated online as new entries are created. In these, everything from the 47 years of *Star Trek* is cross-referenced and recorded in minute detail to give the fans absolute insight into the ever-expanding universe. In effect, much of this desire to record the history of the future resembles what Daniel Boorstin has termed the 'effort to catalogue the whole creation' (1983: 419), whereby since the dawn of time humanity has toiled to record and catalogue its discoveries in order to provide a lasting description of life itself.

The attempts to document a *Star Trek* history of the future, essentially fashioning the 'taxonomy of *Star Trek*', encompassing everything that has ever existed in its world and will ever exist in ours, is similar to Jorge Luis Borges' short story 'The Library of Babel' taken from his collection entitled *Fictions* (1998: 72–80). In it he describes a library collection comprised of the entire knowledge of the universe (a fictional one) from 'the minute history of the future' to 'the veridical account of your death'. The library is infinite, 'limitless and periodic', allowing the reader a lifetime of searching for what they desire, just as *Star Trek* fans endeavour to pursue their dreams and desires through the fictional, but documented and limitless, universe compounded by books such as *Encyclopaedia* or *Chronology*. What is more, as Michael Jindra states, 'this universe is much larger and more complex than any other fictional universe' (2000: 174), including that of J. R. R. Tolkien's Middle Earth novels and even of *Star Wars*.

Several episodes and short story arcs deal with fictional events in the past which are still set in our future, literally going 'back to the future' to create an original historical narrative. The main plot of *Star Trek: First Contact* concerns events intrinsic to the creation of Starfleet and the Federation along with the discovery of warp drive, yet these developments are still in advance of our time period – even set after the yet-to-happen WWIII. Nevertheless, because they have been eulogized by *Star Trek*'s chronology of the future, fans are well aware of these events and see them as part of a 'real' history. They provide a narrative background to many of the popular characters and stories, at the same time 'filling in the syntagmatic gaps in the original narrative' (Fiske 1992: 39).

Greg Cox's novel *Star Trek: The Eugenics Wars* (2001) is described as Volume One in the history of Khan Noonien Singh – a popular character recently reimagined in *Star Trek: Into Darkness* (2013) – and recounts how he rose to power in the late twentieth century during the Eugenics Wars. The author intertwines contemporary figures from history and incidents from the *Star Trek* mythos with real historical events such as the fall of the Berlin Wall, creating a story that endorses *Star Trek* history, both canonically and in the contexts of world events. The Eugenics Wars were supposedly to have lasted between 1990 and 1996, started by a genetically engineered Singh and a group of his supermen acolytes who wanted to take over the world. Cox followed up with Volume Two (2002) which charted Singh's life during the war, how he was defeated, and exiled – leading right up until his appearance in the episode 'Space Seed' (1.22). A third book, *To Reign in Hell* (2005), serves as a prequel to Khan's eventual demise seen in *Star Trek II: The Wrath of Khan* (1982) by filling in what happened while he was trapped on an alien planet by Captain Kirk. The following quotation from the editor of the official *Star Trek* magazine highlights the balance the franchise strikes between fact and fiction and how the fans respond to its future history:

> For continuity freaks, a show like *Star Trek* is a godsend. Each new episode brings yet another small detail that will potentially help fill in the gaps in *Star Trek*'s labyrinthine future history. There are, of course, entire books devoted to mapping the *Star Trek* timeline, but books can only get you so far in the search for previously-unknown little titbits. Only new episodes can provide that extra thrill derived from learning something new about *Star Trek*'s chronology, reinforcing the show's status as a living, breathing, developing entity, fleshing out and colouring in its past as it moves ever forward. (Jones 2002a: 56)

In a number of ways *Star Trek*'s use of history to breathe life into its storylines provides multiple avenues which writers can explore. As a narrative strategy it resembles what has been termed the 'multiform story'. Recognized by Janet H.

Murray, the multiform story is a term that describes 'a written or dramatic narrative that presents a single situation or plotline in multiple versions, versions that would be mutually exclusive in our ordinary experience' (1997: 30). This structure is seen in *Star Trek* as many of its stories are based on the premise that there is more than one alternative timeline. In the original episode 'Mirror Mirror' (2.4), Captain Kirk is accidentally transported onto an alternate version of the Enterprise where the normally peace-loving Federation is a war-mongering barbaric empire. He tries to persuade the opposite version of Spock to change in order for that timeline to be more like his own. This obviously brings about a short-term improvement for the alternate Enterprise but unfortunately, in the long term, Kirk's message of change proves to be the downfall of the Federation. We see the results of this in *DS9* crossover episodes where humans have become galactic slaves to the Klingon, Bajoran, and Cardassian alliance: 'Crossover' (2.23), 'Through the Looking Glass' (3.19), 'Shattered Mirror' (4.20), 'Resurrection' (6.8), and 'The Emperor's New Cloak' (7.12). These episodes play out separate plotlines in which regular characters are presented differently as they have taken different career paths or made alternate life choices, providing an equivalent but upside-down version of the *Star Trek* universe in which the normal characters can be exchanged to accommodate an exciting story.

The multiform story is also used in such episodes as *Star Trek: The Next Generation*'s 'Parallels' (7.11), where Worf shifts through a number of alternative timelines, after he accidentally enters a fissure in time upon returning to the ship from leave. Cut scenes where Worf leaves his quarters or enters a turbo-lift act as transition points when he shifts between parallel time streams without warning. The timelines he experiences range from having a family with his crewmate Deanna Troi to realizing that his friends have been killed in the battle with the Borg from 'The Best of Both Worlds' (3.26, 4.1). 'Yesterday's Enterprise' (3.15) also involves a multiform story, only this time it deals with *Star Trek* lore. The crew of Picard's *Enterprise* is transported into another time, where they are at war with the Klingons because a previous incarnation of the famous ship was not destroyed and henceforth did not go down in history as the catalyst for forging peace between Klingons and humans. Picard decides to sacrifice himself, and the *Enterprise* that should have made history, in order for the proper timeline to be restored. *Voyager* also uses this plot device to similar effect. In the two-part episode 'Year of Hell' (4.8,9) Captain Janeway and her crew fight to survive the attacks of an alien race intent on destroying the ship because they want to change history. Each time the ship survives an attack the timeline is altered slightly, killing many of the main characters and destroying entire planets. At the end of the episode, however, the original timeline is repaired so that it is as if the crew experienced nothing.

Star Trek uses this method of storytelling because it allows for a mode of expression that can accommodate different possibilities, so fundamental in the science-fiction genre. In contemporary media culture, where audiences are used to complex and long-running narrative television series, the multiform story provides a suitable framework, as it allows for various alternative plots and outcomes using the same narrative structure. As Murray states in *Hamlet on the Holodeck: The Future of Narrative in Cyberspace*:

> [The multiform narrative's] alternate versions of reality are now part of the way we think, part of the way we experience the world. To be alive in the twentieth century is to be aware of the alternative possible selves, of alternative possible worlds, and of the limitless intersecting stories of the actual world. (1997: 38)

With *Star Trek* the multiform story works because it has a narrative history which serves as a basis for many of its episodes; there is already a narrative framework in place for multiple plots to expand upon and characters to harmonize with. For fans its 'alternate versions of reality' are part of the way they experience their own world and, as a result, part of how they identify themselves and want to imagine the future. *Star Trek: Enterprise*, the last series to appear on television to date, used *Star Trek*'s historical canon most often. Set before the stories of Kirk and his crew from *TOS*, *Enterprise*'s timeline was almost entirely predetermined. Episodes such as 'Carbon Creek' (2.2) (which revealed first contact with Vulcans actually happened on Earth in 1957), 'Minefield' (2.3) (which had the crew encountering Romulans for the first time) and 'Regeneration' (2.23) (where the Borg make a surprise appearance without being named) concentrated on unpicking the real and fictional history of human space exploration from the beginning of the twenty-first century and the birth of the Federation in 2161.

The defining premise of *Enterprise* was the pioneer spirit, space exploration at its most rudimentary level, not much more advanced than it is today. The show charted the history of Roddenberry's future, where fan favourites such as the transporter and warp drive were in their infancy. *Enterprise* provided definitive fan interaction and appreciation because it catered to a fascination with *Star Trek* continuity and the franchise's penchant for describing the history of the future. The first few episodes exemplified this development by concentrating on key events in *Star Trek* lore; for example, the pilot episode 'Broken Bow' (1.1) revealed new secrets behind the birth of Starfleet and recounted how the Vulcans opposed humanity's first steps toward the final frontier. 'The Andorian Incident' (1.7) expanded upon this trend by concentrating on the Andorian species first seen in the original series, but not regularly used in more recent episodes, and built up a whole new social and cultural history around their characters. Most controversially, in the final episode 'These Are The Voyages' 4.22), the previous four seasons are reduced to historical re-enactment as *Star Trek: The Next Generation*'s Riker and Troi on the holodeck of the Enterprise-D are seen watching Admiral Archer and his crew help forge the first agreement to create the Federation. What these episodes actually do is called 'retconning', an 'abbreviated term for the act of retroactively adjusting continuity', and 'is a long-established staple in the world of comics, where characters' origins are forever being raked over, fleshed out and sometimes adjusted for perceived "newer" audiences' (Jones 2002b: 19). In other words, *Enterprise* used retcons (an insertion into the fictional narrative chronology) as a means to construct the future history that both fascinated fans and kept the series going over a long period of real time.

Enterprise's reappropriation of an overtly celebratory version of *Star Trek* history indicates that it tried to ground its vision of the future in a mythic retelling of its own narrative past. This is part of a process of 'reinterpretation' or 're-visioning' of history which Sarah Neely describes as a 'retrovision'. A 'retrovision is a "vision into or of the past" and implies an act of possessing the ability to read the past, in the way that one would possess a prophetic vision' (2001: 74). For Deborah Cartmell and I. Q. Hunter retrovisions are 'makeovers of history' (2001: 7). A sentiment relevant to *Enterprise* since it tried to re-fashion *Star Trek*'s universal history by making it part of a very specific mythic history. Overall, the retrovisioning of *Star Trek* history is an appealing component of America's return to its exceptional past. Deborah L. Madsen believes 'exceptionalism has always offered a mythological refuge from the chaos of history and the uncertainty of life... it *was* the legacy of the Old World for the New' (1998: 166). *Enterprise* offered an American society unsure of the future the very same refuge through a re-visioning of a celebratory past:

> *Star Trek* creates a future world where the glories of the past are pristine and the failures and doubts of the present have been overcome. It gives us our past as our future, while making our present the past which, like any historical event for the future-orientated American, is safely over and forgotten. (Tyrrell 1977: 713)

Even though *Star Trek* employs a fantastic version of the future in which to set its allegorical stories, it looks to the past as means of broadcasting its messages. The use and manipulation of real and fictional time in this storytelling process further entrenches *Star Trek* as history; it is not a fictional view of a brighter future but rather an ideological view of a real past. Vivian Sobchack, in her book *Screening Space: The American Science Fiction Film*, describes the *Star Trek* films as backward looking, nostalgic, and basically old-fashioned: 'Despite all their "futurist" gadgetry and special effects, then, the *Star Trek* films are conservative and nostalgic, imaging the future by looking backward to the imagination of a textual past' (1998: 277).

Similarly, if we see the *Star Trek* television series as a historical pastiche of the future than we can also view the stories, the fictional narrative, as some sort of history – albeit a history set in the fictional representations of a contemporary North American reality. *Star Trek* looks 'backward to the imagination of a textual past', and projects that history forward through the depiction of a utopian, futuristic version of modern day America.

The Narrative Story Arc

The narrative universe in which *Deep Space Nine* was set was an ambiguous one in comparison with previous series. The writers and producers stressed that the characters were to be fallible, have obvious faults, and, most important of all, would face complex situations in space that no longer had easy answers (Richards 1998: 173). The look and feel of the show would prove to be far darker and more serious than its contemporary *Star Trek: The Next Generation*; for example, being set on a space station meant that if any exploring was to be done, then the unknown would have to come to them. This confined setting implied that there would be more chance for character development across the entire length of the show's run. They would be allowed to grow as the stories they were involved in became more complicated and less resolvable in a single weekly episode. As Chris Gregory argues, '*DS9* concentrates more on the growth the characters experience as a result of the unfolding narratives of the series itself' (2000: 69) rather than their individual actions in separate and varied storylines. For Gregory, *Star Trek: Deep Space Nine* bore a striking resemblance to a soap opera since it incorporated narrative structures very similar to those used in soap television such as complicated and involved character back-stories and interwoven story arcs over time, plus the highly developed historical narrative outlined in the previous section:

> The stories are linked by continuing 'soap opera'-type subplots such as Bashir's ineffectual attempts to romance Jadzia, Sisko's difficulties with his adolescent son, Jake, and Odo's continual pursuit of Quark. It is emphasized that *DS9* is a multicultural community in which there will be less focus on the 'military' life of Starfleet as seen on *TNG*'s Enterprise, and in which relationships between characters will be less bound by their rank and position. (Gregory 2000: 74)

According to the historian Kerwin Lee Klein, '[Hayden] White followed the lead of formalist literary critics Northrop Frye and Kenneth Burke, arguing that a limited number of plot forms and tropes characterized historical narratives' (1997: 53). For Frye this meant that there were four archetypal plot modes or *mythoi*, as he liked to call them, that characterized Western literature. Following on from Frye's and Burke's analysis of literary plot forms, Klein recognises that White read the usage of plots as a form of historical explanation. Historians had no experience or empirical evidence of what actually happened in history, so they inadvertently borrowed from the common plots and narrative forms already present in literature to help manifest a coherent discourse from their material. Klein goes further in his breakdown of White's theories by recounting the four master tropes described in *Metahistory* (1973), White's first and most influential piece. There is a typology of rhetorical figures of speech made up of four tropes; they, in turn, govern the way we operate language and therefore construct a narrative: metaphor, metonymy, synecdoche, and irony (54). The construction and telling of a story in *Star Trek* was crucial to its success over the course of its time on television:

> Narrative focuses our attention onto a story, a sequence of events, through the direct mediation of a 'telling' which we both stare at and through, which is at once central and peripheral to the experience of the story, both absent and present in the consciousness of those being told the story. (Hawthorn 1985: vii)

DS9's overall narrative relied heavily on the use of one of White's tropes to tell its story over the course of its seven year run, specifically metonymy. Metonymy is the trope of contiguity, part-part relationships, where a single event may provide a causal link in a chain of events. With this trope there is no determined end but rather an incomplete and continuous series of events that form an unfinished narrative. This particular trait is best identified in *DS9* where the last season in particular was devoted to the culmination of a war that was first brought to viewers' attention at the end of the second season. The last nine episodes of *DS9* in 1999 concerned the final developments of the 'Dominion War', and they also signalled the farewell to major characters. This meant that all nine had to adequately finish off storylines that had been going on for a number of years; there was no time for introducing new plots or characters: see 'Penumbra' (7.17), ''Til Death Do Us Part' (7.18), 'Strange Bedfellows' (7.19), 'The Changing Face of Evil' (7.20), 'When it Rains . . . ' (7.21), 'Tacking Into the Wind' (7.22), 'Extreme Measures' (7.23), 'The Dogs of War' (7.24), and 'What You Leave Behind' (7.25,26).

DS9 was created to be different from the more explorative ethos of the original *Star Trek* and its later offspring *Star Trek: The Next Generation*. What characterized *DS9* was the inner conflicts and social turmoil found on the space station that could also then be found in the different alien societies encountered in each episode. The larger story arcs concerned the religious, cultural, and political ideologies of entire empires and the personal conflicts initiated when races collided in war. But individual episodes would also be concerned with those issues on a smaller scale – perhaps looking at certain key characters, their backgrounds, and how they were affected by conflict – enabling the audience to fully understand the complexities of the larger story lines and become familiar with 'who's who.' *DS9* is metonymic because some of its story arcs were not finalized and completed when the last episode, 'What You Leave Behind' (7.25, 7.26), was aired. The war may have ended but many plotlines remained unfinished and the audience was left wondering what would happen to some of their favourite characters. For example, Captain Benjamin Sisko left the station to pursue his destiny as religious emissary to the people of Bajor. Originally he was wary of assuming this important religious role and, throughout the seven years, the very secular character was shown to be at odds with his religious duties. In the last episode, however, Sisko decided to continue as emissary and live with the Wormhole Prophets that all Bajorans looked to for spiritual guidance; they would teach him how to lead his newfound people to salvation. In undertaking this spiritual quest in a non-corporeal universe Sisko had left his son Jake and pregnant wife Kasidy on board the station wondering whether he would ever return. Sisko tells Kasidy that they may not be together for a long time but when he returns it might seem as if he were only gone a day. The Prophets do not live in human linear time but rather live outside of time and can therefore deliver Sisko back to Kasidy before he had even left. Without the concept of linear time the Prophets do not understand history and do not understand humanity's preoccupation with memory, remembering, and eulogising the past. When Sisko says to the Prophet Sarah (his mother) that his time as emissary is nearly at an end she responds, 'Your journey's end lies not before you but behind you,' and he finally realises his position as religious messenger for the prophets: his time on the station was only the beginning. This ambiguous ending illustrates the nature of *Star Trek: DS9*'s continued narrative stretched over time and is indicative of its manipulation of the *Star Trek* mythos. Besides Worf, who continued to appear in the *Star Trek: The Next Generation* movies, every *DS9* character had an open-ended future within the franchise's canonical timeline.

Conclusion

Star Trek is more than just good televisual entertainment – it is history. *Star Trek* offers a historical, narrative discourse that not only feeds our passion for what the future might bring, but also forms a relationship with the past mediated through television and film. The stories and characters have captured imaginations and offered life lessons based on the reworking and retracing of human history – albeit an American version of world history: 'In effect, the series have mapped out a chronology within which fans can further engross themselves, a fictional universe complete with its own documented history ripe for Jenkins' "textual poaching"' (Geraghty 2007: 33). As a result, the mythic and future times offered by all series in the franchise offer a way out of dealing with contemporary life; it is not because audiences want to live in a mythic past but rather history and myth offer a better template to fantasize about and create the future. Brooks Landon's claim that science-fiction is not about 'what the future might hold, but the inevitable hold of the present over the future' (1991: 239) makes clear that it is the present that determines what constitutes our science-fiction. Therefore I would argue that *Star Trek* depicts historical time as a means to counteract the turmoil and uncertainty of the present.

History is a representation of the past; it is information transformed into story, which, over time, becomes part of a shared mythology. These stories and myths are retold by *Star Trek* as futuristic narratives; sometimes they are embedded in symbols and tropes or, as in the case of 'going back in time', in stories concerning the dilemma between right and wrong. The stories they recount about the past in the future produce images that, at the micro level, we use to perceive ourselves as individuals both separate from and within society, and, at a macro level, we use to recognize America as a nation. By telling the right stories, the popular science-fiction franchise helped the audience imagine itself acting as a community, pulling together to resolve social problems tackled in weekly episodes, ultimately overcoming a national anxiety deeply rooted in the conception of its own history.

Notes

1. The series are: *Star Trek* (TOS) [1966–1969], *Star Trek: The Next Generation* (*TNG*) [1987–1994], *Star Trek: Deep Space Nine* (*DS9*) [1993–1999], *Star Trek: Voyager* [1995–2001], *Star Trek: Enterprise* [2001–2005].
2. The Dominion, an alliance of alien species from the Gamma Quadrant led by a race of Changelings, was introduced early on in season two of *Star Trek: Deep Space Nine* – mentioned in conversation as potential partners for trade with the Federation from the Alpha Quadrant. Hostilities began between the Federation and Dominion at the end of that season and, by the third, tensions started to clearly have an effect on the crew of *DS9*. By end of season four, the Dominion had invaded the Alpha Quadrant and all-out war was inevitable, with Earth a target of infiltration and terrorism. Seasons five and six featured regular episodes that focussed on the conflict and in season seven almost all the episodes concerned attempts to stop the war and bring peace to the Alpha Quadrant.

3

Reality Resets: Changing the Past in *Eureka*

Stan Beeler

The doxology of the Anglican church ends with the phrase 'as it was in the beginning is now and ever shall be, world without end', reaffirming the immutable nature of reality in a divinely controlled universe. As one might suspect, the nature of reality in genre television is somewhat less firm. In fact, there are some series that habitually play fast and loose with the audience's expectations concerning the relationship of the past, present and future. Sometimes, time travel is employed to simply present contemporary characters in an historical setting, adding an exotic aspect to a tired story line. It can also be used to explain the appearance of characters of historical significance in modern times. However, time travel can be most interesting when it is used to reconfigure the parameters of a developing fictional world. The US/Canadian production *Eureka* is an example of science-fiction TV that employs the trope of time travel to radically alter the established dynamics of its plotline.

Eureka and Time Travel

Considering its genre and venue, *Eureka* was remarkably successful during its five year run (2006–2012) and the pilot episode was 'the highest-rated series telecast in the network's [Sci-Fi] history (as it was then called), netting 4.1 million viewers' (Martin). The pilot episode introduces US Marshal Jack Carter and his daughter Zoe who are stranded by a car accident in a small town – Eureka – in the Pacific NorthWest of the United States. Carter discovers that the town is the home of a secret US government research facility, General Dynamics or GD, with projects and gadgets worthy of the best Bond film. While waiting for his car to be repaired,

Carter finds out that events related to one of the town's research projects are the reason for the car accident that has stranded them in Eureka. A scientist, Walter Perkins, has developed a machine which alters the fabric of time in a very localized fashion. This disruption of time results in the destruction of property, animals and the crippling of Eureka's incumbent Sheriff, William Cobb, by vaporizing his legs. Carter assists in the search for the source of the time disruption and, because he is so effective, finds himself dragooned into the position of the new Sheriff of Eureka. Over the course of the first season, Carter develops a close relationship with Allison Blake, a government agent who is head of security at General Dynamics.

At this point it should be noted that the show develops in a more or less episodic fashion during the first season. There are a series of weekly disasters that result from the town's cutting edge research, but, by the end of each episode, Carter has managed to overcome the problem. Nevertheless, the time travel conundrum that is initiated in the pilot episode is never really resolved. By the end of the first season, references to this event form a narrative plot structure that enhances the serial aspects of the show. In the final episode of the first season 'Once in a Lifetime' (1.12) these narrative threads concerning time travel, which were established in the pilot, are reintroduced to the main plot. Carter wakes up one day and, from the perspective of the audience, the world seems to have changed – Allison has married Carter and they are expecting a child. Moreover, one of the other central characters of the series, Henry Deacon, is married to his research partner, Kim Yamazaki. As the episode progresses a series of strange occurrences indicate that there is some other reality impinging upon this happy state of affairs. Henry has used the time travel technology from the first episode to go back and prevent the accidental death of his (then) girlfriend Kim as she performs an experiment for Allison's ex-husband Nathan Stark. This has caused deadly distortion of the normal flow of time that has introduced an extra four years, and Carter is forced to use the same technology to go back and prevent Henry from rescuing Kim in order to prevent a catastrophic time paradox. The time line is successfully repaired, and a catastrophe of cosmic proportions is prevented. Unfortunately, this change rewrites the happy results of the last four years of Carter's life. As the season ends Carter is living alone with his daughter and Allison is renewing her relationship with Nathan Stark. Since Henry and Carter are the only time travellers, they are the only people aware that they have lost the stable relationships developed over the four years of the distorted timeline. (Throughout the series Jack Carter is normally referenced by his last name by both friends and enemies while Henry Deacon goes by his first. This is probably related to Carter's identification with his official function of Sheriff of Eureka.)

This narrative line in *Eureka* is a relatively new take on the traditional science-fiction story of time travel. Instead of a mind-bending paradox in which the protagonist kills his father or marries his mother we have a more contained domestic tragedy in which one man – Henry – loses the love of his life and the other – Carter – loses his relationship to his wife and family. There are, of course, precedents for time travel's emotional impact to be found in the *Star Trek* episode 'City on the Edge of Forever' (1.28), (which was partially written by the famous science-fiction author Harlan Ellison) as well as in the *Angel* episode 'I Will Remember You' (1.8). 'City On the Edge of Forever' represents a time traveling Captain Kirk falling in love with a doomed woman who cannot be rescued without damaging the timeline. In 'I Will Remember You' Angel first gains a happy life as a mortal with Buffy and then gives it up for the good of humanity. The interlude is removed from the timeline and Angel is the only one who remembers the lost relationship. *Star Trek* is primarily episodic in nature and the events in 'City on the Edge of Forever' do not have far reaching ramifications upon the further development of the plot or the characters of the show. *Angel*, although much more serialized than *Star Trek*, does not directly incorporate the tragic situation of 'I Will Remember You' into the further development of the central plot of the series. However, this episode does add to the emotional depth of the protagonist and may be considered a partial justification of Angel's subsequent relationship with Buffy. Although these two episodes incorporate domestic tragedy in their plotlines, they do not work against each other in the same way as the elements of the *Eureka* plotline. *Eureka* makes these two interrelated events into a centrepiece of the serialized plot and character development of the show.

Because Carter is instrumental in the erasure of the time distortion, his relationship with Henry becomes strained. In the first episode of season two, 'Phoenix Rising', Carter and Henry explore the tragic consequences of their missing four years of history. Henry gives Carter the option of having his memory of the missing four years erased. When Carter hesitates, Henry simply wipes his memory before Carter can decide if he wants to accept the offer. However, Henry chooses to keep his own memories and therefore he still harbours resentment of Carter's intervention. This event sets up a dynamic tension between Carter and Henry that affects the plot structure of following episodes. Because Henry chooses not to forget, we are never sure that Henry is acting in Carter's best interests in any given situation. This is conveyed through the use of short clips of Henry looking at video footage of Kim at times when he is asked to help Carter. The clips, combined with Henry's bitter expression, lead us to believe that he may not be completely honest with his friend.

Time and the TV

This brief introduction to the use of time travel in *Eureka* can provide us with a general idea of how the device is employed to enhance the plot structure of the show. The reason that time travel is such an effective device as it is used in the show depends upon some aspects of the basic nature of television. John Fiske notes that television narrative, in general, has a special relationship with time:

Television's sense of time is unique in its feel of the present and its assumption of the future. In soap opera, the narrative time is a metaphorical equivalent of real time, and the audiences are constantly engaged in remembering the past, enjoying the present, and predicting the future. In series, the future may not be part of the diegetic world of the narrative, but it is inscribed into the institution of television itself: the characters may not act as though they will be back with us next week, but we, the viewers, know that they will. The sense of the future, of the existence of as yet unwritten events, is a specifically televisual characteristic, and one that works to resist narrative closure. (Fiske 145)

Fiske goes on to point out that television's sense of 'newness' may be contrasted with the impression of reportage that may be found in other media. Television viewers do not have the feeling that events have already occurred; they are invited to, '"live" the experience of solving the enigma, rather than be told the process of its already achieved and recorded resolution' (Fiske 145). *Eureka* employs the narrative device of time travel in order to exploit these unique televisual characteristics. The audience follows the events of the first season with a sense of real time, enjoying the swift progression to the culmination of the eternal question: will the hero find happiness with the female protagonist? However, despite the indications that this narrative enigma has been resolved, in its first season the show undercuts our expectations of an analogue of real time by resetting the 'past' and installing a new structure for the viewer's expectations of the future. Narrative closure is firmly rejected; the audience realizes that there will be no quick and clear ending to this tale of a disrupted romance. In partial recompense we are given the pleasurable experience of a temporary, mini-closure, followed by a resetting of the initial quest for a happy relationship. In a film or a novel, this would leave the reader with an uncomfortable sense of waiting for something that will never happen. In television, we know that, barring sudden cancellation, Carter will have a second chance to find happiness with his beloved Allison.

A Brief History of Time Travel

As is the case with any plot device, time travel can be employed by writers in a number of ways. It can be used to provide 'trick' endings that surprise and delight the audience or it can be used to develop profound philosophical commentary on the nature of human existence. Often time travel is simply used as a way for writers to get out of untenable plot developments.

In the early days of television Rod Serling's seminal science-fiction and fantasy anthology series, *The Twilight Zone* (1959–1964), used time travel as a narrative device to provide a science-fiction 'surprise' ending in a number of its most famous episodes. For example, 'The Last Flight' (1.18) – which was penned by Richard Matheson – tells the story of World War I pilot Terry Decker, who abandons a comrade and escapes a German attack by flying through a mysterious cloud. Decker arrives in 1959 where he is held in custody for trespassing on a military airfield. When he discovers that his comrade, Alexander Mackaye, played a pivotal role in World War II, Decker escapes custody and flies back through the cloud to save his friend. The final scene of the episode is a meeting between the future version Mackaye and the man who allowed Decker to escape. It is revealed that Decker died bravely while defending Mackaye and that the personal effects left in the future were never recovered after the battle.

Stanislaw Lem (author of the novel *Solaris*) believes that stories of time travel should be used for intellectual experimentation and representation of complex philosophical positions. He is, therefore, contemptuous of writers who use the trope to enhance the artistic quality of the narrative: 'They try to bring about the conversion of SF to the "creed of normal literature" through articulating, by fantastic means, such non-fantastic content which is already old-fashioned in an ethical, axiological, philosophical sense' (Lem, Hoisington, and Suvin 153). Lem would have considered the use of time travel in *Eureka* as a misuse of science-fiction concepts to further the 'creed of normal literature.' However, *Eureka* develops parallel tragedies through the use of time travel narratives that are far more effective in an artistic sense, than Lem's more cerebral conceptions of the true purpose of science-fiction.

In contrast to 'smart' endings, or intellectual puzzles, we may find a more literary use of time travel in Audrey Niffenegger's novel (and the 2009 film of the same name) *The Time Traveler's Wife*. This is a romantic tale of time traveller Henry DeTamble and his wife Clare Abshire. DeTamble is afflicted with a genetic disease that forces him to time travel to different times and places during his own lifetime. He meets and woos his wife over the entire course of her life during his time trips. Unfortunately, since he cannot control the situation of his arrival during his time jaunts, he dies tragically. The novel is designed as a complex artistic representation of the vicissitudes of human relationships. It would appear that *Eureka*'s writers have followed this methodology in the application of time travel to their own narrative constructs.

Time Travel and Narrative Complexity

Another aspect of the artistic goals of *Eureka*'s writers may be found in the development of strongly connected season-long plot constructs. *Eureka* is an example of the growing tendency towards complexity in modern television narrative and its writers' use of time travel has a special significance in the development of this signature complexity. As indicated above, *Eureka*, like many modern TV shows, combines elements of both episodic and serialized narrative structure. Jason Mittell frames this tendency as follows: 'At its most basic level, narrative complexity is a redefinition of episodic forms under the influence of serial narration – not necessarily a complete merger of episodic and serial forms but a shifting balance' (Mittell 32).

In each episode of *Eureka*, Sheriff Carter is faced with a disastrous malfunction of the cutting-edge technology developed in the local research facility. Yet, in each episode, Carter manages to surmount his intellectual limitations (he has an average IQ in a town full of geniuses) and resolve the problem through a combination of folksy wisdom and somewhat reluctant derring-do. This is the standard structure of traditional, episodic TV. A problem is presented at the beginning of each episode, and, by the end, this problem is resolved and the situation returns to the static situation necessary for the continuation of the series. In *Eureka*, however, as these seemingly unrelated episodes play out we notice that there are underlying connections between the events that provide the audience a much broader serialized narrative that can last for a whole season or even longer. Time travel, in season one of *Eureka*, is the narrative glue that sticks all of the episodes together. Moreover, it is not simply – as Lem would recommend – an intellectual puzzle that must be resolved. Time travel in *Eureka* gives rise to situations with a strong, emotional impact that affects the lives and character development of the central protagonists. Carter has a successful love affair that results in marriage and a new family and, when this is wiped out, he is left with deep feelings for someone who cannot be expected to reciprocate. In the first few episodes after the time paradox has been resolved Allison is constantly surprised by Carter's unexpected use of affectionate nicknames and informal attitude to her. In the same sense, after Carter's memory of the time travel event has been erased, he often asserts that Henry is his best and most trusted friend. This trust seems to irritate Henry who can remember Carter's 'betrayal' of their friendship.

Mittell points out that early attempts to integrate serial and episodic plot structures used the standards of earlier televisual forms: 'These early programs tend to allocate episodic and serial stories as tied to typical generic norms – relationship stories carry over between episodes, as in soap operas, but the police and medical cases are generally bound within one episode or serialized as a two-parter' (Mittell 33). As the tendency to narrative complexity in TV increased, shows like *The X-Files* (1993–2002) incorporated non-romantic narrative lines that last for numerous episodes or seasons. A continuing plotline is known as a narrative arc and it is an important component of modern, complex TV narrative. The arc has a number of functions to aid in the transition from simple, episodic TV. One of the most important of these functions in science-fiction and fantasy TV is that the arc aids in developing an alternate world with believable characters:

> The story arc . . . resists closure and maintains continuity, thus shifting attention
> from plot to character . . . Characters act as if they have been going about their

daily lives from one primetime evening's programme to the following week's episode. And writers often encourage the notion that the characters lead off-screen lives. (Porter *et al.* 24)

It is not only time paradoxes that provide *Eureka* with its unique structural elements supporting the development of well-defined, believable characters. *Eureka* seems to take the middle ground with its application of the time travel device, falling somewhere between a method of extending romantic anticipation and a science-fiction-based logical puzzle. Although the aborted timeline is a scientific puzzle that has physical effects upon the plot structure of the series, its primary interest to the viewer is the disruption of two romantic relationships and one friendship. We are convinced that Henry's romance with Kim can never come back and Carter will have to be very patient in his attempts to regain Allison. Resolution of the romance has been delayed and closure, once given, has been withdrawn. Moreover, the time travel event in season one of *Eureka* reveals a conspiracy that is the backbone of the narrative arc in season two. We discover that Kim's fatal accident in season one is actually the result of sabotage by the town's psychotherapist, Beverly Barlowe, and the narrative follows the puzzle of her motives and the extent of her actions. This interlocking of story arcs (in this case, time travel and conspiracy theory) is another characteristic of modern complex TV narrative. Writers employ several puzzles and relationship trajectories throughout the course of a show so that, as one element is resolved, another can take its place. The audience is rewarded for its attention with the gratification of a mystery solved, while other, potentially more intriguing problems, are introduced. Michael Z. Neuman presents an interesting theory for the presence of multiple arcs in modern TV narrative. He posits that multiple arcs are an effective response to the 'sweeps' structure of US television. Sweeps are the Nielsen ratings periods (November, February, May and July) in which intensive analysis of viewing habits are used to set advertising rates for US TV. This means that the networks are very eager to have high points in their plot structures at these times to encourage viewers to watch their shows (Newman 24). Although the sweeps may have been the initial reason for developing story arcs that end before the final show of a season, the timing may not be so important in this day of DVD, PVR and cable rebroadcasts. *Eureka*, for example, does not necessarily fit into the traditional pattern as it is one of the new breed of cable shows that are not shown in the traditional fall to spring cycle; its broadcast cycle started in July for all five seasons. The 'high points' in the narrative seem to be timed at roughly bi-monthly intervals in the season schedule rather than in the Nielsen sweep months.

Eureka as a Science-Fiction Drama

Eureka incorporates a number of science-fiction tropes that appear to be unrelated to time travel in its narrative, but they are not primary signifiers of the narrative.

For example, in 'Games People Play' (2.4) Carter is accidentally immersed in a virtual reality in which all of the people important to him disappear from the town. Although it is not a time travel story, this narrative structure uses the same technique of mutability to reveal the emotional core of the protagonist. Jack learns that he must accept that he depends upon his daughter and his friends for his sense of self and wellbeing. We may contrast this with a standard episodic narrative in which the protagonist's reality is more or less fixed and the character can rarely undergo change. Jane Feuer believes that this is true even for serial forms: 'It is not correct to say that characters change in prime-time continuing serials. More often they perpetuate the narrative by continuing to make the same mistakes. Rather, owing to the multiple plot structure, characters' positions shift in relation to other characters' (Feuer 127–8). The audience is subject to constant variability in elements that are, in other series, fixed. In *Eureka*, the underlying principle seems to invite the viewer to accept that Carter cannot rely on any aspect of his existence to remain stable. This is, in fact, a good technique to represent life in contemporary society. In this episode, the basic environmental changes are withdrawn as soon as Carter realizes that he is living in a virtual reality, but afterwards he says to Henry that it is terrible to remember events that did not really happen. Ironically, for Henry this is the truth, since he chose to keep his memories of the aborted time line of season one. Indeed, this episode, although it does not actually use the trope of time travel, serves as an extended commentary upon the impact of the time loop upon the character's lives.

This episode additionally serves as a paradigm for the fifth and final season of *Eureka*, which also employs the trope of virtual reality to explore the possibilities of emotional changes in the primary characters' lives. In season five, the central protagonists are trapped in a computer generated virtual world that leaves them to believe that they have lost four years of their lives. The similarity to the time loop of season two is inescapable. The plot structures of *Eureka* tend to have their own loops based on variations upon a theme. One of the primary aspects of the narrative complexity of *Eureka* is the long-term emotional development of Jack Carter. Like time travel, the wacky, science-fiction happenings in the town of Eureka only serve to motivate and illuminate his journey to emotional maturity. Virtual reality is just another device that serves to rewrite the basic premise of the series and give Carter a chance to mature without altering his basic, nice guy character.

Why Time Travel?

The basic idea of a mutable narrative line in which characters and events can be rewritten is not new to television and it is one of the reasons why time travel stories are so popular. Steven Moffat, showrunner for *Doctor Who*, points this out in an interview in 2010 in which he is discussing the *Doctor Who* Christmas special 'A Christmas Carol':

I love 'A Christmas Carol', it's a fantastic story. Even 'It's a Wonderful Life' is really sort of 'A Christmas Carol'. Time travel at Christmas says 'A Christmas Carol' and it says 'Doctor Who'. The moment you think of it, if you have the Doctor as the Ghost of Christmas Past, it sort of makes sense. ('Christmases Past, Present and Sci-Fi')

Moffat is pointing out that Dickens' novella *A Christmas Carol* is really a time travel story, in which Scrooge is given the option of choosing the future and that Frank Capra's film *It's A Wonderful Life* (1946) uses the same mechanism. In *It's A Wonderful Life*, James Stewart's character, George Bailey, is shown a possible world in which he has never existed. As in Dickens' *A Christmas Carol* or the *Eureka* episode, 'The Games People Play', the important aspect is not the mechanism of the change, be it time travel, virtual reality, or the fiat of an angel, it is the inherent mutability of life's narrative. From time to time we all wonder what would happen if we had decided to do things differently. In these works of fiction, we are given the option to carry these speculations to their logical conclusions.

Variations Upon a Theme of Time Travel

In the episode entitled 'I Do Over' (3.4), *Eureka*'s plot follows a time loop again. On the day that Allison is to remarry her ex-husband, Nathan, Carter is stuck in a plot structure resembling the 1993 Harold Ramis film *Groundhog Day*. Like Bill Murray's *Groundhog Day* character, Phil, Carter relives the same experiences of a single day over and over. Carter is the only person aware that time is repeating and he has the nightmarish experience of trying to convince people that he knows what will happen later in the day. As the iterations of the day increase, Carter discovers that the time loop has been caused by Leo Weinbrenner, a researcher attempting to prevent the end of his employment. Carter is finally able to convince Nathan of the time loop and offers to manually change the machine that is creating the disturbance. Nathan points out that Carter is not technically capable of making the necessary changes and sacrifices himself to finally correct the time loop. The episode ends with a tragic scene in which Carter informs Allison that Nathan will not be marrying her because he has disappeared into the time fault.

The *Eureka* writers have developed a number of the primary variations upon the theme of time travel as an effective method for furthering their narrative goals. 'I Do Over' uses time travel as a device to develop strong tragic themes in a fashion similar to the series' first example of time travel in which the romantic tension between the two chief protagonists of the series, Carter and Allison, is resolved and then eradicated. Contemporary serial television often uses romantic tension between two characters in order to maintain the interest of the audience. For example, both *The X-Files* and *Buffy the Vampire Slayer* (1997–2003) employ difficult romantic relationships as part of the serialized structure of their narratives.

In the first, protagonists Scully and Mulder develop a relationship that slowly and inevitably progresses towards the romantic conclusion. The second develops a relationship between title character, Buffy, and Angel that results in disaster, and eventual separation through spinoff. *Eureka*'s writers have hit upon a solution to the narrative conundrum of an inevitable relationship; they use time travel to reset the situation. The tension between Carter and Allison is released, then tragically reset, which allows the writers to employ the developing relationship as a narrative arc that lasts throughout the entire series without ever devolving into a situation in which the audience gives up all hope of a happy end. 'I Do Over' cleverly shifts Carter's struggle against an obvious antagonist (Nathan) to a framework in which he must comfort his beloved for the heroic sacrifice of his rival.

The Never Ending Character

In season three we see another variation upon the science-fiction trope of time travel, when an efficiency expert, Eva Thorne, is placed in control of General Dynamics. Thorne wreaks havoc in the tightly-knit community, by cutting jobs and benefits in order to turn the research facility into a viable profit-making company. However, it seems that beyond her desire to reform General Dynamics' business practices, she has a peculiar interest in the history of the community. While the narrative arc concerning Allison's marriage to her ex-husband is being resolved in 'I Do Over,' Thorne discovers and reopens an underground research facility beneath Eureka that has been closed since 1937. By the end of 'From Fear to Eternity' (3.8), Thorne's narrative arc is finished. She is revealed as a former worker at the old facility that predates Eureka. In the accident that resulted in the sealing of the facility Eva was made immortal and is now 107 years old. At the end of the episode she leaves Eureka to take up a new identity and Carter is fired for aiding in her escape. This arc introduces a common science-fiction trope that is closely related to time travel: the immortal person. Rather than hinging upon paths not taken and unresolved paradoxes, stories about immortals present the audience with a narrative that can contrast the past with the present in a very concrete way. Human mortality is foregrounded and the mutable nature of our physical bodies is emphasized.

Time Enough for Love

As the series progresses *Eureka* continues to develop a pattern of using time travel as a device for altering the course of romantic relationships. In the eleventh episode of season three 'Insane in the P-Brain' a new character, Tess Fontana, is introduced. She becomes an alternate love interest for Carter and adds emotional complication to the time travel-related disruption of Carter and Allison's series-long romance. By the final episode of the third season Carter's relationship with Tess appears to be at an end as she has decided to leave Eureka and take a job in Australia. This device enables the audience to spend the season hiatus waiting for the reestablishment of the Carter/Allison romance that has been a core arc of the series plot structure, but, instead of fulfilling these expectations, the writers choose to introduce another instance of time travel and reset the romantic arc yet again. 'Founders Day,' the first episode of the fourth and penultimate season of Eureka, has Carter, Henry, Allison and two other members of the central cast of the show transported back to 1947. This instance of time travel is mechanically different than the plot device used in the first season. In the first instance, Henry and Carter's consciousness are transported to their already existing bodies four years in the past. When this happens, Henry and Carter are suddenly aware of things that have happened in their own futures and behave accordingly. In 'Founder's Day' the five protagonists are physically transported to a time in which they do not yet exist. This means that they are strangers to the people in the military base that is Eureka in 1947 and, given the Cold War environment of the time, they are arrested. They manage to escape custody and return to the future with the assistance of Dr Trevor Grant, but find that the timeline has been significantly altered by their interference in Eureka's past. Since Trevor manages to come along with them there are now six time travellers who have had an effect upon the past (the five original cast members through their presence in 1947 and Trevor Grant through his absence after 1947). Some of the changes wrought by the journey are relatively minor, but the personal and romantic situations of the five original travellers have changed significantly. Carter's renewed relationship with Allison becomes difficult because, in this altered reality, Tess does not take the job in Australia and she is moving in with Carter. Although Allison regrets that Carter is again out of her reach, because her autistic son is a normal, outgoing teenager in this new reality she resists any effort to go back and repair the damage to the timeline. Henry arrives in the new reality to discover that he is happily married to a woman that he only knows by name in his original timeline. Both of the other two time travellers, Deputy Jo Lupo and Douglas Fargo, have also lost significant romantic relationships in the shuffle.

In this altered reality all of the time travellers manage to maintain their memories of the original time line. In fact, many of the plot structures for season four are based upon the fact that the travellers do not know their new roles in the altered time line. Carter needs to find out about his relationship to Tess; Allison is constantly irritating her son because she treats him like the invalid he was in the original time line; Lupo mourns her lost romance; and Fargo finds it hard to go from flunky to boss of General Dynamics. The impending disaster of the altered time line in season one is, in this instance of time travel, conveniently ignored. As a plot device it is, therefore, quite different. In the first and second seasons, time travel is a cosmic taboo and Carter is required to go back and correct the error that Henry has made. In this season, the alterations to the time line seem to be unimportant to the world as a whole and all of the significant consequences are personal. This is in keeping with the idea that serialized plots traditionally focus upon relationships in order to maintain continuity. However, time travel in this later instance does provide a wealth of comic devices for the writers. The fact that the five primary characters of the series are thrust into roles for which they do not have an appropriate background parallels the plots of a traditional comic farce.[1] At first it appears that the deadly serious and tragic consequences of time travel in season one have been replaced by rather more light-hearted emotional considerations, although some aspects of the altered roles are unpleasant for the characters involved. For example, in episode nine of season four, 'I'll be Seeing You', Trevor Grant's efforts to return to his own time result in Allison's death. This tragic event occurs just after Carter and Allison have finally renewed their romantic involvement, so the audience is led to believe that the love will never be successful. Carter manages to save the day by going back in time with Grant to a few moments before his first visit to 1947. This time he manages to plant an audio recording in which he warns himself to protect Allison and the romantic happy end is again possible.

This time travel device is incredibly complex as a narrative structure. The audience must be aware of the entire serial plot structure of *Eureka* in order to fully appreciate the recursive nature of the story. The section of 'I'll be Seeing You' that takes place in 1947 uses numerous clips directly lifted from 'Founder's Day', but they have been cleverly spliced in with new footage showing a second instance of Carter lurking around the military base that will become Eureka. The audience must understand the future that Carter wishes to modify is his *personal* past.

Conclusion

The complex narrative structure of *Eureka* could have failed miserably if the audience did not care enough about the characters and the created world of the series to keep the various plot elements in mind. However, the fourth season of the show was quite successful with 'more than three million total viewers per week' (Seidman). In fact, I believe the narrative excursions based upon time travel are instrumental in *Eureka*'s development of a cult audience. There have been a number of shows in recent times that have employed the device of time travel to reset plot structures (such as *Heroes* 2006–2010, the UK series *Primeval* 2007–2011 and its Canadian spinoff *Primeval: New World* 2012–2013), but none of them have managed to successfully incorporate plot structures of such complexity. One of the reasons for *Eureka*'s success in this effort is the fact that the characters have remained relatively stable throughout the entire exercise, although their relationships with one another have altered. Carter and Henry are positive characters and Allison is a dedicated mother with a strong interest in Carter. The audience does not have to change its opinions concerning Carter, Henry and Allison; they simply have to acknowledge a change in their physical relationships. In this aspect, *Eureka* is more similar to a soap opera than many other shows in its ostensible genre. Moreover, because the show maintains hope for a reestablishment of the desired relationships, it would seem that it is at least partially focused upon a female target audience, rather like CW's long-running Superman story, *Smallville* (2001–2011). *Eureka*, unlike most science-fiction television, is not so much about the wonders of science as it is a story about believable characters and their relationships.

Notes

1. For example, in Shakespeare's *Twelfth Night*, Viola must learn to behave like a man while dealing with romantic longings that are 'inappropriate' considering the role she is playing.

4

Timeslip: Putting Aside Childish Things

Pete Boss

In 1970 ATV aired the first series of *Timeslip*, the channel's entry into children's science-fiction, and a self-conscious effort to compete with the BBC's output, in particular *Doctor Who*[1]. After the success of the pilot, it was eventually extended to four series, comprising 26 episodes which were shown in the early evening (5.30pm on Mondays) over 1970–1971 and repeated over 1973–1974. A novelization of the first two stories was written by Bruce Stewart in 1970.[2]

Despite strong fan interest evidenced in its excellent official website, *Timeslip.org.uk*, the series has received only passing reference in scholarly accounts of television science-fiction. Possibly one of the contributing factors to this dearth of analysis is the industrial dispute which prevented some of the 26 episodes being filmed in colour, and the subsequent loss of colour masters for all but one episode; the series being available today only from 16mm transfers in black and white with the exception of episode six of season two.[3]

However, *Timeslip* deserves closer examination, both as a successful and challenging example of children's television science-fiction in its own right, and for its remarkably complex approach to issues of science and technology unusual for children's programming of the time. Today one is struck by its relentless scepticism about the consequences of scientific progress, running counter to contemporary educationalist approaches to science and technology (see Robins, 11). This chapter will concentrate on the ways that *Timeslip* offers an education for its young protagonists, almost wholly at odds with the more technophile discourse of children's television of the day, developed though critically dystopian encounters with possible futures, as well as the past. Of particular concern will be the way that *Timeslip*'s technophobic future nightmares are established in relation to the protagonists in their present of 1970, as well as within the wartime national past of 1940, to form a coherently critical view of technocracy and intellectual elitism.

The story centres on the adventures of two holidaying adolescents, Liz Skinner (Cheryl Burfield) and Simon Randall (Spencer Banks), whose discovery of an invisible Time Barrier leads them to experience alternative possible futures and also to visit the past. These transports include disturbing future dystopian visions of a world dominated by authoritarian and technocratic rule, but crucially begin with a journey into the wartime past at a nearby military research base. Here they meet the charismatic figure of Commander Traynor (Dennis Quilley), a soldier/technocrat whose hubris and manipulation of the children contributes to what becomes an often brutal *rite de passage* for the children as they seek to return to their family life in the 1970s, while helping to avert future disasters. All of these stories are bound together by the personal connections of the central characters (Liz's father is revealed to have been a victim of wartime scientific research at the base) as they encounter alternative versions of themselves and others playing key roles in each future scenario, and which forms the basis of the series' cautionary perspective on attitudes to science and technology.

In the first story 'The Wrong End of Time', the Skinner family, comprising father Frank, mother Jean, and daughter Liz are taking Simon Randall, the son of Frank's recently-widowed best friend, on holiday with them. Exploring a nearby derelict Ministry of Defence site, a former naval research station near St Oswald in Rutland, the children slip through an invisible 'time barrier' into 1940 when the station was still active, and are caught up in an attempted Nazi commando raid to steal secret scientific research and technology. The Nazi leader, officer and scientist Gottfried, is in many ways characterized as the opposite number of the manipulative British scientist and project chief Commander Traynor. This is the beginning of a series of adventures in time for the children, during which they experience two alternate and heavily dystopian near futures set in 1990. Here, technological research and its unrestrained application are shown to have horrific consequences, as we witness experiments upon helpless human 'volunteers' (Story 2: 'The Time of the Ice Box') and the destruction of the environment (Story 3: 'The Year of the Burn Up'). Returning from these futures, the children discover their origins in secret research programmes of the recent past and the present (Story 4: 'The Day of the Clone').

Although *Timeslip* was conceived originally as a single story, the resultant series is surprisingly coherent due to consistent narrative and thematic elements. The unremarkable plotline in which the children try to avert future disasters is rendered more compelling and politically interesting here, by the simultaneous attempt to avoid the children themselves becoming, in those futures, victims or agents of the various technological nightmares they encounter. It is this issue of their participation and of agency which gives the series its more critically dystopian edge.

Moreover, these issues are given a wider historical and national context through the first story and its setting in 1940; British wartime military research is here given a more sinister countenance than its customary 'backroom boys' mythology encourages, and it is suggested, ultimately, to be inseparable from the technological dystopianism we go on to witness in the future, and indeed the present.

Science and Children's TV

Timeslip's main science-related discourses tend to be split, in a relatively traditional formulation, between more speculative arguments explaining the show's central narrative device of time-slippage, and its presentation of the applied scientific research and technology which provide the basis for its technophobia. The former is constructed first of all through the appeal to scientific wonder common to many children's television programmes of the time (see below) not to mention the various magazines (including the children's spin-off from the *TV Times*, *Look-In*, in which the series appeared in comic strip form). As well as the supporting references to scientific advisor Geoffrey Hoyle, the first two episodes featured a brief introductory piece-to-camera by well-known science journalist Peter Fairley who, as news science editor for *ITN* and *TV Times*, was well-known to viewers (including youth audiences) from his coverage of the Apollo missions in the Sixties: 'It's fiction, of course, but it's very close to a new theory scientists are now working on to explain the universe, and time. Today's science-fiction so often becomes tomorrow's science fact' (Introduction to 'The Wrong End of Time').

Fairley's endorsement establishes a comfortably familiar viewing framework for the early evening family audience, who were, by then, regularly entertained by programmes featuring strong scientific components of 'how things work' interest. These included *How* (1966–1981), *Blue Peter* (1958–) and *Magpie* (1968–1980), and there was a parallel market in magazines such as *Look and Learn* (1962–1982), as well as a weekly TV spinoff of the Gerry Anderson technophile adventure series *TV Century 21* (1965–1971)[4]. This mirrored the general surge of confidence in a newly modernized nation where technological mastery and change featured strongly in Britain's national self-image in which:

> future generations were going to be different not only because they never had to know the hardships of economic poverty and war, but because they would be entirely familiar and at ease with the coming technologic world of the space age: the future of rockets, computers, plastics and all the myriad electronic gadgets and marvels of 'Tomorrow's World'. (Cook 95)[5]

This pro-technological content was reinforced by science documentary programming which comprised a strong component of the BBC's Reithian mandate.

Timothy Boon discerns that by the end of the 1950s some of the prominent debate about science broadcasting had now focussed rather narrowly on science in and for itself to the exclusion of wider issues:

> [T]here was nothing that looked at all like the science in the service of social welfare ... and which had come to be associated with the political left. There is a hint here of Cold War attitudes affecting what types of science were to be represented ... [Scientific experts and commentators] may have differed on what the precise focus of television science should be, but they all emphasized the transmission of the content of modern science, rather than its effects. (Boon 221)[6]

Breaking with much of the contemporary television discourse of scientific wonder directed at children, *Timeslip* constructs a classic technophobic vision of human society and values imperilled by overreaching scientists. Ironically, the series is unusually far-sighted in the range of technology depicted, which includes lasers, drug testing, cloning, tidal barriers and environmental issues, all of which are misused and co-opted by the technocratic Whitehall elite. A refusal simply to readmit technology as the solution to technologically created problems is a clear concern of writer Bruce Stewart who criticized:

> political philosophers and social engineers who work out a theory and then require the race to be fitted to it. I remember when high-rise flats started in England there was a marked increase in the incidence of neurosis among the dwellers. The answer was not that we should go back to living on the ground as we had (mostly) done, but that there should be an increase in psychiatric facilities to assist the afflicted. (in Robins 10)

Timeslip's central plot device – time slippage – crucially evades the instrumental use of technology embodied by a time machine. The techno-mastery and relative sanctuary of *Doctor Who*'s *avant la lettre* steampunk TARDIS is rejected. Roland Barthes comments, suggestively, on Jules Verne's appeal to children through the security of the vessel which always promises resolution and that while:

> the ship may well be a symbol for departure; it is, at a deeper level, the emblem of closure ... To like ships is first and foremost to like a house, a superlative one since it is unremittingly closed, and not at all vague sailings into the unknown: a ship is a habitat before being a means of transport. (Barthes 66)

Such a sense of secure enclosure and of control is virtually absent as the children simply pass through the invisible barrier which may, or may not, send or return them to their desired destination in time, including their own present of

1970; the various technologically-determined spaces encountered are, in general, nightmarishly claustrophobic and it is only the domestic space of home and its echo in the community of misfits in 'The Year of the Burn Up' which offer such security.

The Home Audience and Intimacy

Broadcast just after 5pm, *Timeslip* addressed a substantial family audience for whom the protagonists might appear unremarkable or typical, within the rather middle-class conventions of extensive TV performance at the time. The cosy familiarity of the present in 1970 is established through the reassuring iconography of the village hostelry in St Oswald (ostensibly Rutland via Ambridge) and the Skinner's home; while offering a schematic rather than dense level of mise en scène, these are effective enough as a clear point of social and cultural anchorage. Though functioning largely to establish the family's typical qualities, it nevertheless reinforces thematic issues through artwork on the wall of Liz's bedroom, marking her interests as less bookish than Simon's, and that of the living room which contrasts with later pictures in a Whitehall office that appear to be inspired by scientific subjects. In a similar vein, the gypsy caravan and the presence of Borrow's *Lavengro* also hint, in the first episode, at a lifestyle opposed to the world of the Technocrats.

Cook and Wright argue that such an intimate context for British science-fiction TV was advantageous, enabling its ideas-led approach to work in relative freedom and with a potency specific to it as a medium:

> SF TV practitioners were able to reach right inside the home, communicating powerful messages and where necessary manipulating audiences' fears, because programmes were watched by viewers in their own private space with all their public defences down and so in that sense they became personal. (Cook and Wright 3)

Timeslip takes this audience and establishes spaces familiar enough to have featured in the everyday goings-on of the soap opera *Crossroads* (1964–1988), which preceded it by half an hour, then contrasts them with visions of a Britain past and present. Though initially appearing distanced and detached from 1970, both wartime past and technocratic future are ultimately drawn together in ways that effectively construct critically dystopian perspectives on *Timeslip*'s present. Much debate exists about the concept of the 'critical dystopia', and I wish to argue that *Timeslip* may be accurately described as one, as a text which, in Constance Penley's words, moves beyond providing the mere spectacle of future disaster 'to suggest causes rather than merely reveal symptoms' (122).

Such causes are established through implicating the series' present, and the wartime past in scientific atrocities of the near future, revealing the consequences of unquestioning attitudes to the use of science and technology, and through the ways that its characters, especially the children, are obliged to reflect on their own potential for complicity. The show comprises a series of juxtaposed and related moments of past, present and possible futures in which the protagonists are potential agents rather than simply witnesses. *Timeslip*'s nightmare future visions resonate with the technological imperatives of the Cold War sublime; fantasies of scientific mastery in clandestine research establishments, sanctioned and enforced by a Technocrat government. Counter to the flow of the educationalist discourse of children's programming, *Timeslip*'s critical and oppositional account is constructed around three main axes. The first establishes future dystopianism firmly within the familiar terrain of the British wartime past and the present of 1970; the second is a sustained criticism of technocratic elitism which is strongly marked as patriarchal; and the third is through the alternative, if tentative, utopian community established in 'The Year of the Burn Up'.

The Wartime Past and the Cold War

The Ministry of Defence base, derelict in 1970, nevertheless conveys an aura of Cold War military secrecy in its dilapidated but potent iconography of fences and bunkers and 'Keep Out' signs. Thrown back to 1940, just prior to the night-time German commando raid, the children are interrogated by the military whose classified work is 'too important for policemen' and where we establish a consistent theme of scientific imperatives liberated from ethical constraints, which lead to ordinary people being patronized and abused. The myth of humble backroom labs, where distracted but brilliant boffins earnestly toil like Santa's elves to save the nation, is soon deflated[7]. Though we see white-coated lab workers earnestly staring at radar monitors, they are marginalized and the drama soon centres on Traynor and his German counterpart Gottfried as a brilliant warrior/scientist. The German soldiers are portrayed largely within wartime thriller conventions through unnecessary brutality, while Gottfried is given a more urbane and rational portrayal; the soldiers speak in untranslated German, but Gottfried has perfect English, having studied at Cambridge before the war. As well as having the Cold War resonance of spying, this characterization serves to place the two naval officers as part of an elite, and future dialogue and events confirm this. Discussing, over cigars and brandy, their pre-war research correspondence it becomes clear that they see themselves as naturally apart from the other characters. This elitism is soon extended to Simon, whose 1970s knowledge and natural ability appeals to both the officers; each will try to manipulate Simon by appealing to his fascination with science – Gottfried soon has him at work with a soldering iron.

Though featuring some elements of the Cold War thriller (the pub landlord is exposed in the present as a German fifth columnist; Gottfried is feared to now be 'with the Russians'), later episodes defuse such anxieties with several references to collaboration with the Russians. Tony Shaw notes that spy fiction peaked in the early 1960s, and that there was the beginning of a 'new phase from the early 1960s in which the cinema's overall support for Cold War orthodoxy mingled with cynical asides about the lamentable dimensions of an increasingly claustrophobic and authoritarian conflict' (2001: 194).

It is this relationship of Cold War science and authoritarianism that *Timeslip* addresses, and the Ministry of Defence base serves, in tandem with its ghostly deserted twin in the present, as a master template for a series of heterotopic spaces which, echoing each other, function ultimately as cautionary variations upon the same theme. The research station establishes ideas of wartime scientific experimentation that take on a more sinister cast for a later generation: less backroom wizardry than *Brave New World* (1932).

Gottfried's pan-scientific appeals cast a long shadow over future episodes featuring enforced prosthetic implants in 'The Day of the Icebox'[8], and Technocratic elites trying to eliminate communities of 'Misfits' in 'The Year of the Burn Up'. In the final 'Year of the Clone' the images of elderly people being marched along for the latest in a series of failed drug tests are genuinely disturbing in their echoes of the Holocaust.

According to series creator Ruth Boswell, *Timeslip* consciously played down the hardware elements typical to science-fiction, focussing instead on imaginative content (2013), and this was no doubt an advantage given the low budget constraints visible in the studio sets and restricted use of location. Yet there is some genuine benefit from the hermetic quality of these sets, which intensifies our sense of the claustrophobia and totality of the dystopian world they seek to represent.

Writing of such constraints, Cook and Wright argue for their capacity to make a 'virtue of necessity' and that British science-fiction television:

> was ideas-led, though on the level of plot, character and situation rather than having the luxury of detailed descriptive re-creations of alternative worlds axiomatic of literary science-fiction. Its plots often functioned as metaphors or allegories, reflecting wider social and cultural preoccupations at the time of their production, particularly political tensions, or anxieties about the effects of new technology. (Cook and Wright 3)

It is not the modest mise en scène of future technology that is effective here, but the relations of the various time-shifted 'variations on a theme' that generate their critical value, crucially feeding back on the narrative's present of the 1970s, and not merely constructing reified and frozen visions of future catastrophes. For Frederic Jameson such a vision would 'not seriously attempt to imagine the "real" future of our social system. Rather, its multiple mock futures serve the quite different function of transforming our own present into the determinate past of something yet to come' (2005: 288).

Thus *Timeslip*'s dystopian episodes reflect back on each other, implicating present and past, and the momentum and secrecy of scientific research appears driven from within Britain, rather than in response to external threats typical of Cold War discourse (the series is notably free from two symptomatic elements: invasion and nuclear threat).

The Scientist and Intellectual Elitism

While future stories introduce the stereotypically unhinged figure of scientist Morgan C. Devereux (John Barron, speaking in what sounds like mid-Atlantic Dalek), he functions to confirm Traynor as a far more nuanced and plausible figure. Ultimately technological disaster is attributed less to the hubris of rogue scientists than to the establishment as a whole; an establishment, moreover, which at times involves the future participation of our protagonists.

We first encounter Commander Traynor at ease in the local hotel bar at St Oswald, dressed in a style suggestive of a middle class milieu somewhat above that of the children and their families and amongst the horse-brasses and log fire mise en scène he appears every inch a member of the local gentry. Though an establishment figure *par excellence,* he is nevertheless a figure of some complexity and ambivalence, as we encounter him at different moments throughout his career as naval commander: Whitehall scientific mandarin, fugitive, prisoner and even clone. While smugly patrician, authoritarian and advocating extreme technocratic positions, he is neither conventional egghead nor boffin, and the main concession to the iconography of mad science is a rather bouffant hairstyle evocative of large foreheads in 1950's science-fiction movies such as *This Island Earth* (1955). Significantly, his character also undergoes experiences in which he is victim and fugitive from a world created in part by his own actions.

Though Andrew Tudor identifies mad scientists to be in some decline in 1970s horror cinema, television was arguably the beneficiary: *Quatermass*, the character and the trilogy of original BBC dramas, 'helped establish two of the key characteristics of British TV SF: the centrality of the scientist and the reflection of Cold War fears' (Cook and Wright 2006: 7), and their increasing adoption of an 'anti-establishment stance'. The figure of Professor Bernard Quatermass played a pivotal role in establishing the scientist as integrated into society, or at least the establishment[9] and images of mad scientists, as lone maniacs in exotic and isolated locales, gave way in the postwar years to narratives in which 'scientific discovery has simply become part of the order of things' (Cook and Wright 146).

Partly in the tradition of a Bernard Quatermass, Traynor is less heroic; as antagonist, his representation of establishment science is that of urbane and self-sufficient scientific mandarin ('answerable only to the Prime Minister') and this well-groomed image of masculine authority evokes Fred Inglis' description of political establishment mouthpieces during the Cold War: 'They acted out in public and for our benefit those qualities of manly and womanly character on which our great nations so depend: niceness, resolution, efficacity, decisiveness, calm, charm, courage, and a dapper suit' (1992: 437).

Laura Forster also notes changes taking place in 1970s series such as *Doomwatch* (1970–1972) and *Survivors* (1975–1977), in the emerging characters of 'the 1970s "dropout" scientists ... [who] ... in tune with issues of contemporary Britain, split their profession and can be seen in direct opposition to the ambitious, driven, Faustian over-reacher seen in other science-fiction' (Forster, 2009: 90). Such representations of the scientist, less melodramatically performed and written (less 'mad') were also appropriate, in Forster's view, to the televisual space:

> [W]ith fewer special effects at a television director's disposal, smaller budgets, and pressure to make use of 'free' studio space rather than expensive location shooting, scientists were necessarily less outlandish characters. Televisual practices lent themselves to the close-up and the medium shot, the domestic or small-scope setting, and fixed-camera techniques. This, I suggest, necessitated a different kind of portrayal of the scientist (79).

The scientific intellectual elite's indifference to the feelings and interests of everyone else is marked by increasingly extreme abuses of ordinary citizens. Frank Skinner, a rating at the base during the war, is lastingly traumatized by the effects of technology Traynor orders him to sabotage; the scientist's lack of compassion is emphasized as the events of 1940 are intercut with Traynor's lofty rationalizations to the Skinners in the present and to which Frank angrily replies: 'And what did our little investigations into 1940 teach me? Only that I'd been mug enough to get in the way of one of your "new developments", and been made to suffer for it ever since.'[10]

Stewart's script consistently underlines the arrogance of scientific elites and their potential to play God and this critique of intellectual superiority surfaces early on. Furthermore it is consistently structured across gender discourses as well as a technocratic class hierarchy; later, this informs some bitter jokes between Simon and Liz who are established as a fairly conventional 'chalk and cheese' mismatch. Liz is given a more emotionally-defined, girl-next-door role versus Simon's rather withdrawn 'science geek'; even Liz's father suggests, in response to Liz's negative view of Simon's bookishness that she could read a few more herself. In 1940, Simon's ability and interests earn him special attention from the scientists and his helpfulness with the equipment (or collaboration, from another perspective) is pointedly contrasted in one well-composed shot with Liz doing the dishes in the foreground; though herself marginalized by performing domestic duties, she also participates in these hierarchies by commenting on Sarah, the mentally handicapped and visibly distressed farm girl, as 'not very bright'. Meanwhile, in the present Traynor has been enjoying his superiority over the Skinners with complex scientific speculations about the Time Barrier; when Jean protests he says, smugly, 'what would you suggest?' knowing she does not know.

Superior intellect and IQ resurface constantly in future stories as the justification for callous indifference to actual human beings, and in 'The Time of the Icebox' the children meet the first of their possible future selves in 1990 in which Dr Joynton defers to things she doesn't need to know, but which 'various superbrains would'. More significantly, a grown-up Liz, now calling herself Beth, has been given an intelligence-enhancing drug rendering her as aloof and heartless as the rest of the scientists, telling Liz (in an effective reversal of her earlier comments about the farm girl) 'I was a little idiot when I was you'. By 'The Day of the Burn Up' Liz's intellectual ability is given a more extended treatment as the infallible computer has decided that she and Simon's future selves are intellectually incompatible and thus non-viable as a couple: she a 'D minus' to his 'A Plus'. Complaining furiously to Beth that it's 'the worst thing I've ever heard', Beth replies sarcastically 'No, Liz. It's progress.' Beth refuses the machine's judgements, and, as a future Liz, begins to enlighten her past self. This initiates a series of running and bitter ripostes to Simon's insensitivity on the subject, for example: 'Sorry Simon – didn't realise it was A Plus stuff'.

Traynor manipulates the children, and his decisiveness, status and confidence suggest the kind of assertive and successful father figure absent from their backgrounds. Both fathers (best of friends) are 'absent' in some sense: Simon's, an amiable unassuming character, appears fleetingly when they go back five years to 1965 and Frank is established, through both plot and Derek Benfield's sensitive performance, as a man whose wartime trauma caused a breakdown. His distracted manner exemplifies a consistent sense of his ineffectuality as he fails constantly to grasp the nature of the children's experiences (functioning partly as the 'disbeliever,' common in science-fiction stories), and his business ventures are unsuccessful. Traynor is, by contrast, the very image of the successful male; however, his relationship with the two children is inflected in different ways. Significantly Liz is more sceptical about him and his works, while Simon's knowledge of science is easily exploited through Traynor's flattery. Ruth Boswell's initial vision of the project was centred on the idea of Liz's encounter with her own father (2013) and this strand of the narrative is one of two main threads, along with the relationship of Simon and Traynor, which work rather in counterpoint. Liz is distinguished by more intuitive qualities through her mother's psychic ability to link with her daughter across time, and she is, throughout, more sympathetic to the circumstances and feelings of individuals. Her relationship with her father, Traynor's victim, is positive by contrast with Simon's initial fascination with the scientist's work; as the classic stereotype of the young male nerd, appealing constantly to logic and prodigiously familiar with science and technology, he is something of a *Joe 90* (1968–1969) lookalike, bookish and with large spectacles. His ability to grasp new developments in technology and science, while reasoning aloud, serves to deliver expository material to the viewer, but this initial wonder diminishes as he is steadily caught up in the negative consequences of Traynor's world. Simon's relationship with Traynor reveals the dangers and illusions of an uncritical fascination with technology.

At first glance, this split of emotionally-sensitive women versus cool and rational men appears simply to reproduce some of the classic gender stereotypes of popular science-fiction, yet they provide the mainspring for one of *Timeslip*'s more potent critiques. Joy Leman has discussed how changes in women's social roles during the 1960s began to provoke a shift in serious television science-fiction drama, arguing, for instance, that by the time of *A for Andromeda* (1961) the female characters were given more central roles within the actual scientific, rather than domestic, discourses of the drama and that, though flawed, they were 'no longer the groupies of Quatermass' found in the three *Quatermass* serials of the 1950s (Leman 1991: 122). *Timeslip* takes rather a different tack as Liz encounters her IQ-boosted scientist future Other, Beth, whose unpleasantness and insensitivity reveal her simply to have adopted the worst aspects of the male-dominated technocracy. The final critical perspective on this is established through *Timeslip*'s questioning of traditional educational philosophy as part of the Misfits' alternative vision of society.

The Counterculture as Utopia

In 'The Year of the Burn Up' the zeitgeist is most acutely evident as the children are thrown into an alternate 1990 Britain pitched somewhere between the Wellsian and the Orwellian. Sanctuary is found in a rebel community of so-called Misfits being persecuted by Technocrats whose Technological Master Plan again evokes fantasies of Cold War technological mastery; maps of grids and infrastructures echo the civil defence measures so witheringly exposed as ineffective in Peter Watkins' *The War Game* (1965) five years earlier. In this future, international collaborations involve the Russians melting their sections of the polar ice caps in a global effort to subdue Nature once and for all: 'There are few things as wasteful, cumbersome and unproductive as a flower . . . something had to be done about natural forms in general.'

The ensuing global catastrophe of the 'Burn Up'[11] is the cause of the tropical jungle[12] at which the children arrive, soon revealed to be 'darkest Buckinghamshire'. Here the children encounter alternate selves whose dissent from the Technocracy forms part of their ongoing education. In Simon's case it is 2957, and he is a technocrat controller of wavering commitment, while Liz once again meets Beth who, in this future, is not a scientist but an artist leading the Misfit commune. Dominated by women and children (a young David Thewlis among them) the commune is Bruce Stewart's countercultural riposte to the patriarchal Technocrats; its collectivist activities dedicated to art and self-fulfilment while subsisting off the land in the face of impending eco-disaster. The Misfits' ethos is strongly suggestive of holistic educationalist philosophy which formed part of the 1960s counterculture and the machine's pronouncements about Liz/Beth's abilities are rejected as she says to Simon that 'all the computer's test result told me was that I was myself and not somebody else'. This individualist defiance is directed both to the standardization of the Technocracy's cloning programme and to contemporary education when she later tells Liz her 'D plus' is because 'your teachers didn't know how to encourage your talents – let it flow'.

The Misfits' community, however rudimentary and fragile it appears in the face of the global catastrophe, completes the critique of technological and intellectual elitism. Not self-consciously Luddite, it simply shows a society existing happily in adversity and against the technological grain; it is such broadly Utopian qualities that give *Timeslip* much of its unusually critical dystopian force. Following Tom Moylan, Frederic Jameson distinguishes between those dystopias which are anti-utopian 'given the way in which they are informed by a central passion to denounce and to warn against utopian programs in the political realm' (2005: 199), and those which still retain a sense of utopian potential: 'The critical dystopia is a negative cousin of the utopia proper, for it is in the light of some positive conception of human social possibilities that its effects are generated and from utopian ideals its politically enabling stance derives' (2005: 198).

Conclusion

Timeslip's pessimism about technology and scientific elites is hardly unusual in science-fiction, but its place in children's television is a unique one, as is its relentless *rite de passage* which visibly takes its toll on the children who return to their own time and their families so much the wiser. Aided by the noticeable changes in the actors over the production – especially Spencer Banks as Simon – we are struck by how much the principal characters develop due to experiences formed through debate and encounters with their possible future selves. There is little time for the sentimental and the childish, as tough choices and grim experiences make this a harsh coming-of-age tale. This quality places the show's account of technological dystopianism, quite properly, within the terms of Darko Suvin's famous account of the science fiction *novum* and particularly in the terms he offers below:

> if SF is organized around an irreversible and significant change in its world and agents, then a simple addition of adventures, where *plus ça change plus c'est la, même chose*, is an abuse of SF for purposes of trivial sensationalism . . . On the contrary, the easiest narrative way of driving a significant change home is to have the hero or heroine grow into it (or better, to have the hero or heroine define it for the reader by growing with it), and much valid SF uses the plot structure of the

'education novel,' with its initially naive protagonist who by degrees arrives at some understanding of the novum for her/himself and for the readers (79).

Significantly this 'education' draws upon countercultural and anti-establishment attitudes of the time, challenging uncritical technophilia not only through environmental perspectives, but prompting the children to re-evaluate their own attitudes; even Traynor himself appears chastened by events resolved neither through *Deus* nor *machina* the series offering neither metaphysical nor technological solutions to the problems encountered, and emphasising instead the crucial role of human actions and accountability. Our parting shot is a moving one, set once again at the Ministry of Defence base. A somewhat dishevelled Traynor stares forlornly after his technocrat double, a clone, despatched into some temporal limbo in search of its own destiny. Meanwhile in long shot we see the Skinners and Simon walking away in the opposite direction, staged as two couples, but with Simon and Liz subdued and sobered by experience.

Notes

1. See also Stewart, B., 'Timeslip Memories Part Two' and *timeslip.org.uk*: for the most detailed and comprehensive account of the series' complex narrative.
2. Currently available in complete (though largely black and white) form, as a 10 hrs 50 mins DVD set from *A & E Television Networks* with retrospective documentary.
3. Much of this vision is clearly evident in the views of principal writer Bruce Stewart. See Robins, T. 'Timeslip' *Starburst* No 91: Time Travel Special, *8*(7) (March 1986) pp. 8–11.
4. Fairley's popular science books include *Project X: The Exciting Story of British Invention* (1970) with a foreword from Harold Wilson whose 1963 'White Heat' speech famously codified the technological optimism of British society's modernizing aspirations.
5. *Tomorrow's World* used a similar title font to *Timeslip* (*Data 70* as opposed to what appears to be *Moore Computer* for the latter), sharing connotations of technology; their Magnetic Ink Character Recognition format being designed for computers.
6. According to Boon: 'The petitioning by scientific organizations of the BBC in the quarter century from 1941 and especially from 1949 was second only to their approaches to government.' This lobbying peaked by time of the Pilkington Committee in 1960, but as he points out 'the scientific elite need not have been concerned about how broadcast showed science because, far from representing it incompetently or in a negative fashion, television producers were keen to convey a view of science that scientists approved of' (237).
7. Popular narrative tropes of 'backroom boys' magically producing technological wonders from minimal resources have also been contradicted by revisionist work which persuasively argues that Britain was, on the contrary, a powerfully well-resourced nation led by a technocratic elite whose prime minister considered technical innovation paramount. See Edgerton, David, *Britain's War Machine* (London, Penguin, 2012).

8. Simon's horror of being the 'first man-machine in the history of the world' is notably the reverse of the concept's heroic reinvention for Lee Majors in *The Six Million Dollar Man* (1974–1978).

9. A development also identified by Christopher Frayling in *Mad, Bad and Dangerous? The Scientist and the Cinema* (London: Reaktion, 2005). See p. 224.

10. The demystification of postwar consensus myths such as 'Blitz Spirit' has been undertaken by Angus Calder in *The Myth of the Blitz*, (London, Jonathan Cape, 1991) but had already surfaced in SF films as noted by I. Q. Hunter regarding *The Day the Earth Caught Fire*'s (1962) questioning of 'the Dunkirk spirit' in Hunter, I. Q. ed., *British Science Fiction Cinema* (London: Routledge, 1999). See also Daniel O'Brien's 'Forward to the Past: Anti-Fascist Allegory and "Blitz Spirit" Revisionism in Daleks' Invasion Earth 2150' A.D. In 'Neighbors', R.C. ed. *The Galaxy is rated G: Essays on Children's Science Fiction and Television* (Jefferson NC: McFarland & Company, Inc., 2011) pp. 97–110.

11. Kim Newman, drawing on Brian Aldiss's term 'cosy catastrophes', notes how many British SF dystopias from Wyndham to Ballard are 'about that national obsession, the weather', Introduction to O'Brien, Daniel SF:UK *How British Science Fiction Changed the World* (London: Reynolds & Hearn Ltd., 2000).

12. One of several unfortunate colonial tropes, as the jungle also provides the setting for *Timeslip*'s only black character, Vera.

5

The *Primeval* Anomaly

John Jeffrey

In a deserted supermarket car park on the edge of a wood, late at night, a woman runs in desperation as a sabre-toothed creature emerges from among the trees. She takes shelter in a large, cylindrical metal bin and, as she shelters, holes appear in it, as if made by giant teeth. She runs on and bangs on the locked sliding doors of an Asda store but the night cleaner has his headphones on, and, although aware of her, ignores her, preferring to carry on polishing the floor and listening to his music. She flees as first trolleys and then cars are overturned behind her by the creature. Her pursuer is a long extinct predator, a mammal-like reptile from the Permian era.

These are the opening moments of the first episode of *Primeval*, a show initially aired on ITV 1 in the UK at Saturday teatime early in 2007, almost inevitably earning it the unenviable reputation of being the commercial channel's answer to the BBC's highly successful *Doctor Who* reboot. *Primeval*'s co-creator, Tim Haines, had previously been a director and producer of the BBC's *Walking with Dinosaurs* (1999) so clearly knew the popular appeal of CGI dinosaurs and their habitat for the TV audience. *Jurassic Park* (1993) had shown that bringing CGI dinosaurs and people together in an adventure could be box office gold. How then to bring these together, on a TV budget, in a popular science-fiction series? The *Primeval* solution to this was the 'anomaly': a portal through which creatures from the pre-human world could enter the present and humans could visit long-vanished versions of Earth's past. The stories played out over the show's five UK series are, to a large extent, all about attempts to contain, understand or exploit these phenomena. In terms of the show's distinctive identity, the anomaly's design provides the wallpaper for the title sequence and the backs of the trading cards that kids were encouraged to buy during its first run on terrestrial TV. Cameron McAllister, the first series' producer, describes them as 'wormholes'...little tiny rips in time [that] have opened up in the worst possible places and creatures from the past and the future have managed to break through and...rampage' ('The Making of...(Season One)'). The loose narrative arc followed by the five seasons of the show is built on the idea, established at the end of the first season, that anomalies in the present might be doorways to future versions of Earth as well as its past. This offers the potential for fantastical creatures from the future in addition to archeologically documented beasts from the past to invade. It also gives a glimpse into a devastated world from which humanity has become extinct and for which human activity may well be responsible. The different kinds of stories accompanying this central arc and the lack of coherence that its developing mythos presents ultimately pose difficulties for the viewer that the final season of the show may not fully resolve.

The first episode of *Primeval* establishes the essential properties of the anomaly, including its look, and positions it in a way that becomes fundamental to many episodes of the show. The first anomaly presented to the viewer appears in the middle of the Forest of Dean. The relatively remote location hides the anomaly from most prying eyes and it becomes one of the norms of the show that the anomaly manifestations, the inciting events of nearly every episode, occur in places that are unlikely to be noticed by very large numbers of people. It is implicit that the anomaly seen here is the one that the creature seen in the opening moments of the show had emerged from. The first episode makes clear, however, that the woman being chased by the creature, Helen Cutter, had disappeared eight years prior to the main events unfolded in the episode and that her absence was as a result of her entering the anomaly and going into the past. This anomaly, then, has either been open for at least eight years continuously or it is a recurring phenomenon at the same location. Its event horizon is revealed to the viewer for the first time in a telling way. A young boy has been keeping a flying reptile, known as Rex, as a pet, having mistaken it for an exotic lizard. It is, in reality, a member of a long extinct species from the Permian era. The disparate individuals who will become the ARC (Anomaly Research Centre) team, and *Primeval*'s principal characters, separately become aware of strange creature sightings in the area and one, Abby Maitland, a zoologist, tries to find out where Rex came from. Searching the woods, it is the boy rather than any of the adult characters who first encounters the anomaly. Rather than reacting to it with terror, he responds with curiosity and a sense of wonder. He explores and leans forward into it. Instead of emerging the other side to see more English woodland, he finds himself looking out into an arid and unfamiliar landscape with a group of the flying reptiles, like Rex, fluttering around a scrubby tree. While he does not step through into this world, his face, framed by the anomaly shows his astonishment and delight at the spectacle. For the viewer and the series, then, the intended preferred reading of the anomalies appears to be established: they are literally wonderful.

Like similar 'magic doorways' in other science-fiction shows, such as the Einstein-Rosen Bridge of *Sliders* (1995–2000) and gates of *Stargate SG-1* (1997–2007), the *Primeval* anomaly is a two-way door with the potential to offer near-instantaneous travel to another place, in this case, in time rather than to another dimension or planet elsewhere in space. Similarly, it has a distinctive, signature look. The portals of *Sliders* appear to show space-time collapsing into its well and look like a vortex that noisily sucks people and objects in, hurls them through its exotic matter tunnel and ejects them into wherever is on the other side. The journey by Stargate presents entry as a plunge into a gravity defying pool, followed by a break-neck careering through space-time until the traveller finally emerges, fairly unruffled given the tumult of the trip, on the other side. In keeping with the scientific premise, the immense gravity implicit in the concept of creating an artificial wormhole big enough and stable enough to travel through, the whole process is presented in both programmes as loud, disconcerting and fairly violent, if not physically dangerous to the traveller. As Jan Johnson-Smith has noted, the 'combination of innovative camera mobilization and the constructive use of C.G.I. ensures that the 'impossible' cinematic images are foregrounded and remarked upon by the audience' (2005: 179). The television production technology thereby makes the Stargate traveller's experience a centrepiece of the spectacle of the show and, hence, audience pleasure. *Primeval*, by contrast, presents the repositioning from 'here' to 'there' as a much more sedate affair. Time travel is presented less as a journey over distance than an easy and immediate transition between adjoining spaces: there is no distinct intermediate space or sense of movement. In his script, series writer and creator Adrian Hodges describes his vague initial concept as something 'shimmering in the air' but observes that the final effect used in the series was 'really rather mystical and rather beautiful...almost like a decoration' and Haines has stressed the stealthy nature of the anomaly manifestation, observing that because it does not 'appear with a crackle of lightning', no one 'in the vicinity goes "What the hell's that?"' ('The Making of...(Season One)').

A journey through an anomaly is more like stepping through a doorway or, in the case of the boy in the first episode, looking through a window into an adjacent space. Unlike the examples from US television cited, the *Primeval* anomaly is a usually silent, hovering golden light orbited by translucent shapes like pieces of broken mirror. Its designer, Mike Milne, *Primeval*'s director of computer animation, explains that the underlying idea for the final anomaly 'look' is that 'the doorway to [the other world] is fragmented over three dimensional space...and as you step through it, you start off with small shards of the other world until eventually you come to large, jagged fragments and then finally you're through into the other world' ('The Making of...(Season One)'). As tears in the fabric of the universe go, this is a very mild-mannered one; as a marker of the *Primeval* 'brand' it is highly distinctive. Above all, it makes time-travel look easy, possibly not technological at all and seemingly, not inherently perilous.

For much of the show's run, the origins and true nature of the anomalies remains mysterious, although speculation by Professor Nick Cutter, the first two seasons' lead character and voice of authority, offers some ideas. When he and Connor Temple first examine the anomaly in the Forest of Dean, Connor discovers that it has a powerful magnetic field. The team's compasses go wild in its vicinity, and metal objects near its event horizon are pulled in. In keeping with the roughly sketched conspiracy theorist, SF-geek attributes ascribed to the character in his first moments on screen, Connor speculates, to much derision, that it may have something to do with an alien spaceship. Later, Cutter enters the Permian era through the anomaly in search of a final resolution to his fears that his missing wife, Helen, may be dead, and of clarification about why these holes in time are appearing. He finds neither, only more questions. In the dust of the Permian era he uncovers a human male's remains and signs of a camp, but not Helen, although her camera is discovered. Nothing is found to suggest that the anomaly is the product of any kind of technology. When it begins to shimmer and dim as though losing energy, he and his military escort, Captain Ryan, barely manage to return before the anomaly closes, apparently, of its own accord. Near the end of the first episode Cutter wonders aloud whether this has happened before or if this is the first occurrence of this phenomenon and, if so, what has changed to make it happen. He has no clear hypothesis about the cause of the event or whether it is a one-off. When he returns to his office, however, he hears a noise and finds that someone has left a living ammonite on his desk: he realises that Helen has returned and left this as some kind of message for him. If she has returned, of course, then there must be more than one anomalous time event – and the series is up and running with the mystery of the anomalies intact. Only in season five's penultimate episode is an explanation given.

The first season of *Primeval* builds on this initial introduction. As more anomalies appear, Cutter becomes emboldened in his speculation about what they are and how they might occur and the narrative pattern of the show becomes more clear-cut. Each episode sees a new anomaly appear with a fresh danger emerging from a distant era of the Earth's history. By the third episode, however, the appearance of a pattern in the manifestation of a series of anomalies allows Cutter enough evidence to advance an idea. An anomaly appears in a swimming pool, it disappears and another appears in a reservoir near London, raising the temperature of the water by bringing with it some of the physical environment of an earlier, hotter, sea. Cutter suggests that prediction may be possible and that the phenomena are 'time's equivalent of an earthquake, strong enough to rip apart the boundaries of dimensions'. He continues that his 'guess is that the fault line ruptured at the swimming pool, then ran to the reservoir: it could crash its way through into our time again anywhere along ... [a predictable] line' (1.3). When one appears in a basement of a suburban house which is flooded by the water that flows out of it and finally one at sea, near the southern English coast, both along his predicted trajectory, the hypothesis appears to be confirmed. The terms used and the methodology suggested reinforce the idea that the anomalies are natural occurrences and that, although the exact forces behind them might remain unclear, they follow physical laws akin to more conventional terrestrial phenomena such as seismology and geology and, therefore, that their mysteries might be unravelled by careful scientific observation.

Ambiguity about the anomalies is maintained, however, despite Cutter's apparent breakthrough. Near the end of the third episode, Cutter ventures into the ancient water-world to which the anomaly leads and finds his wife, Helen, apparently waiting for him on the other side. Far from needing to be rescued, she seems at home in the late Cretaceous, swimming in a pool surrounded by a Hesperornis rookery and shooing the creatures away like annoying gulls. Helen Cutter's role over the first three seasons of the show creates a problem for the viewer. The idea that the anomalies appear as part of some, as yet unexplained, natural process is at odds with the way in which she is able to use them. When she is snatched by soldiers from special forces, sent by Sir James Lester without Cutter's knowledge, she is able to predict what will happen at the next anomalous event (an incursion by sabre-toothed cats in the next episode) and threatens that preventing it may be contingent on her release. This suggests that, by some mysterious and presumably technological means, she is in control of these events or, at least, has extensive foreknowledge of them.

As a narrative strategy, the lack of clarification as to why the anomalies have started appearing and what they are suggests that the viewer is being given glimpses of a range of possible resolutions akin to those outlined by Tzvetan Todorov in his structural examination of the fantastic in literature. According to Todorov, science-fiction texts constitute part of the fantastic (more precisely, the 'instrumental marvelous' [sic]) and the fantastic text must make the reader 'hesitate between a natural and a supernatural explanation of the events described' (1975: 33). The hesitation is part of the pleasure of engaging with the fantastic text as well as a condition of its being fantastic. The long suspension of an explanation for the anomalies in *Primeval* fulfils a similar function to what Todorov calls the 'ambiguous vision' of both character and reader in fantastic literature. Not that the viewer is ever encouraged to think that a 'supernatural' explanation in its purest sense is likely: Cutter's empiricist language and faith in rationalism and even Helen's straightforward use of blackmail to escape Lester suggest a world with wonders but without magic.[1] Rather, its modalities are analogous to Todorov's differentiation between the uncanny and the marvellous text. The uncanny text will ultimately offer an explanation that does not challenge long-held views about the nature of the world, whereas the marvellous text will shake the foundations of belief. The oscillation in *Primeval* is between two possibilities. The first is that these phenomena appeared because people with insights into and control of time (Helen and others) are using temporal technology to disrupt the laws of the world we know. The second is that these occurrences are part of the natural cycle and nothing to do with human agency. If so, any confidence the ARC scientists have in their understanding of the laws of nature is misplaced as this new world is a much stranger place than contemporary science would have it.

Helen Cutter's part in the show rapidly develops from damsel in distress to super-villain. She pops up, apparently at will, over the first three seasons, to taunt, torment and eventually assault various members of the ARC team, some with fatal consequences – Cutter is dramatically killed by her at the end of the second season. With each return to the present, it becomes apparent that Helen has acquired ever more exotic technologies from the future to create clones, disguise her appearance, to plot the position of anomalies and even to create anomalies at will with a hand-held remote control. Hanging over the show, as always, is a lack of clarification about what the anomalies really are: conflicting hints about what they could be tantalize the viewer throughout. While Helen's technologies strongly hint that the anomalies are products of advanced technology themselves – that time travel has been achieved by human ingenuity at some future time rather than as a consequence of a natural process – in contrast to the conception of them as natural phenomena, suggested by Cutter's earlier Earth-science analogies, her cryptic hints about her 'mission' suggest an alternative 'third way'.

Helen is convinced that the devastated future that she has visited is connected to the anomalies and in particular, to the activities of the ARC team. From her perspective, the temporal anomalies seem akin to events attributed to man's mishandling of the planetary environment. Like holes in the ozone layer over Earth's southern pole, freak weather events, rising sea levels and global average temperatures, they appear to be evidence of yet more man-made disruption of the natural world. Helen is clearly convinced that this is the case, and her attack on the ARC at the end of the second season presents her as a misguided, if well intentioned, eco-warrior who has crossed a line into terrorism. In an improbable twist, her demise is at the claws of a velociraptor that has strayed from its own time period and encounters her in Africa's Great Rift Valley in four million BC, where she is attempting to change the timeline by killing the early ancestors of the human race, whom she has finally come to see as irredeemable (3.10). In her final moments, Helen is presented as the ultimate crazed animal rights activist, willing to wipe out her own 'toxic' species to save the rest, the paradox involved notwithstanding. All through this series of events, however, no one apart from Helen, the viewer included, has a very strong sense that this explanation is definitive, or even partially true. Helen's absolute confidence and mastery of advanced technologies early in her storyline may aid the credibility of an understanding of the anomalies as being the unintended effects of some form of temporal pollution that the ARC team would cause at a point in the future, but her final unravelling into a psychotic poisoner has the opposite effect. The fact that she succeeds in slaughtering a group of pre-humans, and that this has had no apparent effect on the contemporary world that the ARC personnel return to suggests that time is resistant to such attempts to alter it and that she does not grasp this. By the time the threat she poses has been neutralized then, neither the viewer nor the ARC team are more certain of the underlying causes of the anomalies than at the start of the show. The viewer is also no clearer about how the show wishes us to conceive the nature of time.

As her involvement with the work of the ARC team becomes more directly confrontational and her array of technologies more fantastic, Helen sparks a type of arms race in anomaly-related gadgets. Connor and the ARC team develop more ways to interact with the anomalies, culminating in creating one in the ARC laboratory in the final season. Early in season two, Connor develops an anomaly detector that registers and pinpoints the FM radio wave spikes that appear when an anomaly opens. He goes on to design a field generator that acts as a locking mechanism to seal an anomaly, stopping anything entering or leaving through it and, by season four, a device that can remotely sense where each one leads to. He discovers properties of the anomalies: if an anomaly opens inside another anomaly, for instance, it cannot be locked and projects mini-anomalies that are weaker versions of itself until the two can be separated and then separately locked (4.7). While Helen becomes the arch terrorist of post-anomaly Britain, Connor becomes its boffin, its key researcher and also a latter-day Barnes Wallis[2]. The credibility of Cutter's 'geeky' student morphing into the country's leading expert on anomalies and anomaly-related tech designer in a matter of months aside, Connor's role, like that of the rest of the ARC team, becomes one of protecting national security.

This represents the other main way in which the anomalies are understood in the show: while, for the scientist they may be principally objects of wonder and doorways to adventure and knowledge, and to Helen they are evidence of the destructive nature of the human race's overreaching and meddling with the natural world, to the British government they are always perceived as potentially a serious threat to the nation's security and also an acute embarrassment to its conventional security and civil services.[3] From the first episode, it is clear that knowledge of the anomalies is not something that is going to be widely or democratically disseminated. As soon as Cutter and Stephen Hart make their way to the Forest of Dean, a government department begins to take an interest in their activities. In the evening after their initial reconnoitre of the area, Cutter is approached by Claudia Brown, a Home Office civil servant, in a bar. When, afterwards, he is introduced to her superior, Sir James Lester, it soon becomes apparent that any investigation or interaction with the anomalies must take place under the auspices of representatives of the British government. By the end of the first episode, everyone who will become a member of the ARC team has sat down in front of Lester and been forced to sign the Official Secrets Act, binding them by the same rules as the service personnel who will now accompany them to each new anomaly incursion, whether they like it or not. The anomalies and what they represent are an official secret from the public, whatever they may be. The relationship between the Anomaly Research Centre and the government is somewhat hazy: it is not a Ministry of Defence research facility, but, at the same time, it is closer to the centres of power than a quango, having at its head a rather mysterious figure in Lester. He dresses as a senior civil servant might but is quite adept with firearms (2.6), even if the pen and sarcasm are his weapons of choice. When pressed by Cutter, he describes himself as a 'trouble shooter without portfolio in the PM's office', and, when called a 'hatchet man', describes this as 'colourful but surprisingly accurate'; indeed, when Cutter says that he will have to be shot if he is to be stopped in his search for Helen, Lester's response – 'Let's hope it won't come to that' – is ambiguously positioned between the wryly amusing and the downright sinister (1.1).

Lester's aloof and bureaucratic manner, his scepticism and not-very-well-hidden agendas set him in direct contrast to the more wide-eyed adventurers of the ARC team. Unlike them, he is not fascinated by the anomalies' nature or learning about them. Rather, when presented by Cutter with the idea that the Forest of Dean anomaly is a 'doorway between time-zones in the world's history', his only concern is 'the immediate risks' posed by it. His relationship with both the Home Office and military intelligence is repeatedly suggested by the twin strategies used to deal either proactively or reactively with anomalous events. Firstly, the potential threat posed by Helen Cutter is met by sending in a special-forces team to snatch her and then holding her *incommunicado* and interrogating her in the ARC. Secondly, Lester has to deal with information 'spills' and does so by sending in Claudia Brown to put in place a *cordon sanitaire* followed by news management mopping-up operations after anomalies have affected members of the public, sometimes in spectacular ways, such as the incursion into the London Underground by gigantic Carboniferous Era arthropods in the second ever episode. The mundane cover stories for the disruption such as gas leaks and chemical spills are all the more believable because of the banal world they suggest those not in-the-know, the general public, expect to live in. The world of spin, government deception and extraordinary rendition evoked, thanks to news items in the contemporary mass media such as growing unease over the legality of the US government's holding prisoners in Guantanamo Bay, is a plausible one.

While the Britain presented by the show is not necessarily the version of Blair-ite Britain into which the series was first released, there are striking parallels to it and to other popular fictions such as the BBC's *Spooks* (2002–2011). The state apparatus as presented here is entirely concerned with control, both of events and information. Warning the public that rips in time are appearing and should be avoided is never an option as it would entail admitting that these events are happening in the first place. When, in the fourth season of the show, entrepreneur Philip Burton effectively becomes the boss of the ARC and the direction of its research, with Lester still in the picture as government liaison and watchdog, the much maligned public-private initiatives so vilified in the NHS around the time has found its way into the regulation and exploration of wormholes. In post-austerity Britain, even the scientific discovery of the century apparently has to seek private sources of funding or go under. Given the reputation of such partnerships in the real world and Lester's and Abby's constant mistrust of Burton's motives, it is unlikely from the start that any good would come of it.

The first five episodes of Season One of *Primeval* have at their core straightforward 'meet-a-monster, beat-a-monster' storylines. The season finale does something slightly different. In the sixth episode a predator from the future, a blind superfast killer that has evolved from bats, emerges to cause havoc in the present day, its power to kill without being seen seeming supernatural. A creature from the future is something new for the show, but what make this storyline strikingly different from those preceding it is that it presents time in a way that the viewer has not been prepared for. Previously, no one in the ARC team has shown much concern about the possibility of changes effected in the past altering the future. When a future predator enters the Forest of Dean anomaly and escapes into the Permian era, all that changes. Cutter pursues it into the past where it dies, but, unknown to him, leaves several of its young behind. He also finds that this and his own actions have created a time-loop paradox[4]. The human remains he found on his first visit to the Permian era are the bones of Ryan, who is killed on this, his second visit. When Cutter returns to the present he finds that Claudia Brown has ceased to exist and only he knows this because, for everyone else, the timeline has altered. Lester's concerns about the threat posed by the anomalies are apparently justified. Lester could not know this, of course, because his memories have changed along with the timeline itself and the only evidence of corruption of the timeline is Cutter's insistence that a catastrophic change has happened and that a member of the team has ceased to be. This abrupt shift in the presentation of time's nature provides a cliffhanger at the end of the first season and might herald a much more complex kind of plotting than hitherto. That this is not the principal kind of threat that the show suggests that we should be interested in is apparent from the inconsistent way in which the idea is dealt with subsequently.

The first season of *Primeval* sets up a range of possibilities about the anomalies for the audience to speculate about, but it is the creatures that emerge from them that are the main antagonists for the ARC team and their job is to deal with them and keep the general public safe and oblivious. Other time periods are dealt with geographically, as though they are a 'where' rather than a 'when': a place from which creatures and even some climate can come. The incursion can be dealt with by ushering the escapee back or by killing it in the present, without any harm being done to the present. Time simply goes on as normal and all this is as it should be. Although the final episode offers the viewer the possibility that the timeline is not fixed and immutable, it is not an idea that is lingered on or presented as especially important prior to this episode, and is only fitfully important afterwards. Joan-Pau Rubiés warns that the everyday 'assumption that time is an absolute dimension that always points toward the future may be suspended for the sake of speculation, but then that speculation had better be good – that is, logically coherent' (1997: 81). The treatment of this idea in *Primeval* does not bear close scrutiny. A consistent version of how time 'works' is never striven for: there is no real attempt to explain why Helen's interventions in pre-history apparently made no difference to the world of the present as understood in the early episodes. When Cutter discovers another version of Claudia Brown at the start of season two (her alternative-timeline name is Jenny Lewis and she is apparently not even a relative of Claudia Brown, despite being identical in all but hair colour), this is swiftly accepted and the new character drafted into the team. Indeed, the improbability of Helen's death as she tries to change the course of human evolution suggests that she has been thwarted by temporal determinism rather than just a happy accident, although her intentions are in keeping with her conviction that the timeline can indeed be altered.

Later seasons, however, come to centre on the idea that somehow the anomalies are connected to the disastrous future and ultimate mass-extinction event that Helen feared. Characters come back from the early part of the blighted future to try to put things right, without knowing exactly what it is they need to fix. One of them, Matt Anderson, even infiltrates the ARC team, with surprising ease, and becomes its leader in the final season. In addition, the idea that the anomaly is something new in human history is challenged by the appearance of anomalies that lead to the nineteenth century and medieval England in the third and fourth seasons. They may be rare events and presumably rare enough not to have been noticed by many people, but they are not unprecedented. The two versions of time (as another country and as a stream that may be diverted) coexist uneasily until, near the end of the show's run, an explanation is advanced for the appearance of the anomalies and an attempt is made to unify them.

In the final season of *Primeval*, in the tradition of the overreaching mad scientist, Burton tries to create a limitless source of clean energy by harnessing the natural anomalies that are beginning to appear all over the world and turning them into one huge artificial super anomaly. This is the event that Matt has come back from the future to prevent: it will block a process known as 'convergence' and bring about the apocalyptic future that has been promised since early in *Primeval*'s run. By the penultimate episode of the show, Lester's job is no longer about news management: the anomalies are everywhere and sightings of mysterious 'golden lights' are being discussed on the TV news along with reports of a Tyrannosaurus Rex that is eating shoppers in a busy London street. The man from the future, Anderson, is given the job of providing the definitive explanation of what the anomalies are. He explains that they are a natural phenomenon that heralds the reversal of the Earth's magnetic fields roughly every million years. The increasing anomaly activity is a normal part of the process, known as convergence, which has happened every time that this reversal has occurred. Convergence has to be allowed to run its course, however, for life to be able to adapt to the new conditions. Burton's machine will stop this process in its tracks for the first time in Earth's history with devastating results. Exactly how Matt knows this is unclear, but the explanation offers a tidy connection to the magnetic field that robbed Connor of his flat keys in the first episode and just enough popular science-fact to give it a frame of reference within contemporary science-related panics.[5] In Matt's explanation, presented to the viewer as the authorized one, the anomalies are not anomalous at all: over a geological time-frame, they mark a shift in the planetary electro-magnetic climate. They are, as a character remarks about them in the fourth season, 'natural, like the weather' (4.7).

The *Primeval* anomalies are finally demystified in one sense, but the ideas that they represent are not. The writers' refusal to try to resolve paradoxes or to establish and stick to a set of rules about how time might work may be seen as a major flaw in the series as a whole. This could be an unreasonable position with respect to popular science-fiction narratives, and this series in particular, however. Brooks Landon argues that 'thematic and symbolic ambivalence is neither accidental in the SF movie, nor only a reflection of culturally inadequate response; it is in fact the basic or distinguishing pattern of those SF movies we most cherish and discuss' (1992: 21–22); however, sometimes a glaring error of logic goes beyond a point where it can be accepted or overlooked. Perhaps, in a serial drama, such gross ambiguities are more acceptable than they would be in a more condensed narrative. The variety of attitudes towards the anomalies articulated by the key players, the multiplicity of theories and even the final episode's cliffhanger ending (Matt is confronted by a version of himself from the future and warned that he will need to 'go back') might simply underline the show's serial nature, its makers' desire for continuance and a lack of joined-up thinking in the plotting of its story arc. It might also, however, be evidence of a more fundamental problem: the problem science-fiction has when dealing with time and time travel. It can offer a definitive view and create a mythos about what time is and how it works and stick to it, or, as in this case, it can opt for a fudge in order to create different kinds of plots for different types of viewers. Allowing that time and thus history may be fixed, and time travel is part of a natural process, means that crossing into another time cannot rupture the continuum and therefore has no consequences for those not directly affected. This is useful for simple adventure stories, in this case, the stories of human-versus-creature that are the staples of the show and principal appeal for the young trading-card collectors in its teatime audience. Allowing that the timeline is alterable and that time travel can be destructive to the timeline itself complicates matters, but provides a longer-term storyline rooted in conspiracy and super-villainy more satisfying for older viewers. It would be difficult for these two different and contradictory conceptualizations of time to coexist without loss of coherence. When dismissing Cutter's 'earthquake' theory of how anomalies spread, Lester complains that they are 'trying a little bit too hard'. *Primeval*'s treatment of the nature of time might be another example of this.

Notes

1. Todorov employs the term 'supernatural' broadly, using it to embrace many of the tropes of science-fiction as well as horror etc.' (1975: 172). The relationship between Todorov's discussion of the fantastic and the science-fiction genre is interestingly outlined by J. P. Telotte (2001: 10–16).
2. Sir Barnes Neville Wallis (1887–1979) – principally known as the inventor of the 'bouncing bomb', used by the Royal Air Force in raids on dams in Germany during World War II.
3. This mirrors J. P. Telotte's (1989) idea of the 'double focus' inherent in some science-fiction texts, where the often technological object of wonder is simultaneously recoiled from as monstrous and threatening.
4. Constance Penley (1990: 119–120) cites Ray Bradbury's story 1952, 'A Sound of Thunder', as the seminal time-loop paradox story and one that embodies the 'essential elements of time travel and its consequences'.
5. For instance, Bryan Nelson (2011) published a piece online on the shift in magnetic North two months before the final season was aired in the U.K.

6

'There Is a Corridor': *Sapphire & Steel, Torchwood* and the Time Topography of P. J. Hammond

Kevin Lee Robinson

Foreword

During the course of writing this chapter I was in correspondence with Peter Hammond and, where appropriate, I have included his direct responses to my questions. I have chosen not to include a transcript of the email interview and rather include his comments in the body of the text as I felt they provided better insight into his approach when in the context of examples. I would like to thank Mr Hammond for taking the time to help with this work as his input hopefully made this a more relevant and apposite chapter on the subject of writing about time in television productions.

Peter J. Hammond is a British television writer with a long and varied pedigree. His early work included scripts for shows such as *Dixon of Dock Green* (1955–1976) and *Z-Cars* (1962–1978). Hammond also contributed multiple episodes to long running police drama, *The Bill* (1984–2010) and latterly to *Midsomer Murders* (1997–). While P. J. Hammond is clearly an accomplished writer of crime and police procedural drama he is most likely to be remembered for his telefantasy writing. As well as contributing to *Torchwood* (2006–), Hammond was the creator/writer of the challenging, occasionally bewildering and arguably seminal cross-genre series *Sapphire & Steel* (1979–1982). It was in *Sapphire & Steel* that Hammond developed an unusual perspective on the use of time in his narrative construction. Rather than a sort of river of events to be travelled or a causal chain, Hammond portrays time as both a tangible place and, seemingly, an anthropomorphized presence.

Starring Joanna Lumley and David McCallum as the eponymous main characters, *Sapphire & Steel* revolved around the adventures of two mysterious agents who
appeared to travel through time and space with the purpose of cleaning up reality
when time (or, indeed, the creatures that inhabited it) broke through to wreak
havoc in the material world. *Sapphire & Steel* was an enigmatic show, steeped in the
uncanny, wrapped in layers of the supernatural, and constructed around a plethora
of science-fiction and horror tropes.

Titled *The Time Menders*, in P. J. Hammond's original pitch the show was turned
down by several UK production companies until an executive at ATV saw the
original episode and, having been terrified by it, picked up the first season without
any requirement for further treatments. Like *Doctor Who* (1963–), *Sapphire & Steel*
was initially designed to be a show aimed at children but it was soon upgraded
to a 7pm adult-orientated time slot in the schedules. Considering the high level
of sustained menace, supernatural otherness and domestic based-horror on display
in the first season the reason for this change seems quite clear and appropriate.
While Peter Hammond had previously worked on a modern fantasy for children,
Ace of Wands (1970–1972) which also had a supernatural element, *Sapphire & Steel*
was much more aggressive in the use of horror as a narrative device. Hammond
describes the ethos of the show in the short documentary 'Counting Out Time':
'We never showed blood, we never used knives, we never used guns, we just
provided fear' (2007). This ethos of providing fear and mystery over visual shocks
or gore is integral to Hammond's writing, as I will discuss later. For *Sapphire &
Steel* the enigmatic backdrop to the action is set up immediately.

Each episode opens with either a set up scene for a new story or a recap of
the previous episode's cliffhanger before filling the screen with stars. From these
stars we see a winding ladder or pathway that weaves through the screen to
produce a web-like lattice. On this lattice we are presented with a green graph
line, reminiscent of a heart monitor, which causes the web to melt like a burning
fuse. Then we see a shifting shape that may or may not be a face, over which
meteor-like representations of elements fly though the screen before finally settling
on sapphire and steel. All this is accompanied by an authoritative, God-like, voice
that declares in a speech conceived by showrunner Shaun O'Riordan:

> All irregularities will be handled by the forces controlling each dimension.
> Transuranic heavy elements may not be used where there is life. Medium atomic
> weights are available: Gold, Lead, Copper, Jet, Diamond, Radium, Sapphire,
> Silver and Steel. Sapphire and Steel have been assigned.

The show opens in a flurry of big concepts against a seemingly transcendent
or possibly divine backdrop. One is left with questions to be answered from the
beginning of each episode. Who is the voice? What directs the assigning of agents,
what causes these irregularities, and so on? Yet these questions are rarely addressed,

let alone resolved. At no point are we given any real backstory or exposition to inform the viewer who Sapphire and Steel are, who dispatches them on their adventures (known as assignments for the purposes of the show), or, indeed, who or what the enemy actually is. Rather than expose the viewer to the world of the heroes, Hammond chooses to avoid extended exposition in favour of small mysterious hints about the *Sapphire & Steel* universe. Throughout each assignment we are presented with vague indications of the milieu of the show, but we are told very little of the actual background story that acts as a catalyst for the constant sparring between Sapphire and Steel and the mysterious enemy. When we are given any indication of the backstory it is enigmatic and steeped in the mystery of the two central characters. We learn little of who they are and not much more of the world they come from. Probably the most notable example of this is the final assignment during which Sapphire and Steel are confronted by 'transient beings', who, we assume, are agents of time in the anthropomorphic antagonist sense. At the end of the adventure we know little of what or who they are beyond they have been sent to trap the two central characters. In the main it is Sapphire who will occasionally try explaining to human characters, often to the disapproval of the superior and occasionally arrogant Steel, who they are and what their goals are. In episode one of the first assignment she explains her perspective of time to a young boy, Robert, who is trying to make sense of the disappearance of his parents.

Sapphire: 'There is a corridor...
(Steel interrupts through some form of ESP)
Steel: <it cannot be explained to him>
Sapphire: <it can in a way, but not by you perhaps>
Sapphire: 'There is a corridor, and the corridor is time. It surrounds all things and it passes through all things. Oh, you can't see it, only sometimes when it's dangerous' (1:1)

She goes on to confirm when questioned by Robert that time can break through weak points in the fabric of the corridor and take what it wants.

Here Hammond is presenting time as a character. He gives us time as an entity, presumably a God-like being that is in some form of cosmic opposition to the dispatching voice from the opening credits. However, this is never expanded upon to any degree and it remains a mystery how time manages to operate as both antagonist and concept throughout the show. Certainly the character 'Time' seems to dispatch entities to combat Sapphire and Steel, as seen in the final assignment where a service station is taken over by antagonists known simply as transient beings. Hammond discusses this in an interview with journalist Guy Haley where he simply states that: 'I've never known. A lot of people have asked over the years where they came from. But I've no idea' (Hayley, 2007).

Here there may be a hint at the method Hammond employs throughout his writing when dealing with the fantastic or the uncanny. He holds information back from the viewer and effectively renders them as clueless or as informed as the protagonists in his scripts. Additionally he will then weave a further conundrum around the backstory of the central character to increase the sense of disassociation from the norm for the viewer. This combination of the unfolding mystery of the assignment, which we see in the same relative time frame as the protagonists, and the persistent restating that Sapphire and Steel, and in his later work for *Torchwood*, Jack Harkness, are not earthly in origin, presents the viewer with a perpetual mystery to be solved.

This would seem, on the face of it, to run contra to the expectations of a television science-fiction narrative in terms of the presentation of characters. With other mysterious 'genre' characters, the Doctor, Number Six in *The Prisoner* (1967–1968) and so on, we are presented with the enigma of who or what they are as part of the plot of the show and, indeed, in *The Prisoner* it could be argued that the backstory of Number Six is the main plot of the series. The *Doctor Who* franchise is so entrenched in this fascination with backstory that in a total reversal of the approach taken by Hammond a recent arc has been based purely around the Doctor's real name. In *Sapphire & Steel* Hammond purposely chooses to almost entirely pass over backstory in favour of presenting his story in the narrative of the present. When there is expositional discussion of events from the characters' past, such as in the opening assignment where it is revealed that Steel sank the original *Marie Celeste* and replaced it with an uninhabited copy, it is used briefly and only to highlight the suspense of the narrative present. The reference to the *Marie Celeste* is there to warn us that Steel is capable of being a hugely destructive force if required.

Sapphire & Steel, with its detective show undertones and its unusual characters, flew in the face of traditional expectations of the hero figure. Hammond had, at the time of writing the show, been involved with several police procedural style drama series such as *Z-Cars*, and *Sapphire & Steel* often edges towards this format. Clues are pieced together and the scene of the crime is deconstructed in a forensic manner. This technique places a rather analytical facade on the action and suggests a science behind the paranormal presentation of other areas of the narrative. Steel is not an extension of Campbell's *Hero with a Thousand Faces*, in point of fact his backstory seems to hint at a less than heroic character. While retaining a traditional good versus evil structural narrative, *Sapphire & Steel* refused to adhere to the conventions of the questing knight hero. Instead the show offered a rather distorted mirror reflection of the traditional hero. The presentation of Steel as the hero is not that of the clean-cut heroic figure and, as described earlier in what we assume was his callous sinking of the *Marie Celeste*, we know he is capable of killing without mercy to complete his mission.

There is certainly cause to also consider Steel as a character who reflects the times in which he appeared. One can see Steel as a reflection of the Thatcherite era. As pointed out by Peter Wright, Sapphire and Steel do indeed seem to embody the concept of freedom through order and order through governance that underpins conservatism. The opening credits speak to this and it is clear that irregularities are to be controlled. Steel dresses in a grey businesslike suit and is commanding and direct. Sapphire tells Robert in assignment one that Steel objects to her using time as if it was some sort of wardrobe. It is, as Wright observes, hardly surprising that Sapphire and Steel were 'acceptable as heroic figures for the period' (2006: 195). Hammond, as discussed in the same chapter, denies knowingly engaging with the political climate during the writing of the series however and, while we must accept that the influence of daily life does often resonate in a writer's work, there may be more of a narrative imperative in operation. Regardless of the political or social zeitgeist, television producers are not ones for radical changes to show formats. With *Sapphire & Steel* Hammond was taking a chance by presenting the audience with these unknown, often ruthless, and potentially unsympathetic characters. During our correspondence in answering a question on the ruthless nature of his central characters, Hammond stated that:

> I knew at the time that I was taking a chance with such a fanciful subject, and with leading characters whom some may have considered to be unsympathetic. But thankfully it was not a problem with the commissioning team and they in turn were prepared to take that chance.

Clearly the creative team behind *Sapphire & Steel* were well aware of the unusual nature of the show in terms of both the setting and the characters. At *Sapphire & Steel*'s creative core was the acceptance that this was a show that would be taking chances with the audience's sympathetic and emotional attachment to the central characters. Add to that the heightened degree of horror, such as the plague victim emerging from a child's bedroom wall and the faceless landlord of Assignment 3; the lack of back-story and the unusual nature of the show, with its unsympathetic heroes and blatantly enigmatic nature, and one begins to understand the level of the risk taken by ATV in producing *Sapphire & Steel*. In effect, this was a narrative about the unknown.

Throughout *Sapphire & Steel* there is a requirement for the viewer to accept the presence of the uncanny and that we are rarely given explanations of what this means. We do know, however, that the characters in the show are powerful and have knowledge beyond our ken. It is made perfectly clear that humankind is powerless in the face of these time travelling giants from beyond our plane of existence. Sapphire regularly demonstrates her supernatural control over time and Steel is often in possession of superior knowledge, such as his deduction that the owner of the junk shop in assignment four has released an entity hidden in every photograph ever taken – a deduction only possible with knowledge outside human understanding. In Hammond's scripts for *Sapphire & Steel* and *Torchwood* the titans and gods of time stride the Earth, subject only to their own laws. They destroy or create chaos on a whim or at the demands of a war we do not understand and we become involved at our peril.

This unearthly quality and inhuman nature is nowhere more evident than in Assignment 2. Here Sapphire and Steel are investigating a presence in an abandoned railway station where they encounter psychic investigator Tully. From the opening scenes Tully is presented as a rather bumbling but well-meaning character who has become embroiled in the events of the episode. The supernatural entities he seeks are actually something totally outside his experience, which he tries to explain by rooting them in his perceived notions of the supernatural. To Tully the events in the railway station are the result of ghosts and spirits. Early in the opening episode of assignment two we are given what appears to be a throwaway comedy moment that sums up the ineffectual nature of the human protagonists when dealing with these superior beings. The show begins with a series of clearly paranormal-related paraphernalia being set up around the disused station. For the viewer tension builds through a series of shots of darkened platforms, deserted stairways and half-lit rooms. After setting up an intricate series of detection methods, including tape recorders and tripwires, Tully's attention is attracted by the eerie sound of approaching footsteps and, clutching his candle for light, he is confronted by a ghostly apparition who declares himself to be from 'the other side'. Confused and apprehensive at seeing what he seems to assume is some form of paranormal activity Tully stammers, 'What?' and the apparition (who viewers will have by now recognized as Steel) replies 'The down platform' before apparently blowing out Tully's candle and then casually and uncaringly disrupting all his carefully set out trip wires and devices. As a result of this encounter Steel is presented as uncaring and dismissive of the rather frail Tully, and even when the more amicable Sapphire joins the investigation she is, in turn, manipulative and also slightly amused by the bumbling psychic. Sapphire manipulates Tully with flattery and displays of friendly flirting, while simultaneously breaking down everything about him, from his chemical composition to foreshadowing the resolution by giving his precise life expectancy.

There is yet further evidence of Sapphire and Steel's superiority and air of god-like power when it is revealed that the entity in the station is using various aggrieved apparitions such as a World War I soldier killed after the Armistice, or a crew of submariners drowned in a submarine test, as a supply of resentment. Steel, again wielding unearthly knowledge of the uncanny, seems to instinctively understand the needs of the shadowy entity. Needing to feed the monster something as a trade for ending the problem, Steel barters the remaining five years of Tully's life in exchange for the entity releasing the summoned ghosts. The deal struck, Steel sends Tully over the bridge and we hear his agonized scream as he is devoured by the waiting presence. The hapless Tully is sacrificed to the monster and neither protagonist displays more than a passing regret at their actions. In fact, Steel refers to Tully as negotiable goods at one point and, before sending Tully to his death, he assures him that they are winning. The episode ends, not with any discussion of the actions taken to defeat the entity, but with Steel, in a rare moment of emotion, appearing to jump joyfully into the air before vanishing.

It would seem then that there is almost an undercurrent of divinity to Sapphire and Steel. The otherworldliness of their existence puts them beyond the moral questions of right and wrong, and clearly this is a game of 'ends' not 'means' for these superior beings. Contrast this with the caring, moralistic and often self-sacrificing characters of other contemporary science-fiction shows such as *Doctor Who* and we clearly see that Hammond was creating a shift in the expected paradigm of the hero character. Sapphire and Steel were a new kind of protagonist: cold, ruthless, and most of all, superior, beings with little interest in human kind. *Sapphire & Steel* introduced two questionable heroes with ambiguous morals to prime time.

I questioned this approach during our exchange and Hammond confided, 'Yes. I feel that people from outside time have every right to be above human concerns and therefore appear to be ruthless. Although every so often they will show an act of kindness, however much it may seem begrudged.' The question this raises, however, is the impetus behind the choice of character employed in *Sapphire & Steel*. Clearly this cannot have been to appeal to industry. Television is generally accepted to be a devourer of repetition, so to offer a show of unprecedented complexity and narrative legerdemain was a wild gamble. We are left with the conclusion then that this choice was a matter of authorship. Hammond was creating a new kind of hero based not on a desire to do something different but by following his notion of what the narrative required.

Indeed Hammond is so fond of the unusual and the strange that, when questioned about the difference in approach needed for crime drama and science-fiction, he responded:

Although my first love has always been fantasy-cum-sci-fi, writing for TV on a regular basis has proved that there are very few opportunities to pen such material unless one is allowed to write one's own show, which is rare. Therefore I was lucky that ATV, as it was then known, took a chance on *Sapphire & Steel*. I was also invited to contribute fantasy scripts for *Ace of Wands, Shadows, Space Island One*, and, much later, *Torchwood*.

For those unfamiliar with the show, *Ace of Wands* (1970–1972) was an episodic children's television presentation featuring the adventures of Tarot, a mystical and apparently magical figure and his two assistants. Hammond wrote several episodes for the show and his contributions feature many elements which he later seemingly developed for *Sapphire & Steel*. His episode 'The Meddlers' featured a threatening musician which could easily be an early incarnation of the menacing 'Johnny Jack' from assignment six of *Sapphire & Steel*. Following on from his previous comment, Hammond goes on to explain his fondness for inserting the strange and uncanny in the mundane:

l often tried my best to incorporate strange goings-on in many of the other more down-to-earth series that I wrote for, especially as l have always liked writing character. So when working on police shows I tried to avoid straightforward crime stories by concentrating on unusual happenings and the odd quirky character or two. I suppose it could best be described as people and events on the edge of crime, or involved in crime against their wishes. And you were right to mention *Z-Cars*, because l managed to work a few weird stories into that show as well. It was the same with *The Bill*. I enjoyed writing for it when it had single thirty minute episodes. Or twenty-four minutes without the ads. In other words, short stories that had to have a beginning, middle and end within that framework. I found that ideal for writing some odd little tales. By its very nature the *Midsomer Murders* landscape is an eccentric one, but the show's fixed, golden rule is that, however dotty their stories may seem, they must always be anchored in reality. So I will be forever grateful to the original producer Brian True-May and his team for allowing me one indulgence. Out of the nine episodes I had written for them, the eighth was my favourite. It was called 'The Silent Land', and in an odd way it played with time. But, most important of all, it provided one genuine supernatural moment.

A glance through the plotlines for Hammond's work on *Midsomer Murders* confirms his recurring use of the supernatural and his fondness for the unusual and bizarre. The episodes he penned are replete with corpses in model villages, sightings of murder victims, spiritualist churches and undertakers found dead with a rictus of fear on their face. Episode titles such as 'Dance with the Dead' and 'The Silent Land' again reflect this interest.

This leads rather neatly to Hammond's return to time-based narrative in *Torchwood*. Here Hammond wrote the episode 'Small Worlds' for the first season of the show and 'Out of the Rain' for the second. *Doctor Who* spin-off *Torchwood* was pitched at the adult viewer, and, indeed, several episodes contained adult or sexual scenes and the show leant towards content usually associated with the horror genre. One of the most notable examples of *Torchwood* adopting a familiar horror trope is the episode 'Countrycide' (1.6) first broadcast in 2006. Where other episodes of *Torchwood* are based around the concept of alien or transdimensional intrusion, 'Countrycide' is set in a remote Welsh village where the inhabitants have adopted a cannibalistic ritual. Although the show is a departure from the regular narratives in that it features no alien presence, it is not unusual in that it adopts horror conventions. Episodes of *Torchwood* often feature a supernatural element to alien technology such as gloves with the ability to bring back the dead or devices that project ghostly events from the past. The show featured *Doctor Who* companion, Jack Harkness who, as discussed by Lorna Jowett and Stacey Abbott, is 'coded as monstrous because he blurs the line between living and dead' (2013: 211). In many ways Sapphire and Steel are similarly coded as monstrous by their own actions, their knowledge and intimate relationship with time and the otherworldly creatures within it and because of their distance from humanity. It could be argued that Jack Harkness takes a not dissimilar role to Steel in the *Torchwood* dynamic in that he is a guardian of secret knowledge and different from the humans around him. Harkness is, however, considerably less forbidding and distant than Steel. He is charismatic and charming but, as Hammond portrays him, no less ruthless when getting the job done.

In the *Torchwood* episode 'Small Worlds' (1.5), Hammond returns to his love of the creature from outside time. During the opening scenes of the episode we are introduced to tiny, glowing, rather fairytale-like flittering creatures that are being photographed by Estelle, who will later prove to be an ageing old flame of Jack Harkness. The scene is reminiscent of the Cottingley fairy photographs[1] (which are later integral imagery for the episode) and steeped in traditional fey imagery. As we watch, the harmless fairy folk transmute to snarling humanoid creatures. After a brief expository scene restating the loneliness of Jack Harkness where he dreams of the sound of fluttering wings, which we assume belong to the same fairy creatures, we are introduced to Jasmine, a rather detached and lonely child with a bullying stepfather and few friends. As she leaves her school alone to walk home, we see her being targeted by a man who later is revealed as a predatory paedophile. Jasmine is soon the subject of an attempted abduction, but the fairy folk come to her aid. Repeating the cajoling phrase, 'Come away, Oh human child' from W.B. Yeats' poem 'The Stolen Child' in an ethereal voice, the fairy folk target the antagonist, pursuing him and physically and mentally tormenting him into admitting his guilt to the police. Once in his cell, the fairies return and fill his lungs with rose petals. Torchwood is called in to examine the tortured corpse and Jack reveals he has seen these creatures before. Later Jack describes them as being 'children taken from out of time' and informs us that they are 'the source of nightmares' and refers to the 'Lost Lands' they inhabit.

This rather detailed plot summary is necessary to demonstrate that here Hammond is drawing on a multitude of cultural and mythological sources to establish the premise of the episode. The notion of the 'Lost Lands' with its echoes of *Peter Pan* and resonance of the traditional mythology of the changeling child is clearly considered as existing 'outside time'. Once again Hammond situates time in topography rather than as a concept and he hints at creatures that live on or in it, much as he did in *Sapphire & Steel*.

The resolution to this episode also contains echoes of the highhanded and almost god-like status of the character from outside time. In this instance, while the rest of Torchwood bumble ineffectually to find a way to combat the Mara, Harkness makes a ruthless decision. When the Mara threatens the world with retribution if he refuses, Jack hands Jasmine over to the Mara in front of her grieving mother. Facing the silent protestations of the Torchwood team he asks, 'What else could I have done?' As the episode ends we see Gwen find the face of Jasmine in one of the photographs from the Cottingley hoax and the ethereal voice of the Mara returns, this time to quote more of Yeats' verse:

> Come away, oh Human child, to the waters and the wild.
> With a Fairy hand in hand, for the world's more full of weeping than you can understand

Again here there are echoes of the ruthlessness of Steel in the capitulation of Harkness. He seems, to the viewer, to be defeated and unwilling to look further for a solution. In the wider context of the show, Harkness will repeat this willingness to sacrifice those around him several times, most notably in *Torchwood: Children of Earth* (2009). Hammond writes the character of Harkness as perhaps not totally heartless, but certainly as willing to sacrifice a child for the greater good. When I asked him about his approach to the character he stated that:

> I may be wrong to assume it, but I always saw Jack Harkness as someone who, with all his charm, was conning everyone he came into contact with, including his own colleagues. Maybe this was because he was born to be a loner throughout time.

It would seem that again here the otherness of the time traveller is what drives the actions of Hammond's version of Harkness. It is this otherness, this disconnection with the humanity around him, that allows him to make the decision to simply sacrifice Jasmine as a solution to the problem. Harkness and Steel then seem to be appropriate vehicles for Hammond's affection for the ruthless hero.

Hammond returned to Jack Harkness as the inhabitant of a place outside time in his second script for *Torchwood*. In 'Out of the Rain' (2.10) the Torchwood team see an image of Jack as a travelling performer in some old movie footage. The footage also contains the image of a group of demonically grotesque performers known as the 'Night Travellers', who escape the film to steal the living breath from their unfortunate victims. Jack and the team eventually destroy the film containing their essence and the Night Travellers vanish. Once more Hammond places characters outside the regular flow of time. The Night Travellers seem able to exist in some form of timeless stasis facilitated by celluloid. Once released, much like the transient beings and other denizens that inhabit the 'time lands' of *Sapphire & Steel* and 'Small Worlds', they reach into reality and create havoc.

While many of the *Torchwood* narratives feature the science-fiction notions of encounters with alien technology, trans-dimensional wanderers and traditional time travel tropes mixed liberally with horror conventions, such as return from death and cannibalism, Hammond's episodes are firmly fixed in the supernatural. For Hammond there are always bogeymen in the cupboard and something fey in the dark woods.

The dark woods analogy is a good one to use when considering the portrayal of time in Hammond's screenplays. As discussed earlier in *Sapphire & Steel* and particularly the 'Small Worlds' episode of *Torchwood*, time has an almost physical presence. It is treated as if having the topography of another world or place. In this respect, much like the deep dark forest of traditional fairy tales, time is a dangerous place of otherness. This narrative device of positioning time as a tangible place allows the intrusion of the uncanny into the real world. This intrusion of otherness into reality is, of course, the basis of many traditional fairy tales and ghost stories. Hammond adopts the alternate dimensional otherness often found in the work of dark fantasy writers such as H. P. Lovecraft. Indeed, when considering the timelessness of the Mara in 'Small Worlds' or the transient beings from *Sapphire & Steel,* one is reminded of the Cthulhu mythos of god-like beings who, either sleeping beneath the waves or exiled to the stars, seek to return to the Earth from a timeless dimension. However, and rather surprisingly, considering the similarity of the underlying themes, when I asked Hammond about this he responded that he was not very familiar with Lovecraft's fiction. He did, however, go on to name several other influences which, when taken in the context of this writing, clearly demonstrate the influence of the supernatural in his work: 'I have to confess that I know little of Howard Lovecraft's work. I shall have to read up. But Edgar Allan Poe has been an influence, along with J. B. Priestley, M. R. James, Walter de la Mare, H. G. Wells and Ray Bradbury.'

Hammond is free ranging in his use of genre. Refusing to adhere to the strictures of science-fiction or horror tropes, he liberally draws from all his influences and creates an individual perspective on the presentation of time. Hammond invites us to see time not as a physical or abstract concept but as the land from which all our fears migrate into the real world. It is this use of time as topography which affords Hammond the opportunity to assimilate the principles of the ghost story into the presentation of time travelling elemental avatars or to pit a science-fiction adventurer such as Jack Harkness against creatures from the world of fairy tales. When constructing his narratives Hammond has the deep dark forest, and all the ghosts and goblins within, at his disposal. When asked about using time in this way Hammond confirmed his delight in fairy tales and in morally dubious characters:

As a child I was hooked on Hans Christian Anderson and the Brothers Grimm fairy tales, even though I found them scary and, at times, depressing. Yet I preferred them to stories about sport or action heroes. So I suppose those 'dark forests', as you put it, were the start of my interest in creepy fantasy. At that time I also found the two early Disney films – *Pinocchio* and *Snow White and the Seven*

Dwarfs – entertaining but quite disturbing, although I had made up my mind that the wicked step-mum was much more interesting than soppy Snow White. In fact, I even had an early crush on Hans Christian Anderson's evil Snow Queen.

Fairy tales may well play a major role in the presentation of time in Hammond's writing. Certainly the fear of the unknown and the monsters of the forest are evident in the majority of his work. In many ways this desire to delve into the dark fiction of the fairy tale or the ghost story renders the time travel element subservient to the master horror tropes. Considering the earlier discussion of time travellers as God-like beings it is surprising how minimalist Hammond is in his use of actual temporal displacement. Sapphire, for example, while certainly able to reverse time, seems limited in this capacity. Harkness seems inadequate and small in Hammond's *Torchwood* stories and the depiction of his immortality is subservient to its narrative use, where events in his long history serve as a catalyst for the episode and his time travelling is never discussed. While there is a constant presence of 'time' as entity and topography in Hammond's writing, there is no time travel as we would recognize it from television shows such as *The Time Tunnel*, *Timeslip*, *Doctor Who* or literary sources such as stories by H. G. Wells.

Hammond, in response to my enquiry about this stated:

I'm quite happy writing about characters moving backwards and forwards within small perimeters of time. But I've never wanted to write about people of the present day going back to historical times or into the distant future. Then again, I have nothing against jokey time travel feature films, although they are of no interest to me. And of course there are exceptions, such as the film *Pleasantville*, which is fun yet has a far from funny message. What I can't abide are time travel stories, especially in television, that take themselves too seriously, where people go back in time and just so happen to bump into famous people of the past. It's all so nudge-nudge and reminds me of those naff semi-biographical US films of the Forties where characters delivered lines such as 'Chap upstairs. Calls himself a writer. Name of Dickens.' So with S&S [sic] I decided on things and people from other times arriving unwanted and moving around within those narrow perimeters. And I kept Sapphire's use of time to a minimum because I felt it helped the drama. If she were able to perform all sorts of magical tricks with time I think it would have nullified much of the fear and suspense.

It is in the last statement here that we really see the approach Hammond takes to his writing. There is a clear hierarchy of importance to the narrative. Fear and suspense are paramount to Hammond and this dictates his approach to the depiction of time. To support the need for a landscape conducive to the generation of unease in the viewer, Hammond needs an open cupboard in which to hide his bogeymen. Time, when presented as entity or topography, offers this. There is a further hint at the construction of his particular style in his decision to use 'things and people from other times arriving unwanted and moving around within those narrow perimeters'. By doing so he has access to the mundane. As a result the horror of the creatures that dwell in the dark 'time' forest and the other-worldly knowledge and powers of Sapphire, Steel, Jack Harkness and the other lords of these forbidden realms is played out against the backdrop of a vulnerable and ineffectual humanity.

This enclosing of the powerful and supernaturally remote with the mundane was remarked upon by *Sapphire & Steel* producer Shaun O'Riordan who stated that Hammond had a 'remarkable ability to make everyday things scary.' Curious about this I asked Hammond what he felt this referred to:

My work has usually dealt with ordinary people being mixed up in, and threatened by, extraordinary situations, and therefore being in need of help. And if a main part of this threat comes from the manipulation, by forces unknown, of everyday objects that we take for granted and therefore feel safe with, then the threat can become terrifying. With *Sapphire & Steel* it was clocks, pictures, books, etc. With my *Shadows* episode it was eggs, and in the story I wrote for *Space Island One* it was a child's wrapped gift. I think I may have gone overboard on this theme with my last episode for *Ace of Wands*, where almost every household item under the sun went bananas. It was my least favorite episode because of that. It should have been more subtle. The Peacock Pie episode with its B&B, its kippers for tea, its tiny Austin Ruby car and its mundane suburban setting was, I believe, just about right.

As with many ghost stories it is the horror of the supernatural intrusion into the mundane world that provides the suspense. For Hammond time provides the vehicle to allow this to happen. By depicting time as another realm where creatures seek to harm the real world, or as a God-like creature dispatching its emissaries to wreak havoc, Hammond allows himself a topography of otherness with which to intrude on the everyday world of the humans that stumble into the plans of these malevolent divinities. Time for Hammond is a wild and dangerous place where a great evil lurks waiting to do harm. This is an unusual and, in terms of television narratives, probably unique approach to this trope. This threat requires great powers to thwart its machinations; sadly for the humanity caught in this cosmic crossfire the agents of the cure are sometimes no more sympathetic or any less dangerous than the cause.

Note

1. The Cottingley fairies featured in a series of photographs taken by cousins, Elsie Wright and Frances Griffiths, in the early part of the twentieth century. The photographs

appear to depict a ring of fairy-like creatures dancing around a young girl or bathing in sunlight. They were taken by many, including Arthur Conan Doyle, as potentially being proof of the existence of faery creatures. In 1983 the girls revealed the photographs were a hoax and that they had been too embarrassed to admit their fakery at the time.

Part II

Experiencing Time

7

'No One Can Touch the Gene Genie': The Past as Fantasy Space in *Life on Mars* and *Ashes to Ashes*

Nicola Allen

Life On Mars aired on British television between January 2006 and April 2007[1]. The show depicts the plight of Detective Chief Inspector Sam Tyler, who is hit by a car in 2006 and wakes up having been somehow transported to the same place 33 years earlier; without explanation and without any initial sense that any change has occurred, Tyler slowly realises that there are no mobile phones in his vicinity and that everyone he works with in the present seems to have mysteriously vanished. Tyler learns that he is expected to begin working under DCI Gene Hunt, who has been awaiting a new recruit and who takes Tyler to be his new DI (a demotion for Tyler). During the course of the series the two detectives clash over their differing ideas of what constitutes best practice when it comes to solving crime on the streets of Manchester, with Tyler's more progressive methods conflicting with Hunt's old-school approach to policing. This chapter investigates that discord between old and new ideologies in *Life on Mars* and its sequel *Ashes to Ashes* (2008–2010), as well as exploring the show's presentation of a complex relationship between outmoded and progressive politics, which the show represents through the relationship between Hunt and Tyler (and in *Ashes to Ashes* through Tyler's successor DI Alex Drake). The trajectory of Hunt's characterization is almost Miltonic as he escapes the confines of his original role as backward-looking, apish antagonist to become, by the final show, the unlikely popular hero of the series, and a sex symbol to boot.

The unexpectedly positive audience response to Hunt was not lost on the series' creators and, as *Life on Mars* progressed, the promotional material surrounding the show increasingly emphasized the opportunity afforded by the programme to indulge in the allure of a supposedly forbidden rhetoric, and Hunt was taken up (by some) as a hero of unreconstructed masculinity[2]. The promotional clips and adverts for the show emphasized the fact that he routinely uses violence to elicit confessions from suspects; he frequently tells poor-taste jokes and often takes unilateral decisions that undermine the other officers on his team. In doing so, Hunt represents an old-school TV cop, frequently acting more like a sheriff than a sleuth. This contrasts with Tyler's style, Sam is a '00s TV detective: an intelligent graduate who uses brains over brawn, and who often articulates a respect for the processes of investigation. However, this rather dichotomous characterization, although actively caricatured and thus heightened in the media surrounding the show, should not be taken at face value, and doing so actually risks simplifying the series' depiction of a more subtly nuanced relationship between old and new and progressive and traditional styles of TV cop.

As the show progressed the gap between the dichotomous characterization of Tyler and Hunt in the promotional material and the more complex construction of the two central characters as depicted in the episodes themselves became ever wider. The introduction sequence for episode five of season two (which also became the trailer for the episode) epitomizes the way in which the juxtaposition of Hunt and Tyler was presented in promotional material. In the opening scene the viewer sees the TV screen in Tyler's 1970s flat, which is tuned to BBC One; the opening scene from an episode of *Camberwick Green* (1966) blasts out in front of a drunk and unconscious Tyler:

> Voiceover: This is a box, a magical box, inside this box is a surprise. Do you know who's in it today? It's Sam Tyler. Hello Sam [an animated version of Sam waves to the viewer]. How are you today? [Sam puts his head in his hands] Oh dear, not very happy? Is it Gene Hunt? [Sam nods] Is he kicking in a nonce? [Sam points, and the scene cuts to two Camberwick-style figures brawling in the street; the character of Hunt is clearly the aggressor – he punches, kicks and uses a dustbin lid to incapacitate the suspected felon, before repeatedly kicking him once he's down, then he pauses to wave to the camera]. (2.5)

This represents a crucial moment in the positioning of Hunt as the excesses of violence that are frequently associated with him exist only in representations that emphasise his status as a fantasy character. His violence is made 'safe' through the explicit focus on its status as fantasy/fiction, which is emphasized by the use of the animation, not to mention the comedy created by the concept of a brawl between children's TV characters. Hunt is never actually shown beating up 'real' people (he throws a few punches, but does not launch anything like a real-life version of the kind of violence shown in the *Camberwick* clip); this is as close as he gets to actual sustained violence.

The layers of intertextuality and the metanarratival aspects here work to detract from any symbolic value that Hunt might have had as a figure of real-world, unreconstructed 1980s masculinity, and instead work to situate him within the realm of fantasy and make-believe. Similarly, his reconstructed sexual politics have no real-world application, we only ever see one almost-kiss with Alex, Hunt is otherwise completely neutered in all but words, these factors seem to have contributed to Hunt's formation as a fantasy figure of forbidden outmoded masculinity. However, he was initially positioned as an unreconstructed sexist who wasn't meant to elicit sympathy, let alone desire. Indeed, the popularity of Hunt took many by surprise and led to a certain level of confusion over how to define Hunt's character. The extent of this confusion was indicated in the fiasco surrounding a poster campaign during the British General Election of 2010. An allusion to Hunt appeared in a Labour Party poster campaign in the run up to the election.[3] In the poster Hunt and the Conservative leader David Cameron are merged in an altered version of an advert for *Ashes to Ashes*, in which Hunt sits astride his car (a 1980s Audi Quattro) with the words 'Fire up the Quattro' underneath. The Labour Party poster had the same image but with Cameron's head replacing Hunt's and a new tagline, which reads: 'Don't let him take Britain back to the 1980s.' The Labour Party used Hunt's image in their poster under the mistaken belief that he formed a symbol for outmoded and discredited 1980s Thatcherite politics, but the audience's response to the inherent subtleties and complexities of the actual character meant that this presumption represented something of a misfire, forcing a re-think, and, eventually, the poster was pulled. However, the Conservative Party also mistakenly thought that Hunt's popularity represented a public endorsement of what they regarded as a kind of right-wing radicalism within 1980s Thatcherism, and so they used the same image with another altered tag line: 'Fire up the Quattro: It's time for change'. Again, the assumption that the public understood Hunt in such terms was misjudged. Hunt's politics are never really so clearly defined. Here, both parties misunderstood the complexity of the show, and positioned Hunt too straightforwardly in relation to 1980s right wing politics. When, in fact, the popularity of Hunt represents a much more complex relationship with the audience, one that does not entirely align him with 1980s right-wing rhetoric in its ascendency. This chapter argues that the figure of Hunt (and audience reactions to him) are much more subtle than was perhaps anticipated by the advertising engines of either party.

Hunt's world was always popular; *Life On Mars* elicited positive responses from audiences and critics alike from the very start. It was generally hailed as an intelligent 'science-fiction/cop show for a graduate audience who may have had a yearning for such genres (familiar from their childhood), but who required such shows to be revamped in line with their perceptions of 'quality TV', as well as their more progressive politics. *Life on Mars* and *Ashes to Ashes* filled that gap. *Den of Geek* typified the positive reception that the show received within the 20–30 somethings age group when the website reviewed the first two episodes of the first series thus:

> After the dramatic finish of the opening *Life On Mars* episode, it says something for writers and directors when they can keep the same level of pace, interest and downright confusion for the viewer for the following week. But, as we already know, it's because *Life On Mars* constantly delivers episode after episode of quality drama that we love it. (*Life on Mars*, Series One, Episode Two: Review)

The use of the word quality here is indicative of the response the show received; it was praised by reviewers as a show that took the science fiction and the cop-show formats and did something intelligent and interesting with them. But, despite its eventual popularity, it took over eight years for its creators, Matthew Graham, Tony Jordan and Ashley Pharoah, to bring the series to life. In an interview Pharoah describes the process of the show's creation, which seems to owe much more to the cop show format, than to science-fiction:

> About eight years ago the production company Kudos sent the three of us off to a hotel in Blackpool for a long weekend with the brief to come up with some series ideas. We had all just written on *City Central* and didn't fancy doing another cop show, but somehow we got talking about *The Sweeney* and thought it would be amusing to see a techno modern cop in the Seventies. It all mushroomed from that core idea. (Stack)

However, despite its cop show origins, the popularity of *Life on Mars* coincided with and was often linked to a massive resurgence in interest in science-fiction aimed at a young-adult market. A resurgence brought about by the return of *Doctor Who* (2005–) to British TV screens the year before. Curiously, it wasn't just science-fiction elements that the shows had in common: the new *Who* series immediately saw the franchise regain its 1970s position as an immensely popular, primetime show, but one which, in its rebirth, also prioritized a combination of generic staples and which included an aesthetically 'rougher', visually more working-class characterization of the Doctor himself (not entirely unlike Gene Hunt). The Christopher Eccleston series drew upon the actor's reputation for appearing in shows that dealt with edgy, gritty, social realism, such as *Our Friends in the North* (1996), a series which spanned the entire adult life of its four central characters, but which was chronologically realist in its depiction of the physics of time and space.

In the re-boot of *Who* the Doctor dons a leather jacket and enunciates his lines in a decidedly working-class northern English accent. This Doctor is a departure from previous ideologically dubious attempts to universalize *Doctor Who* in time and space through the appropriation of liberal humanist middle class values masquerading as 'universals'. Thus, if in previous incarnations, the Doctor represented the entire universe through markers of identity that are so hegemonic as to have become invisible, then Eccleston's Doctor does something slightly different, and is more in line with post-modern identity politics which prioritize the singular and dispense with the universal. Oddly, in his explicitly Northern working-classness the re-booted Doctor seems oddly aligned with certain aspects of the characterization of Hunt, whose traditional, working class roots are emphasized, in conflict with Tyler's much less explicit sense of his own working-class status, the nostalgia associated with Hunt may suggest that there is an acknowledgement (even a lamentation) of the fact that such figures have disappeared from television. Thus, in the reboot, the Doctor is contextualized specifically within contemporary northern English, working class history[4]: Rather than being completely exterior to history, Eccleston's Doctor has, despite maintaining the status of Time Lord, the appearance of a more defined singular position within it, but the Doctor embodies aspects of both Hunt and Tyler and demonstrates the closeness between the two. Tyler's dress is almost identical to Eccleston's Doctor, and his working class, northern roots are also clearly prioritized for the audience in his accent.

This near-pastiche style, which sees the show incorporate established realist styles alongside science fictional tropes becomes similarly, but more implicitly, integral to the unique success of *Life on Mars* and *Ashes to Ashes*. The central characters necessarily take on the foibles of the times that they live in, rather than transcending them, as all the while the show demonstrates that the characters' 'truths' are only ever partial and are always fragile.

As hinted at above with the displacing of a single character in time *Life on Mars* also borrows from US shows such as *Quantum Leap* (1989–93) but the show also stretches that format. Like Sam Beckett, his namesake in the earlier series, Sam Tyler solves the 'problem' of each show without attaining resolution for himself, but whereas in *Quantum Leap* Beckett's personal quandary is only rarely alluded to (apart from in the intro sequence), Tyler's situation forms the spine of the narrative, and this lends the series the feel of serial drama. Each week Tyler's journey home drives the narrative (rather than functioning only as the facilitator for what is essentially an episodic narrative). The turmoil that Sam encounters as a result of his desire to return home and the growing sense that should he achieve this he will leave behind an increasingly attractive life (and love affair) in the 1970s begins to function as a key part of the narrative, whereas in *Quantum Leap* Beckett articulates his time-travel at the start of each episode but is then completely emerged in the narrative of the space to which he has jumped before jumping to a new place in time for the next episode, Sam stays in the 1970s, he builds a life there but is constantly reminded that he doesn't belong there.

This conflict between a desire to stay in the past and a pull to return home to the present continues in the sequel, *Ashes to Ashes*, in which Alex Drake also begins to fall in love with her 1980s life. For Drake, this process contains an extra dimension as it is suggested that one of the side-effects of her existence in Hunt's world is that she will experience the passage of time differently, and, in the final episode, it becomes clear that, not only are the officers living in a kind of purgatory that has been created by Hunt, but the longer the dead officers spend in Hunt's limbo the more they become estranged from the circumstances of their actual lives and deaths, and the more slowly they come to experience the passage of time.

The final series reveals that all of the characters have experienced similar 'deaths' to those of Tyler and Drake but the other officers have forgotten their previous lives altogether. However, this scientific paradigm phenomena does not form the crux of the show's drama, nor indeed do the lives of those who live in the time period to which the protagonist has 'jumped' (as happens in each episode of *Quantum Leap*). Instead, it is the particular personal circumstances of the main protagonists of *Life on Mars* and *Ashes to Ashes* that informs the action and the characterization within both series. Nowhere is the centrality of the protagonist to this narrative made clearer than in reactions to the switch between Tyler and Drake as central character. The huge success of *Life On Mars*, and the departure of John Simm as Tyler after just a year in the role meant that *Ashes to Ashes* aired with huge expectation and a sense that it was going to be difficult to emulate the success of its parent show. Reviews for *Ashes to Ashes* were initially mixed, to say the least. The *Guardian*'s Mhairi McFarlane complained after the first episode of *Ashes* that:

> There's something about *Ashes to Ashes* I find dispiriting, and I'm not talking about Keeley Hawes turning up for work at Met HQ dressed like a member of The Human League. Although that too. In last night's episode, DCI Alex Drake (Hawes) fairly cheerfully submitted to an induction into her new workplace that involved allowing her male colleagues to gather round and rubber stamp her backside. It was all right to take part, she reasoned, because her life in 1981 is only a creation of her subconscious. By the same token, she could've stuffed the inkpad up DS Ray Carling's rear without fear of professional repercussions.

Indeed, one of the most prominent features of Hunt's characterization as a 1970s and 1980s northern cop is his sexual politics. *Life on Mars* had prioritized the difference between the new man and the old, and had contained a female cop, Annie, who experienced liberation only with Tyler, the enlightened 'new man' from the twenty-first century. In *Ashes to Ashes* the inclusion of a female protagonist provides the opportunity for a different aspect of the unreconstructed masculinity that Hunt embodies to be foregrounded, one that sometimes came close to (but never actually crossed) the blurred lines between post-modern pastiche and actual offence. The show draws, but never oversteps, very definite lines when it comes to Hunt's particular brand of unreconstructed alpha maleness, as noted by John R. Cook and Mary Irwin:

[. . .] for a sector of the female viewing audience in particular, much pleasure is to be had in Alex's very unreconstructed romance with macho, domineering Gene Hunt. As evidenced by a very busy thread on 'Hunt's Housewives', one fan forum on the entertainment website *Digital Spy*, this is a key aspect of the series. Much of the forum's disclosure centres on key 'romantic' scenes that take place between Alex and Gene, on the attractions of Gene Hunt as a fantasy partner and the forum members' desire to be in the same position as Alex, involved with the kind of heroic alpha male hero whom they see embodied in Gene. They make much of a number of occasions in the first series which one poster calls 'heart flutter' moments when Alex faints and is rescued by Gene, and in particular the scene in episode 1.6 where, to the muted strains of Ultravox's 'Vienna', Gene smashes through a plate-glass window in order to carry an unconscious Alex from near death in a deep-freeze, in the manner of the archetypal romance hero. (84–85)

Hunt's role as a substitute for the traditional romantic hero is carefully positioned within the show as that of a fantasy, one that emanates from Drake herself, and is as much a part of the culture that she has imbibed as the cop show elements are of Hunt's. The 'Housewives' reaction to Hunt is in line with the show's final revelation that the time travel element of the series is laced with a heavily intertextual aspect: the past that the characters create is constructed from TV, books and films. Cook and Irwin go on to note that the participants in the 'Hunt's Housewives' thread also post on their shared love of other 'romantic heroes' such as Mr Darcy and Mr Rochester, placing Hunt in a tradition that the show implies has informed Drake's sense of what constitutes a viable partner, and that pervades her subconscious – despite her concomitant desire to be liberated from the patriarchal value systems that confine the heroine to experiencing liberation only tangentially through her relationship with the alpha male, Drake's desire might represent an interpolated response to 1980s media.

Crucially, the narrative of the series itself moderates Drake's desire for the unreconstructed aspects of Hunt's character, and this aspect of Hunt's characterization always stops at the level of rhetoric, a rhetoric that Drake reinforces as being 'safe' because (like the cartoon violence discussed above) the promise of submission is only ever articulated as a fantasy that will never be acted out. The show treads a very thin line when Drake initially seems to accept her role of submissive female to get what she wants:

Alex Drake: Please?
Gene Hunt: No.
Alex Drake: I'll let you stamp my bum.
Gene Hunt: I'll get my coat. (2.1)

The key here lies in the setting and the tone of this exchange. Both Hunt and Drake know that this is a joke that does not (in reality) constitute actual submission, but crucially it is also a joke that occurs in a time that is sufficiently removed from the present, thus permitting Drake (and 'Hunt's Housewives') to indulge in an outmoded, even dangerous, romantic fantasy of the kind that has informed their sexual development, but that they now understand to be flawed. The forum 'Hunt's Housewives' allows female fans of Hunt to indulge this fantasy without compromising or threatening the hard-won freedom of the present day, since the action is 'safely' confined to the past. This is not an unproblematic stance but it helps to articulate a level of nuance that was missed by the advertising teams who tried to ride Hunt's popularity for the Conservative and Labour Party campaigns in the last general election, and that explains why those attempts to evoke aspects of Hunt's perceived appeal backfired. The audience is too acutely aware of Hunt's status as a fantasy, he is thus removed from any real-world application.

The time travel element of the show becomes, in some senses, a statement about the impossibility of creating a show like this outside of a recognition of its own artificiality. There is a performative aspect to nearly all of the exchanges that Hunt is involved in, and this is heavily emphasized in his 'heart flutter' conversations with Drake:

Gene Hunt: DI Bollyknickers, you appear to be drunk in charge of a handbag and dressed like a tart again.
Alex Drake: Oh, piss off, you lardy fascist!
Gene Hunt: We'll make a copper of you yet. (1.2)

Several Freudian concepts, including processes of identification, phylogenetic heritage, and intergenerational process; the notions of transgenerational transmission, 'fantasies of identification' (de Mijolla, 1986), and 'alienating identifications' are also present in the parent and spin off series, as Hunt is bestowed with a knowingly (almost clichéd) Freudian father-figure imagery:

Gene Hunt: [to a young Alex Drake] Bye, little lady. Any problems, you just call the Gene Genie.
Alex Drake: How come you were there, taking the little girl's hand? That couldn't have happened. You weren't there. You're not real.
Gene Hunt: I'm everywhere, Bolly. I was needed and I was there. (1.3)

Here, Drake and Gene encounter Drake as a child who has become unwittingly involved in the case of a suspected terrorist; Drake has no memory of having met Gene at this stage in her life, but the time travel elements of the series allow him to fulfil the Freudian functions of a father-figure role. There is a decidedly Oedipal element to his relationship with Drake, one that in the end he forbids from being fully fulfilled, as the universe that he creates seems to actively conspire against them ever fulfilling their sexual desire. However, the existence of that desire is hinted at throughout *Ashes*; in the third episode of the first series Hunt ends up saving Alex from an attack, but their close proximity is thwarted when Alex recovers consciousness before Gene has the chance to fulfil the role of romantic hero. The patriarchal model is updated and partially rehabilitated in the lack of a kiss; but implicit in both Tyler and Drake is an acknowledgement that they desire and need Hunt; both speculate that he may be a product of their own psyche as they try to work out whether Hunt's world is real or not.

Tyler and Drake's desire for Hunt and his world is key to the show's narrative development, as they both gradually become more attached to Hunt and/or his world and less sure of their original mission to return home. This essential battle that plays out between the protagonist's desire to return home and the undeniable (if unexpected) appeal of Hunt's world is hinted at right from the start. In the first episode the true nature of the *Mars* and *Ashes* universe is hinted at in the scene in which Tyler and Hunt realise that Mrs Raimes' neighbour is the killer: they take a slow-motion leap onto and over a desk, side-by-side. This is a device frequently used in *Starsky and Hutch* (1975–1979), a seminal buddy-cop drama of the mid-1970s starring Paul Michael Glaser and David Soul. Frequently, Starsky and Hutch would be seen leaping over furniture, cars, or any other obstruction in a similar manner to get to the bad guys or the victim. Tyler also mentions *Starsky and Hutch* in episode six of season two. The dream world of Hunt then offers Drake and Tyler a space free from the repression that is necessary in their present lives, one in which they can indulge their fantasies unhindered by the pressures of the present, real world.

The easy assumption is that the appeal here comes from a world free from the constraints of political correctness; the *Guardian*'s Nancy Banks-Smith articulates this notion:

> What no one expected was the roaring success of Philip Glenister's Gene Hunt, who could have gone on without rehearsal as a rhino and had a line of banter like a swung shovel. It would have taken a saint with a soul above ratings to refuse a sequel. Gene Hunt, with Ray and Chris but without Sam and Annie, will move to the Met in a series set in 1981 called *Ashes to Ashes*. It is arguable that nothing on television is as truly in touch with its time as a cop show. It may not mean it; it cannot help it. Dixon of Dock Green in the 50s, Z-Cars in the 60s, The Sweeney in the 70s. *Life On Mars* spoke of nostalgia for a time when PC did not mean politically correct and detectives were seldom mistaken, even in a poor light, for social workers. (Nancy Banks-Smith)

However, this endorsement of a world before political correctness isn't quite how the show presents the phenomena of Hunt's world. The imagery associated with the unrepressed psyche does involve a shedding of what might now be regarded by some as 'political correctness', but this is not the limit or source of its appeal. The care with which Tyler and Drake treat suspects and victims is born out of a training that has involved asking them to think before they act, to overcome any prejudices that they may bring to a case; but any sense that a retreat from this position might be desirable if it involved a return to a world that is more sexist or more racist is always immediately and resolutely undermined by the show itself. Instead, the elements of Hunt's less civilized approach that are presented as appealing to our protagonists are those that challenge the civilizing process on a more basic level. Drake, in particular, is drawn to behaviour that is less civilized, rather than to behaviour that simply represents a non-critical attitude towards colonial, patriarchal or heterosexist ideologies. She is drawn to Hunt as a taboo by her own standards but more specifically the show emphasises an interplay between Drake's cerebral approach to almost every aspect of her life and work, and the complicit allure of Hunt's equally pervasive indulgence of a baser, less cerebral instinct:

Alex Drake: The mind's an amazing organ . . . .
Gene Hunt: I've got an amazing organ.
Alex Drake: . . . capable of much more than you could imagine.
Gene Hunt: Right again. (1.3)

This is not to negate the appeal of a non-politically correct cop show. Nostalgia – particularly for more straightforwardly understood gendered roles and the lost machismo of figures like Hunt – is present, but the show also always complicates these ideas by suggesting finally that the figure of Hunt is himself created out of a fantasy and that his character (and the rest of his world) are the embodiment of the desires of a very inexperienced young man: it is revealed in the final episode that Hunt himself died as a young bobby on the beat on his first job on Coronation Day in 1953. Upon being stranded in limbo Hunt unconsciously created his own persona pastiched from the kind of TV show cops that he had grown up with.

In an interview with The *Guardian*, *Ashes* co-creator Matthew Graham, who wrote the final episode, explained the ideology behind Hunt's world:

When we discussed the philosophy behind it we decided that, seeing as how the cosmos was infinite, everybody who dies can afford to go to some kind of purgatory plane that is relevant and significant to them. So we liked the idea that coppers with issues would go to a place designed for coppers. And a coppers' paradise surely has to be *The Sweeney* or *The French Connection* if you're an American. That's the place where you've got all the freedom and, therefore, all the chances to make all the big mistakes that could lead you to hell. But all the good decisions would lead you to heaven. We both agreed that Gene isn't appointed by anyone. He has done this for himself. He's re-invented himself and built a world that is very potent and real, one that draws others in. But Gene doesn't know he's doing it. He doesn't go off into a room on his own and talk to God. He just obeys some animal spiritual instinct inside him.

This instinctive drive to create a team is crucial to the appeal of Hunt, who, above all else, prizes teamwork over individualism. Both Tyler and Drake get a relief from the burden of being solo detectives, both are demoted to DI in the transition, but both seem to find a release in this lack of responsibility, in part because they have found a partner and are no longer expected to work alone. In the end, Hunt is never guilty of the sexism/racism that the show places firmly at an institutional, rather than individual, level. Indeed, Hunt's escapades trying to catch an escaped heroin addict and petty criminal in the *Blue Peter* garden (and thereby revealing that it was he who is responsible for the famous vandalism of the garden that happened in 1983) represent the limit of his rule breaking, and again emphasize the slightly cartoon nature of Hunt's violence. The show always imposes limits upon the extent of his supposed old school pre-political correctness methods.

Indeed, the series, and in particular the character of Hunt, are never about reinstating a world without political correctness; the series is, in no way, aligned with any sustained criticism of that aspect of modern life; if anything, the viewer is always positioned with the time travelling protagonist's more enlightened and liberal reaction to the lack of representation of minority groups within 1970s and 1980s policing, but like Sam and Alex, the viewer is also asked to interrogate the partiality of their own position. Hunt's world providing a utopian space after the tradition of Thomas More, i.e. one in which alternatives can be played out and evaluated. At the level of specifics, the show seems to be particularly at pains to suggest that what is so appealing about the overtly constructed past of Hunt's world is the level of teamwork and cooperation that the show implies is often missing in the time traveller's contemporary experience of sleuthing (and, more broadly, their experience of twenty-first century existence).

This aspect of *Ashes to Ashes* seemed lost at first, even on those who were willing to place the accusations of sexism in a more subtly nuanced context. The *Guardian* website carried a second review of the show on the same day as McFarlane's, in which Stephen Brook accuses Keeley Hawes' detractors of sexism:

I can't understand the critical mauling that the superb Keeley Hawes has received playing DI Alex Drake on *Ashes to Ashes*. Is it just good old fashioned sexism? I watched last night and thought that Ms Hawes was very good indeed, but the press have taken against her.

However, this assertion did not extend to an approbation of the show itself, which Brook also went on to dismiss as somehow lacking:

My beef with *Ashes to Ashes* is that it doesn't suck us in. We never forget that we are watching a post-modern high concept TV show. Compare this to *The Singing Detective*, for example. Which makes for an enjoyable romp, but the thought that Hawes is ruining it is way over the top. It is not that good to begin with.

It is true that both the original and spin-off series rely rather heavily on what Brook refers to as the show's 'post-modern high concept' aspects. As noted above, both employ a post-modern montaging of several established TV genres, including police drama, sit com and serial, and it could perhaps be argued that the science-fiction and time travel elements of the show are only really ever secondary amongst the many genres alluded to.

After the first episode of *Life On Mars*, each subsequent show is prefaced by a monologue (see below) in which the protagonist re-tells the narrative of how they ended up in Hunt's world and re-affirms their commitment to getting back to the present. This works to prioritize the science-fiction time travel format of the show, even if this is sometimes less obvious in the episode itself. This juxtaposition of the framing monologue and the actual episode is particularly noticeable in *Ashes to Ashes*, in which Drake constantly narrates the effects that the new world is having on her character. Perhaps chief amongst these is the scene that so troubled McFarlane, the one in which Drake submits to the infamous ink-pad stamping that marks her entrance into Hunt's world, and perhaps marks the creation of another Drake – one liberated from the constraints of a 'real' world that would judge her behaviour as that of a victim/whore. Thus, the title sequence monologues of both series work in two ways. Firstly, they prioritize the time travel aspect of the programme. Secondly, in the case of *Ashes*, the opening monologue emphasizes that Alex has left behind a world and an identity that has been created out of the differing expectations and social mores of that time; in Drake's case, her twenty-first century identity is laden with the particular responsibilities of child-rearing and the expectation that as a post-feminist twenty-first century female she should try to have it all, so whereas Tyler simply states that:

My name is Sam Tyler. I had an accident and I woke up in 1973. Am I mad, in a coma, or back in time? Whatever's happened, it's like I've landed on a different planet. Now, maybe if I can work out the reason, I can get home.

Each episode of *Ashes* begins with the slightly longer monologue:

My name is Alex Drake. I've just been shot and that bullet has sent me back to 1981. I may be one second away from life, or one second away from death. They say that as you die your life flashes before you, all those memories and mistakes that form us. Well bring it on, my life can flash away as much as it wants because I'm not going to die. I'm coming back to you, Molly.

If Tyler and Drake have left behind (respectively) the responsibilities of parenthood and the complex sexual politics of twenty-first century relationships, then they have also escaped from a world that holds unpredictable terrors and threats for them as officers, and what they get in return for their services in Hunt's purgatory is to indulge in a dream-world which contains all of the aspects of their psyches that the present has forced them to repress. As Robert Lloyd notes in his review of the series in the *LA Times*: 'Sam belongs both to 2008 and 1973; on screen, the real and the dreamed are equally actual. It's a cop show, a fish-out-of-water comedy, a drama of displacement, a bit of a love story and, like *Mad Men*, a romantic tour of the fashions and social mores of a past era.'

The key aspect that makes this outdated world so attractive for Tyler and Drake, ultimately, is that in the biggest sense they feel it to be entirely known. Both protagonists experience a level of superiority over their fellow officers because of their knowledge of what will happen next on the world stage, and the 'dreamed' past almost always lives up to their reading of it. This isn't true of their individual plight – which remains necessarily contested ground – but over the big things Drake and Tyler know the score and the other characters can only admire their knowledge and acumen. In the second episode of the first series Tyler complains that: 'This place is like Guantanamo Bay', only for Hunt to assert his ignorance of any such place: 'Give over, it's nothing like Spain' (1.2). Drake has a habit of recognizing puns to which her fellow officers are not privy; this culminates when Drake offers New Kids on the Block and The Backstreet Boys as names for a local gang who are new to the drug dealing business (1.8).

Compared to the protagonist's slightly superior knowledge of what will happen next on the world stage, the other characters provide moments in which their naivety is exaggerated to the full:

Sharon 'Shaz' Granger: Several people were looking for Mr Hugh Jarse. And it turned out Mike Rotch was quite popular too.
Alex Drake: Right.
Sharon 'Shaz' Granger: Five or six had chronic asthma and . . . one man had some very imaginative suggestions. (2:3)

This ensures that the audience is constantly reminded of the fact that our protagonist is an outsider in this time, despite the fact that the series only shifts its time setting within recent living memory. But the jokes are always at the expense of the historical (as opposed to the contemporary) characters, and thus, for Drake and Tyler, Hunt's world becomes an empowering dream space. The departure from the present fulfils all of the usual functions that we might expect from a time travel show, we indulge a fantasy in which we are constantly privileged with the gift of hindsight.

Indeed, the fact that this 1970s/1980s world and its inhabitants might be an act of wish fulfilment, nothing more than an ego-fuelled creation of their own psyches does not escape the protagonists of either series. Drake and Tyler constantly refer to their own situation, and, rather than offer scientific explanations for the time travel that they are apparently experiencing, both reiterate their own belief (informed by the psychoanalytical element of modern policing and investigating) that they are experiencing some kind of extended dream, or psychotic episode. Drake complains to Hunt in the first episode of *Ashes*: 'Just look at me! Look at me! I am trained to get inside the criminal mind. And now I'm stuck in my own – with you!' (1.1).

This reiteration of the protagonist's belief in the dreamed (rather than actual) nature of the time travel is an integral part of the show's explanation of events right from the first episode of *Life On Mars*, in which Tyler also favours a Freudian (rather than a Newtonian) explanation for the apparent anomaly in the time/space continuum. Here, Tyler dismisses his new surroundings as a product of his own mind, he even references Freud when uttering what he believes will be his parting shot to his new DCI, he says: 'See you, Gene. Give my regards to the Id'[5]. This continues in *Ashes to Ashes*, the second episode of which sees Drake attempt to take control of her dream space, when she complains to Gene: 'Will you just shut up and listen to me! This is my bloody fantasy, and I will be listened to!' (1.2). However, the show also undermines in its viewer's minds any sense that this approach contains a full and satisfactory explanation for the existence of this alternative world. For each time that Tyler's liberal values force Hunt to rethink his position, there is an equivalent episode in which Tyler's policing seems hesitant, overwrought and over-thought in comparison to Hunt's more neanderthal approach to law and order. The audience is constantly reminded that Tyler is a better policeman and detective, but Hunt is a better TV cop. Thereby, the show implicitly critiques the realist analytical bent of contemporary TV crime thrillers, and asks its audience to acknowledge that what they miss in such TV shows is the indulgence of a form that isn't realist, a form that is overblown and which borrows from the wish fulfilment styles inherent in earlier cop shows, cowboy films, space and time travel narratives. In the first episode comedy arises from the fact that a murder suspect's diary pretty much defies analysis: 'From the diary, quote, 'I killed her. She's been killed. I'm a killer, an ace killer.' That particular entry is not awash with ambiguity' (1.1). This interplay between an almost constant reiteration of a modern Freudian explanation for the *Ashes* and *Mars* worlds, and the simultaneous undermining of this explanation is also emphasized in *Ashes to Ashes*, as Drake is supposedly familiar with Tyler's case and, upon realising that she is in the same world that Tyler entered and that she's met Hunt, she exclaims:

Alex Drake: You're taller than I imagined.
Gene Hunt: I'm bigger in every department.
Alex Drake: [feeling Gene's heartbeat] My God, it's real. (1.1)

Throughout both series the protagonists state repeatedly that they believe that their time travel is a product of their own psyches and that they have created a dream world that they can decode. They only have to identify the correct patterns and symbols. From the start potential patterns and symbols are simultaneously offered and then undermined, this impacts upon the audience's ability to read the show. The only thing that remains constant is the careful balancing of the considered and sensitive policing styles of Drake and Tyler and the brawn of the older television cops that dominate in Hunt's purgatory. This is epitomized in the character of Nelson, the landlord from the pub, who is altered depending upon who is talking to – he speaks in a Jamaican accent to the other characters but reverts to his natural Mancunian accent when talking to Sam, explaining: 'Folks just seem happier with the other Nelson' (1.1). Nelson seems poised between two worlds – he has one identity when he is with Sam and another when he talks to Hunt's team, he doesn't fundamentally change very much but the markers of his identity (particularly his accent) alter.

At the end of the first episode of *Life on Mars*, just when he is sure that he is dreaming, and that jumping off a building will force him to awake from his dream-world, Tyler is confronted with a moment of doubt, a challenge to his own logic, a challenge that will create and sustain a tension throughout both series, but one that is born out of his desire to believe in this new world:

[Sam stands on a building roof, planning to jump to wake up from his coma]

Annie Cartwright: We all feel like jumping sometimes, Sam. But we don't, you and me. Because we're not cowards.

[After taking Annie's hand]

Sam Tyler: What's that on your hand? Is that grit?

Annie Cartwright: Sand. When I was running up here, I tripped and I fell against the fire bucket.

Sam Tyler: See, why would I think of something like that? Why would I put that kind of detail in it?

Annie Cartwright: You wouldn't. (1.1)

Thus, the audience too is always carefully positioned as if they too are torn between two worlds, or rather between the two explanations, one rational (it's all in their heads), one fantastical (Hunt's world is real). This helps to create the drama that the series needs, but it also allows for a hybrid form to emerge – as the characters and the narrative are granted a unique licence to exist equally in both eras. The protagonist does not 'move' to the 1970s/1980s (we have no evidence of anything so concrete), rather the science-fiction time travel ensures that they are always poised between two forms and two eras of police drama. In some ways the show operates as a sort of anti-*Quantum Leap*; the present doesn't help to alleviate the risk of mistakes being made in the past when the two worlds collide, instead what is revealed is the illusory nature of the past, which becomes a place of fantasy and wish fulfilment for the officers stranded there. And this illusion is very much born out of the dying brains of a series of present-day police officers, each transferring their particular TV-inspired fantasies onto Hunt's template.

Notes

1. The show transferred (with limited success) to America in 2008, and, in the UK, a sequel to the series, *Ashes to Ashes*, aired on BBC One in February 2008. This was followed by a second series in 2009, and a third, and final series in 2010.
2. 'Gene Hunt is top cop, says poll'. The *Guardian* 4 July 2008 (London: Guardian News & Media).
3. For more details and discussion of this poster from both sides of the populist political divide, the following websites might be useful: http://www.theguardian.com/politics/ 2010/apr/02/david-cameron-gene-hunt-labour-poster, accessed 2 December 2013; http://www.dailymail.co.uk/news/article-1263244/Cameron-80s-TV-cop-Gene-Hunt-new-Labour-campaign-poster.html, accessed 2 December 2013; http://news .bbc.co.uk/1/hi/uk/8601781.stm, accessed 2 December 2013.
4. In addition to his leather jacket and jeans, the Doctor's accent suggests that he is a product of a specifically working class, Lancashire background.
5. The id is one of the three parts of Sigmund Freud's (1856–1939) model of the psyche, the others being the ego and the super ego. The id is the unorganized part of the personality structure that contains the basic drives. The id acts according to the 'pleasure principle' and is the unconscious seat of our desires.

8

Watchmaking in the Dark: the Intricacy of Intimacy in *Crime Traveller*

David Hipple

Crime Traveller is a 1997 BBC One series of eight 50-minute episodes, released on VHS and (in the UK and the USA) on DVD, but never repeated or continued[1]. Holly Turner is a police Science Officer with a time machine (built by her father) in her flat, which can send her a few hours or perhaps days into the past. (She briskly discounts the future, since it does not yet exist) (1.1). Turner and Detective Jeff Slade collaborate secretly, solving (but not thwarting) recent crimes, the 'Laws of Time' constantly constraining their actions. This discussion opens by sketching some of *Crime Traveller*'s genre-blending antecedents. We then consider the consequences of its design for series/serial character drama, its position amongst contemporary genre texts and others, and its distinctive operation as hybrid genre narrative. This series overtly locates itself primarily between science-fiction, fantasy and the detective story, while secretly operating more as a romance than anything else. Its promotion only cautiously recognizes the most nonchalantly entertaining genres working to rigorous underlying rules. Central to this discussion is *Crime Traveller*'s relentlessly equivocal presentation of time travel as philosophically momentous but historically sterile. Although its promoters actively played down the sense of continuity that would soon become a major selling point for episodic narratives, *Crime Traveller*'s true through-line is a character drama that develops smoothly across the series, enabled by the superficially pointless individual stories: eight entire episodes, nominally about crime-solving time travel, repeatedly and contortedly prove that the protagonists cannot possibly make any historical difference of any kind at all. And yet, this series remains an instructive treatment of 'time' as a trigger for drama.

In the faltering genre TV market discussed below, Jane Killick sensed that *Crime Traveller*'s 'detective-drama-with-a-twist' shtick could be an inheritor of the charm of 'classic series' *The Avengers* (1961–69), *The Champions* (1968–69) and *The Saint* (1962–69), and she reports its first episode gathering a healthy 11.1 million viewers (Killick, 16). On his website, series writer Anthony Horowitz now says of *Crime Traveller* merely that, 'It was liked and disliked in equal measure' (2013). Apparently further episodes once seemed likely ('In the second series we might start the episode with Slade time travelling,' and, 'Horowitz doesn't plan on writing the second series by himself') (Brown, 65), but none appeared. Time travel continues to be a strong science-fiction theme, as evidenced by regular TV and film releases as well as two recent (2013) landmark anthologies: the huge *Mammoth Book of Time Travel SF*, and the even more colossal *Time Traveller's Almanac*[2]. Both books inform my discussion here.

The very few scholarly allusions to *Crime Traveller* typically assess it as insubstantial amusement. Peter Wright's analysis of 1990s British TV science-fiction identifies only *Yellowbacks* (1990), *Chimera* (1991), *Stark* (1993) and *Black Easter* (1995) as 'retain[ing] British TV SF's characteristically reflective stance towards contemporary events', contrasting the techno-action series *Bugs* (1995–99) as typifying the remaining 'marginal SF series or revisions of earlier dramas':

> *Bugs* eschews political comment in favour of attributing the world's troubles to lunatic individuals. As such, it is light entertainment akin to Anthony Horowitz's punningly titled *Crime Traveller* [. . .] Given the obviously limited potential of the concept, the Rules [*sic*] of Time provide convenient dilemmas to what would otherwise be mini-adventures (Wright, 301–302).

We can, however, say more about *Crime Traveller* in relation to other print and screen texts. It mixes science-fiction, fantasy and detective conventions, a generic fusion with a respectable heritage across several media. In three novels from 1951, for example, John Dickson Carr transported twentieth-century characters into challenging historical settings. Another writer of detective fiction enthuses: 'No scientific or other wholly credible explanation is given for such whimsical feats. Yet these historical fantasy/supernatural detective story hybrids are among Carr's most accomplished works' (Pronzini, 1)[3]. P.J. Hammond says of creating the much later *Sapphire & Steel* (1979–1982):

> I've written fantasy in the past, for children's programmes. I'd written a lot of investigative stories for various police shows. I rarely wrote about police procedure itself: I wrote about strange, disturbing stories on the edge of crime. So this was a way of combining the two: an investigative story, which encompassed science-fiction and pure fantasy – and so you had two detectives coming to mend Time (2007).

In its own take on these genres, *Crime Traveller* presents time travel as circumscribed by strict Laws of Time. These are never definitively articulated, but those that Horowitz describes in one interview are as follows (my gloss):

1) Turner: 'If something has happened, it'll happen.' You may directly observe past events, but changing them is impossible (and your observation of an event is somehow part of it).
2) You can't use your 'future' knowledge to cheat: Time will somehow stop you.
3) Having travelled back in time, you must physically return to the machine by the exact moment of setting out or be consigned to the Loop of Infinity, reliving the same short period forever.
4) Meeting yourself would cause a 'temporal schism' (never explained, but sounds disastrous) (Brown, 64–65).

A further law is explicitly introduced in episode eight:

5) You cannot exist in more than two 'time zones', i.e. travel back to (or *through*) a journey you have already made (1.8).

The first episode also establishes Turner's father's disappearance into a Loop of Infinity, after failing to return to the time machine within its operating cycle. This stabilises for harsher science-fiction sensibilities the trope popularized as comic fantasy not much earlier by *Groundhog Day* (1993), strongly enough to make the first episode's title immediately comprehensible.

Kinship with *Bugs* is evident (it is made by the same company, Carnival Films, and produced by *Crime Traveller*'s co-producer Brian Eastman), including *Crime Traveller*'s inaugural self-inscription (although by no means carried consistently through the episodes) as an action-orientated show. The first episode's opening sequence culminates with a villain crashing his car out of a high-rise car park and falling several storeys into the Thames, echoing the hunted baddies driving off an unfinished flyover in *Bugs*' introductory episode (their car then inexplicably explodes in mid-air) (1.1). Carnival Films specifically primes both series' audiences to expect stunt-filled entertainment, but Horowitz's promise of 'lots of explosions and chases!' (Bailey, 24) in *Crime Traveller* is at best a little overinflated.

John Brosnan opposes Wright's evaluation quoted above by claiming that, 'The time travelling angle offers more plot potential than the *Bugs* formula,' but corroborates Wright's charge of political detachment in *Bugs*, and by association in *Crime Traveller*. Brosnan's acquaintance with Carnival's production priorities illuminates a perspective linking genre marketing strategy to narrative style: 'Back in 1995 I sold an idea to *Bugs* and so got the series "bible" which told potential writers that they were to avoid any form of social realism, no police, no hospitals, etc., and the characters were to have no personal lives' (66).

Only Slade, Turner and their boss develop beyond token sketches – although Detective Chief Inspector Kate Grisham nevertheless remains largely a conservative establishment figure. She appreciates smart, conscientious Turner's reputable foundation of scientific discipline, but despairs of Slade's impulsive, disrespectful approach to policing, moving to sack him early in episode one. His worldly effectiveness and Turner's intellect dovetail eccentrically, complemented by Grisham's bewildered support (and in episode seven Slade saves Grisham's career, by a whisker) (1.7); but their culture is blandly middle class, and at least three-quarters of their cases involve wealthy, elite and public figures. In episode five Gareth Oldroyd arrives 'down here', pursuing a criminal with a prominent record 'north of Watford' (a cliché implying parochial southern ignorance of England north of London) (1.5). Successive episodes' carefully-plotted temporal wanderings readily eclipse such cloudy hints of cultural and political context.

The physical environment is also strikingly unspecific. In episode one, Reading railway station's distinctive facade is doggedly anonymized to 'STATION'; and a tangentially significant betting shop is drearily marked 'BOOKMAKERS'. The bookie's window, however, imparts the pun 'A GOOD PAST TIME'. In the same white-on-blue lettering, episode five's laundry truck improbably announces 'LAUNDRY – Laundering time: same day'; and in episode eight a van bizarrely advises 'TIME IS RUNNING OUT: Time to take a break'. Also in episode five, a prison governor's inlaid floor reads 'tempus fugit' – all suitably austere visual jokes (the scripts are far snappier) for miraculous time travel consigned to such a bland context. Clocks commandingly introduce scenes or are smuggled into the mise en scène to reinforce the mainline sequence of linear events, upstaging the flavourless physical settings. This design thread runs throughout the series to the late Professor Hayward's clock-filled quarters in episode eight.

Presentation of the time machine itself is sumptuous in contrast. It is a magnificently ramshackle accretion of ill-matched screens, a laptop and other components, dominated by a digital stopwatch display (duplicated in a portable wristwatch accessory, to stress travellers' countdown-based jeopardy). More baffling is a portable quarter inch tape recorder (a type commonly used in broadcast industries into the 1990s), which Turner is frequently seen finely (and meaninglessly) adjusting to set up time trips. This connects with visual and sound design strategies that generally celebrate this remarkable machine. In episode six Slade sets the tape winding, with the momentary audio cliché of *something* speeding up, one of many subtle implications of time somehow being manipulated, however obscurely. When Slade narrowly (of course) manages his return to the time machine on this occasion, the first detailed shot includes the tape running in the foreground (1.6).

We see during Turner's solo trip in episode one that the time machine is really the whole room. She cranks up a control on the tape deck, and Anne Dudley's gorgeous, dreamy score gives way to a crescendo of clicks, trills and beeps. (During this sequence the frame displays a 1954 Tintin poster, *On a marché sur la lune* [*We Walked on the Moon*], asserting pop-cultural production credentials)[4]. She closes doors and shutters, creating a darkened capsule accentuated by a steep overhead view of the oddly-shaped room as the machine activates. Explosively loud, a band of light encircles the walls at floor level and rises towards the ceiling, replaced and followed by others, to a cacophony of synthesized sounds dominated by a rhythmic *whoosh*. This overlaying of striking visuals with detailed, luxuriant sound design is efficient shorthand for something exceptional yet plausibly mechanical taking place.

Slade's reactions to the machine both anticipate and disarm ridicule. As he first fumbles for what this rickety contraption resembles, Turner interrupts: 'Spare me the inane comparisons, please.' Following this first excursion, with its unnerving noise and sweeping lights, he nervously jokes, 'What did you do? Photocopy us?' Elsewhere, however, *Crime Traveller* establishes measured competence:

> We cannot change the past. There are deterministic webs that stitch up the past and the present. The most obvious example is the man who travels back in time and kills his grandmother. If he did so, he wouldn't have existed in the first place. This, of course, is a paradox. Time, therefore, has to protect the past. This is what Stephen Hawking described in his Chronology Protection Hypothesis. Past events must happen as they have happened. We may not always like it, but unless we learn to accept it, the very notion of time travel will remain forever out of our reach (1.4).

Thus Turner ends a lecture to the Institute of Time, launching episode four. She plays to orthodoxy, referring to Stephen Hawking's suggestion of time travel's impossibility in a 1991 speech[5]. Hawking facetiously imagines a Chronology Protection Agency safeguarding us from the inevitable associated radiation, perhaps enough to warp space-time sufficiently to prevent such travel in any case – or even sufficiently to collapse space-time to a singularity, ending the universe. He playfully concludes:

> The Chronology Protection Hypothesis is supported by some recent calculations that I and other people have done. But the best evidence that we have that time travel is not possible, and never will be, is that we have not been invaded by hordes of tourists from the future (140).

Science-fiction editors and writers retain ideas like this, often in detail. Peter Haining, for example, introduces his anthology *Timescapes* by quoting Hawking's cautious 1995 *retraction*: 'If you combine Einstein's general theory of relativity with quantum theory, time travel does begin to seem a possibility' (7). Paul Levinson also tackles Hawking in his story 'The Chronology Protection Case', itself a notable neo-noir addition to the intersection of time paradox and detective work[6].

Levinson's mismatched possible-couple find that they have in common an interest in convincing a vengeful universe that they will never publish the secret of time travel – a plot not a million miles from the present discussion.

Crime Traveller, then, also acknowledges Hawking and proposes its own solution: time travel is modestly possible within strict boundaries, but a traveller cannot influence events thus witnessed. Interpreted in these terms, attempted intervention in the past has always been visible from the perspective of the present, before (from the characters' point of view) the journey to the past took place. The trip to the past *has already happened*, and its consequences are established, seemingly 'before' the decision is made to undertake it. The challenge is to accept this subtle form of simultaneity: travellers have no second chance to influence events, as it might first appear, but may newly understand a brief slice of history more thoroughly from two simultaneous angles. This structurally formal approach to time travel narrative seems to have engaged Horowitz markedly: 'What happens in those three or four hours, maybe a day, happens twice. You have to dramatize those events twice, from two quite different perspectives – almost parallel worlds. It becomes incredibly complicated and rich and fun!' (Bailey, 24).

Thus the first episode unravels a classic locked-room murder mystery in this spirit, partly through the time travelling Slade being glancingly shot. This turns out not to be an attack at all, but an unintended consequence of the oblivious murderer's plan to mislead witnesses as to the timing of events. The bullet deflected from Slade's skull fortuitously creates a further clue, allowing him and Turner to recognize the attempted misdirection, and therefore to work out how only one person was in a position to try fooling investigators into interpreting the impossible-looking murder as therefore the unarguable suicide of someone with no obvious motive at all.

But if the murder itself cannot be prevented, what dramatically satisfying impact or purpose can time travel have in the first place? This chapter addresses such questions in terms of narrative form, generic function and audience engagement. On that last point, *Crime Traveller* clearly trains its audience into interpreting events from multiple perspectives, without the lengthy flashbacks of its similarly meticulous and more enduring contemporary *Jonathan Creek* (1997–present, following the latest of several production revivals). This underpins Horowitz's structural response to conventional detective series formats, in turn raising questions of generic operation discussed below.

As a product, *Crime Traveller* resonates closely with *Jonathan Creek* as well as its own stablemate *Bugs*, sharing with the latter a usually low-key science-fiction air akin to that of *Mission: Impossible* (1966–73), and to the atmosphere later firmly appropriated in Britain by espionage series *Spooks* (2002–11). *Bugs* had provided mainstream breakout roles for soap-opera actors Jesse Birdsall (*Eldorado*, 1992–93) and Craig McLachlan (following duties in *Neighbours* from 1987 to 1989 and *Home and Away* from 1990 to 1991), with Jaye Griffiths who had appeared in *The Bill* from 1991 to 1995. Another arrival in this marketplace was the ITV series *The Vanishing Man* (1997–98). Like *Crime Traveller* it was science-fiction written by Anthony Horowitz, this time clearly drawing on the American series *The Invisible Man* (1975–76), and (like *Bugs*) portraying a high-tech criminal underworld. *The Vanishing Man*, too, cast a popular face as its lead, in this case Neil Morrissey who had featured since 1987 in the comedy drama *Boon* (1986–95). *Crime Traveller* attempted the same for Michael French (Slade) following his original 1993–96 soap stint in *EastEnders* (1985–). These cases are all instances of 'stunt casting', where producers attempt to brand the product by presenting a reassuringly popular actor in the lead. Of those mentioned here, *Bugs* endured for a while but only *Jonathan Creek* and the considerably later *Spooks* became reliable fixtures, the latter featuring a heavy-duty cast centred on a very serious and established actor (Peter Firth), and the former flamboyantly casting a conspicuously thoughtful stand-up comedian (Alan Davies) in the lead. The others (including *Crime Traveller*) radiate a relative lack of confidence by trying to exploit the comparatively lightweight presence of popular soap stars, indicating considerable hesitancy in promoting science-fiction narrative in general. Promotional confusion was well illustrated in 2006 with ITV's *Eleventh Hour* by Stephen Gallagher (writer of *Chimera*, one of Wright's favoured science-fiction series, above). It starred Patrick Stewart, best known as Jean-Luc Picard in *Star Trek: The Next Generation* (1987–94), who confused audiences by insisting to many interviewers (who did not help by constantly invoking *Star Trek* and suggesting to him that *Eleventh Hour* was ITV's answer to the BBC's new *Doctor Who*) that the new series was not science-fiction at all.

Such confusion characterizes the landscape of British TV science-fiction in the mid-to-late 1990s. This market bemusedly looks back to the long success but eventual disappearance of *Doctor Who* (1963–89), reliably present for decades as a very British mainstay of popular science-fiction, with distinctive and generally admired shows like *Moonbase 3* (1973), *Blake's 7* (1978–81) and *Star Cops* (1987) irregularly swinging by on hyperbolic orbits. Come the 1990s, this familiar expectation had evaporated, a discomfort only exacerbated by overwhelmingly negative reaction to the transatlantic TV movie *Doctor Who* (1996). In 1992 authoritative science-fiction commentators assess *Doctor Who* as 'a notably self-confident series, juggling expertly with many of the great tropes and images of the genre,' while also outlining its latter-day disruptions of format and schedule, leading to indefinite suspension (Brosnan *et al*, 346). Five years later it was sorely missed, partly accounting for these tentatively experimental launches of other shows. Slade's glimpse of a salvaged police box in episode six is, in a 1997 context, affectionately understood as the obsolete emblem of a defunct series fondly remembered by any British television-watching child of the prior 30 years – not today's overwhelmingly iconic feature (a character in itself) of the revitalized mature drama *Doctor Who* (2005–) as cartwheeling Gothic romance. In 1997's environment there was no model for a credible and robust British science-fiction TV series.

The mystery/science-fiction/fantasy/detective space, into which *Crime Traveller* fell, was thus created by commercial conditions in British television, although thanks to exactly these insecure circumstances the creators seem to have been coy about any identification with science-fiction at all. Horowitz approaches an interview reluctantly granted to *SFX* magazine by claiming (without explanation) that, 'There's a nervousness about science-fiction on TV, as it seldom seems to work in England' (Brown, 63).

Stephen Gallagher clarifies the industrial conditions operating at this time. He was invited by *Bugs* co-producer Stuart Doughty to pitch ideas for this BBC adventure series, competitively inspired by a development memo originating in ITV. Admired for *Chimera*, Gallagher could now address contrasting ambitions:

> I had always wanted [. . .] to do something that was fast-moving, and fun, and not too taxing on the intellect, if I can put it that way without actually seeming to run the show down. I wanted to do [. . .] something that just got the target in its sights and absolutely went for it. And I suppose on my CV that's what *Bugs* does for me (2005).

Gallagher claims further that, 'We [i.e. *Bugs*] were the only fast-moving, light-on-its-feet adventure show.' Horowitz's *The Vanishing Man* attempted this for ITV, and Carnival aimed *Crime Traveller* at *Bugs*' BBC audience.

Gallagher describes Carnival Films as being 'basically Brian Eastman'. It is also responsible for the long-running detective series *Agatha Christie: Poirot* (1989–2013), suspended for a while from 1997. Horowitz had written nine episodes for *Poirot* by then. He frequently reports *Crime Traveller*'s inspiration arising from *Poirot*'s format, and he credits the *Poirot* and *Bugs* producer with making his new series possible:

> Brian Eastman, having heard that *Poirot* wasn't going to continue, asked me if I had any ideas for another series. I told him about the idea for *Crime Traveller* and he immediately commissioned me to write a script and the project was suddenly alive and running (Clark, 21).

The serendipitous idea mentioned here is a conceptual twist on conventional TV detective shows:

> TV detective shows tend to have a three act structure: act one, the murder; act two, the investigation; act three, everyone goes into the library and you flashback to the murder [. . .] You time travel back to the murder in the flashback. And I thought, well, why not get rid of the flashback and time travel for real? (Bailey, 24)

Here, then, were the circumstances leading to the optimistic launch of a TV series about a moderately competent and generally idealistic detective with authority issues, and his colleague who spends her private time tinkering with her missing father's time machine.

Crime Traveller allows speculation to arise over a relationship between the leads, initially deflating expectations of any liaison but consolidating the matter into a dignified narrative spine as the series evolves. Episode one sees Turner travelling alone to protect Slade's professional credibility, then beginning to share the machine with him; and episode two shows the pair developing an instinctive working rapport that suggests considerable personal affinity (in a story where her aunt's murder by poison scarcely affects Turner's emotions at all) (1.2). Philippa Sidle argues persuasively that episode three most definitively indicates potential beyond professional cooperation (1.3). Future-Turner must spend a night at Slade's flat to avoid meeting herself in her own, so, 'From an initial polite awkwardness [...] they progress over the evening to the kind of tentative closeness that precedes romantic advances between relative strangers' (Sidle, 2014). Then Turner remembers her belief that Slade's flat is available only because he is sleeping with the soon-to-be victim, and she destroys any romantic atmosphere. They end the episode amiably sharing a bottle of wine and agreeing to 'start again'.

Episode four nevertheless firmly moves this relationship into a slightly enigmatic spotlight. Slade arrests a criminal, who future-Turner later that day learns will shoot Slade. She travels to avert this, against her scientific judgment and refusing to explain why, lecturing him about the ethics of influencing people's actions. Slade *is* nevertheless shot. Narrative convolutions eventually reveal his inevitable survival, but only after Danny (the porter in Turner's residence) has asked what her lecture was about. 'I was outlining a scientific theory. All my work, everything I believe in, is based on it.' Danny asks how the talk went. Stricken, Turner replies, 'I was proved right.' Again, events seem to have demonstrated the futility of attempting to change the past – but this time (and having barely reacted at all to Aunt Mary's poisoning just two episodes earlier) Turner is affected deeply by this presumed personal cost.

Although episode five's main plot scrutinizes Slade's relationship with his father and their respective betrayals by Oldroyd, it also includes *Crime Traveller*'s most spectacular stunt since episode one's crash into the Thames, when Slade and Turner crash a car through a wall to prevent a major arrest from failing. A little later their future-selves are shown in a commandingly lofty concealment, observing their òwn crash. Mise en scène alone demonstrates their distinctively exclusive partnership's extension now to serious shared risk, before presenting them like a pair of superheroes standing guard together over mundane events.

If this should be in any doubt, it is emphatically echoed in the opening sequence of episode six: a gang meets at night to plan a robbery...but high above them, calmly watching, the uniquely equipped duo already wait. *He* whispers something, *she* nods very slightly, and they exchange an understanding glance: they have what they came for.

Episode six's initial surprise is that this gang is arrested just three minutes into the action. The main story emerges as a country house murder, but only after Turner has told Slade that they are wearing the machine out, and that he should return to conventional investigation. Slade (willingly) does so, but he and subordinate Nicky quickly hit a dead end. Slade assigns Nicky some tasks, then catches sight of a police box (evidently reminding him of *Doctor Who*) and with a smile simply says, 'I've got another line of investigation,' but Turner refuses the use of the machine. Undeterred, Slade talks his way past Danny and uses it alone. This becomes the episode's emotional focus, all the more so when future-Slade is captured and Turner (who has realized what he has done) solves the case in order to rescue him and return him to the machine in time to avoid the Loop of Infinity. Slade tells Turner that he used it because he 'wanted to *know*'. 'To know *what*?' she responds. 'That Hawkins was murdered by his illegitimate son? That he was being blackmailed by Kirby? Is that what you wanted to know?' To Slade's amazement at her knowledge, Turner bitterly says, 'I worked it out. It can be done.' By now the time travel seems no better than lazily treacherous: 'How could you? You steal in here, invading my privacy. You use my machine without my permission. And you almost get yourself killed in the bargain. How *could* you?' Turner has solved the case and saved Slade, whose trip only complicates the evidence while jeopardizing both his own safety and Turner's trust.

We have seen these two operate successfully only together. Turner's solo trip in episode one heads off Grisham's attempt to sack Slade – but also alerts the criminal, whose arrest would have led to others but who instead dies while fleeing. In episode four Slade thanks Turner for travelling and saving him, but she disagrees: 'I didn't save your life. I nearly got you killed.' Slade argues that only future-Turner's warning of his own shooting prompted him to pocket the book that stopped the bullet; but she points out that without her interference (impelled only by her own thoughts) he would never have been in harm's way to start with. In episodes five and six we are vividly shown the pair growing together as a team, only for Slade to betray their partnership. At Slade's attempted apology, the incensed Turner says, 'Sorry will *not* do. It won't even start. That's it. You can do whatever you like, but you are never, *never* using my machine again.' The episode ends with this alarming atmosphere accentuated by the bemused but not stupid Grisham, intrigued by Slade's success rate and unimpressed by Morris's efforts (see below), deciding to investigate Slade herself.

In episode seven all pretence of *Crime Traveller* being primarily a detective series is finally dropped. It opens with Turner trying to repair the machine. Slade arrives, with peace offering flowers for her (this relationship providing strong continuity between episodes), and Danny produces a more impressive bunch delivered for an absent tenant. Turner, at first grimly sarcastic, is still adamant about the machine but at least warms to the flowers. Slade convinces her that his scheme to fund the machine's completion by travelling back to win the National Lottery *might* not be 'cheating' (therefore breaking the Second Law of Time), and so he sets off.

Although time travelling Slade is roped in to deal with a robbery, the episode begins and proceeds with principal attention to the lead characters' relationship. In between, Slade's sole motivation for time travel in any case is to fund Turner's research through the titular 'Lottery Experiment'. Horowitz has said of this episode that:

The paradoxes became more fun to write about than who got killed. [...] I thought to myself, 'Why can't Slade win the Lottery? And if he can't win it, why can't he tell someone else the numbers?' Compared to that the actual crime in the story, a gold bullion robbery, became almost a sub-plot (Berkman, 22).

More generally, Horowitz has explained:

I began to realize that the crime was actually less interesting than the whole travel business itself. What it was much more about was paradoxes and riddles, and the puzzles of time which no one has ever dealt with before. That was what was exciting about it (Bailey, 24).

It quickly becomes clear that *Crime Traveller*, however it might be promoted generically, stabilizes naturally on the progress of this central relationship. In terms purely of plot structure, as Horowitz says, time travel is merely an inventive surrogate for the detective show's conventional flashback, with the novel pleasure of seeing each episode's 'flashback' intertwine itself with the mystery itself. Across these narratives, however, we also observe a partnership that is both willed and necessary, developing under the gaze of 'normal' society while also estranged from it. With Slade under suspicion in episode five, Detective Morris tries to ingratiate himself with Oldroyd: 'Slade's in pretty close with Turner, and when I saw her leaving just now I thought, well, it might be worth a try.' In episode six Grisham asks Morris to investigate Slade's prodigious crime solution rate. He is closer to the strange truth than Grisham can accept, when reporting that Slade's double decoys for him while Slade consults 'The Machine', a shadowy band of informers with which Turner is connected.

This relationship's development is entangled with the question of how Time apparently reacts to our heroes' various exploits. This matter has been implicit all along, but comes to the fore in the final two episodes.

Episode seven briefly wonders who or what controls this elaborately ineffectual time travel. Even while assisting Slade in exploiting the National Lottery, Turner continues to object: 'I bet it only gives you two minutes. I bet you it knows what you're doing.' Slade doubts that the machine has a view of any sort, but Turner clarifies, 'I'm not talking about the machine. I'm talking about Time.' Having travelled back, Slade is visibly pleased to find himself with 'more than twelve hours' to play with; but this is exactly what provides scope for the blizzard of diversions that assail him. The cancellations of Slade's training course and Turner's lecture (for which she has already left) are just the beginning.

This is reminiscent of *Sapphire & Steel*, where 'Time' is a wilful and even spiteful entity, quick to crush those unlucky enough to impede it. Sapphire explains, 'You can't see [Time] – only sometimes, and then it's dangerous. [. . .] You cannot enter into Time, but sometimes Time can try to enter into the present: break in; burst through and take things; take people.' Steel elaborates, 'It's very, very big; and it's very, very dangerous. [. . .] Creatures have access to the corridor [of Time]. They are forever moving along it, searching, looking, trying to find a way in' (1.1). Time in *Crime Traveller* is never overtly sinister, but it rectifies or neutralises events in ways that go poetically beyond natural regulatory processes.

Here, Time's first obstruction of Slade's plan occurs when Turner makes space for urgent notes by obliviously erasing the lottery numbers he has left for her. Nicky has forgotten to charge his 'Rolls-Royce of mobile phones' (in an era when almost no one had such a device); and just as Slade arrives at the only nearby public telephone it is occupied by an old lady with an unhurried stack of change to spend on small talk. Slade finally commandeers the phone booth in the name of police business, and calls Turner's now-empty office. The moment she finally enters to answer, Slade must respond to the alarm sounding in the bank to which Grisham has assigned his time travelling self, unaware of his dual presence. The note that Slade orders hand-delivered to Turner remains prominently unregarded on her office door; and a call to her car phone fails as she enters an underpass. Her fax machine is out of paper; and when Slade moves his note from her door to an unmissable space on her desk, it is instantly hidden by a police underling delivering a tray of samples.

Time seems to be manipulating numerous people either to protect its own integrity or to thwart Slade personally. This is not the vengeful force of *Sapphire & Steel*, but more like the sense in *Quantum Leap* (1989–93) of some controlling personality that drives narrative events towards some higher *good*. Slade energetically seeks to use time travel for monetary gain (albeit on Turner's behalf), but through *Time*'s intervention he largely inadvertently but very neatly foils the anticipated robbery, emphatically saving Grisham's reputation along the way and incidentally enriching his altruistic relationship with Turner.

As for the lottery experiment itself: failing to get Turner's attention, and with only minutes to spare, time travelling Slade entrusts his lucky numbers to the absolutely conscientious Nicky – who dutifully buys a ticket. Slade's numbers are 8, 12, 11, 22, 6, 1, rendered by Nicky as 1, 9, 22, 11, 21, 8 because he held Slade's note upside-down. Slade thus gets four out of six numbers correct, so his prize is not the intended millions but £186. This is £14 less than the cost of the laser refractor that Turner has to replace as a result of Slade's little jaunt. Slade is thus granted a few intangible social benefits for his trouble, but a peremptory jolt in purely practical terms. *Time* will not be messed with, but nevertheless somehow repays and/or encourages good intentions. This is the aspect of *Crime Traveller* that operates as fantasy rather than science-fiction: the narrative rewards laudable attitudes, rather than adopting likely consequences of purely empirical considerations.

By episode eight we know that Turner's financial circumstances are modest, her ramshackle time machine a labour of love dedicated to her father's memory and to research for its own sake. Even when the objective is financial, Slade uses the machine conscientiously (attempting to fund Turner's research). Turner maintains her machine through constant effort, inadequately funded by her police salary.

This episode takes shape with Slade and Turner leaving the Renoir Cinema following a screening of *Les Enfants du paradis*[7]. When Turner rejoices at this 'brilliant' and 'timeless' film (subtitles, black and white, three hours long), Slade jokes that it did at least seem 'endless'. We then learn that Turner originally saw it with her first boyfriend. When that very man, Stephen Marlowe, duly appears, Slade responds to him with undisguised jealousy. It is notable that the typically sanguine Slade responds as if threatened by the very idea of a boyfriend who could share with Turner a dense French film, and with whom she could also talk on a level about her science. Slade belittles this presence with uncharacteristically childish petulance, well before Marlowe is revealed as a genuine antagonist.

Marlowe's equivalent (and, we discover, ill-gotten) time machine contrasts strikingly with Turner's. Its sleek surface and engagingly tactile interface are dedicated to the pursuit of wealth (possibly corporate, preferably personal). *Crime Traveller*'s narratives prize human creativity being rightfully consecrated to public good, not committed to capitalistic profit. When about to kill Turner, Marlowe explains his plans for this technology: 'Time travel: it's the most astounding discovery since... well, whenever. Whoever puts their name to it is going to go down in history. And think of the money! Billions! And why should I share that with you?' (1.8)

Naturally Marlowe's scheme goes awry, and he is lost as his time machine disintegrates. That machine, however, yields to Slade the eye-wateringly expensive spare part to fix Turner's. *Crime Traveller*'s final shot is a close-up of her hand at last clasping his, over the 'electromagnetic crystal with niobium casing'. Their Heath Robinson mission (as Marlowe himself describes it) will, it seems, continue in philanthropic personal partnership[8]. *Time* appears to be very much on their side. Sidle drives home this connection's indispensability to the series as a whole: 'What is certain is that their relationship is a triangle, with the time machine forming the third corner. It comes between them and it binds them together' (Sidle). (It seems clearer that *Time* itself is the third participant, but with the machine as its enforcer or Earthly avatar.)

The series thus ends on a fantasy note, while retaining the overall aesthetic of rational science-fiction. It communicates modest but sincere intent to confront commercial and artistic issues across several genres, while competing with many other products to attract and retain an audience in this uncertain market. In this environment, its strategy included easing demand on audience investment by deliberately making each episode generally comprehensible on its own:

> Despite the fact that Slade's learning more about these Laws' effects from week to week, there's no continuity between episodes. 'You can watch them in any order you want,' says Horowitz. 'What's interesting is that the series has developed so that all eight are very different' (Horowitz quoted in Brown, 64–65).

This is disingenuous, and could only endanger *Crime Traveller*'s sense of coherence. True, each episode's surface story stands alone, with only a few continuing characters linking any together. In sequence, however, they constitute a firm arc not particularly concerned with the series' superficial themes; so another promotional own-goal from the same interview is Horowitz saying, 'It's wrong to call it science-fiction, because while there's obviously a big science-fiction element to it, it's about *Crime* and *Travelling*, as the title suggests. It's also just as much about detectives and the police' (quoted in Brown, 63). In attempting to make the episodes individually accessible, this statement draws attention away from the one thing (the evolving connection between Turner and Slade) that unites the continuing series as a greater, single story. For publicity purposes, Horowitz both distances the series from a popular genre despite having been wholly responsible for the adept application of its conventions, and disguises his solidly-written serial arc.

Series episodes need have nothing in common but style: *The Twilight Zone* (1959–64) is an *anthology series*, disparate stories without continuity. *Star Trek* (1966–69) is a *series* with *serial* insinuations: characters persist, *implying* internal chronology, but invariably episodes *stipulate* no sequence at all[9]. In contrast, it is almost ludicrous to contemplate *24* (2001–) except in terms of episodic continuity, epitomising the *serial* format of much modern TV drama, assisted by popular technology. In 1997 *Babylon 5* (1993–98) was verifying audience responsiveness to long story arcs, commonly time-shifting their viewing with VCRs. VHS and DVD sales of full seasons exploded in 2000 with *The X-Files* (1993–2002)[10]. These contemporary comments on *Crime Traveller*, however, actively downplayed its elegant accomplishment of this nascent market's defining structural feature.

The Laws of Time imply continuity at least of narrative discipline, a quality especially relevant to science-fiction and detective sensibilities, both represented in *Crime Traveller*. Introducing an alternate-history detective anthology, Lou Anders considers each genre's fundamental question:

In mystery, [the central] question is traditionally rendered as 'Who dunnit?' A crime has been committed, and the journey of our narrative will be to discover who did what to who, where and why. [...] Unravelling the mystery is at the heart of the story's promise and thrill. In the sister genre of science-fiction, the question is a somewhat broader 'What if?' [...] The mystery here is in figuring out what makes the world of the story different from the world we know and then examining the light that those differences cast on our everyday notions of society and self.

Who and what. Mystery and science-fiction (Anders, 11).

Anders then quotes Robert J. Sawyer, interviewed by John Scalzi: 'I've always thought that science-fiction has way more in common with mystery than it does with fantasy. SF and mystery, after all, both prize rational thinking and both require the reader to pick up artfully salted clues about what is really going on' (Anders, 12).

This persuasive view did not guarantee *Crime Traveller* acceptance. Sidle quickly discerned partisan camps of disapproval: 'Mainstream critical reaction to the first episodes was tinged with incredulity, rejecting the fantastical elements of the scenario, and serious sci-fi followers will probably dislike its lightweight, populist approach' (Sidle). Even deprecation, however, could occur in terms of patient engagement typical of genre fandom. Steve Miller writes to *TV Zone* magazine, for example, cursorily bemoaning the first episode's production qualities before focusing his complaint: 'It wasn't just the acting or the dialogue, or the dreadfully clichéd characters [...] it was the way the time travel aspect was handled that got me' (52). Seemingly Miller would forgive considerable production inelegance if fantastic material were only managed deftly, as his long letter outlines. Next issue, Liane Broadley responds: her letter refutes some of Miller's objections, accepts others (while asking, 'But what do you expect from a pilot?') and proposes both *The Vanishing Man* and *Crime Traveller* as valuable creations by the 'very talented' Horowitz, befitting a world already embracing *Jonathan Creek* (Broadley, 38). Such exchanges indicate and mobilize committed fans' cooperative expertise in science-fiction, fantasy and detective stories.

These magazines also include Dominic May's editorial reviews of all *Crime Traveller* episodes, again speaking to experienced viewers' nuanced evaluation. For example, of the pilot episode he says:

Based on this first episode, *Crime Traveller* is a hybrid of *Dempsey and Makepeace*, *Bugs* and *Poirot* enveloped in an H.G. Wells wrapper, and appears to be trying to appeal to the broadest possible audience. If you're looking for genuine science-fiction, forget it. [...] Overall the story was ludicrous, and this was its joy. I spent 50 minutes in front of this silly little series full of wooden characters in daft situations and loved every moment of it (60).

On reaching episode five, May is less smitten:

> The key to working out how Slade has been framed happens very early in this
> episode and could possibly be detected by a child of three rather than a trip back
> in Time. I look forward to a story when I am actually surprised by what Slade
> and Turner uncover (60).

Episode eight induces May's not-ungenerous summary comment: 'Will there be
a second series? Declining ratings suggest possibly not, but if renewal occurs a more
diverse take on the subject matter is required' (61). However these commentaries
evaluate the series overall and its individual episodes, they highlight fans' and critics'
standards for confidently successful fantastic material, standing up for both boldness
and consistency in unabashedly impossible narratives. Such observations expose
as inexpert and self-limiting the cautious production and promotional attitudes
outlined above.

This boldness/consistency balance is elucidated usefully by prolific author
and critic Isaac Asimov, who always sternly insisted that science-fiction, while
inevitably counterfactual, must cleave to plausibility. Usefully for this discussion
he wrote mysteries as well as his more famous science fiction, while also being
receptive to ingenious narratives' more general pleasures:

> I have often said [...] that the qualified science-fiction writer avoids the
> scientifically impossible. Yet I can't bring myself to make that rule an absolute
> one, because there are some plot devices that offer such dramatic possibilities that
> we are forced to overlook the utter implausibilities that are involved. The most
> glaring example of this is time travel (1995, 235).

Asimov first comprehensively invalidates time travel on various empirical
grounds, and then nevertheless embraces it as too fertile and entertaining to lose.
Malcolm J. Edwards and Brian Stableford essentially concur, persuasively stationing
time travel unsteadily between science-fiction and fantasy thanks to its inherent
logical contradictions (1228).

Ann and Jeff VanderMeer's landmark 2013 anthology declares a liberal stance
as to time travel's generic boundaries:

> Most prior [anthologies] have zeroed in on excellent yet decidedly science-
> fictional tales in which the focus has been on the dreaded 'time paradox' –
> otherwise known as either 'And Then I Found Out I Was My Own Father'
> or 'Will I Be Kissing My Mother By Mistake?' That may be the bedrock of time
> travel fiction, but there is so much more (viii).

The VanderMeers happily embrace fantasy and horror deployments of time travel[11], splitting their collection into four sections of which only one honours 'stories in which the paradox of time travel is front-and-center' (ix). Rian Johnson's Introduction also locates time travel narratives ambivalently. He first notes their affinity with science-fiction's rationality-based allure: 'A good time travel story will have an interior logic that encourages and stands up to untangling.' He also qualifies this point, though:

> When we're talking about whether or not a story's 'time travel logic' makes sense, it is important to remember that every story builds its own framework for its own logic. In that sense, time travel is more of a fantasy-based story element than a science-based one (xi).

Johnson goes on to compare the joys of a time travel story with those of an Escher illustration: *knowing* that a staircase cannot really do *that* does not stop us enjoying the drawing in its own terms. Untangling its impossible ramifications is its essential intellectual appeal.

Farah Mendlesohn and Edward James draw a succinctly systematic distinction between science-fiction and fantasy: 'The most obvious construction of fantasy in literature and art is the presence of the impossible and unexplainable. This helps to cut out most science-fiction which, while it may deal with the impossible, regards everything as explicable' (3).

This is a cleft stick for *Crime Traveller*. Its science-fiction trappings decisively regulate consistent stories, avoiding amateurish condescension. (*Babylon 5*'s producer and main writer, J. Michael Straczynski, excoriates TV professionals who believe that, 'As long as we have aliens, ray guns and spaceships, we're *guaranteed the sci-fi audience automatically*,' or, 'It's Sci-Fi. There are no rules. You can do whatever you want').[12] On the other hand, John Grant characterizes 'the timeslip detective mystery' (citing Carr's aforementioned novels) as a recognizable flavour of fantasy narratives that address mysteries by means inspiring little rational credulity (821–823). *Crime Traveller* teeters between romantically arbitrary timeslips and drily technical projections.

Horowitz, cursorily aware of fantastic TV history, tried to fit his stories to respect viewers' mature expectations and acumen: 'It wasn't meant to be *Doctor Who* or anything like that. It was meant to be more intelligent and complicated in its own little way.' He expands on this:

> There is a sort of extraordinary jigsaw element going on. These are incredibly complicated stories. They may seem occasionally daft or dumb or whatever, but underneath it all the idea of repetitive action, all the rules of time [. . .] all these rules which we created we then obeyed rigorously (2004).

Similar discipline later informed creation of the audacious time travel riffs in *Life on Mars* (2006–07), also stabilized in audience understanding by knowing roughly how the police might work:

We'd always have to sit down now and again and have a discussion about, 'Right, what's the science of this show? What's the logic of this show?' Now we *understand* the logic of the show; and when you see it onscreen the logic of the show is pretty straightforward (Naryan, 2006).

Like *Crime Traveller*, *Life on Mars* projects firmly rules-based science-fiction rationality. Its sequel *Ashes to Ashes* (2008–10) eventually resolved the overall story as supernatural fantasy, but the US remake of *Life on Mars* (2008–09) maintained an intact science-fiction scenario throughout. Like *Crime Traveller*, these creations all (initially) espouse ideals of science-fiction plausibility, venerating clear evidence and reasoning. Introducing a collection of his own mystery stories, Asimov sets out the basics of fair play with one's audience, whether dealing with science fiction or detective stories:

You explain all facets of the future background well in advance so the reader may have a decent chance to see the solution. The fictional detective can make use only of facts known to the reader *in the present* or of 'facts' of the fictional future, which will be carefully explained beforehand (1968, 10).

It was Asimov's stricture (however unwittingly) that made *Crime Traveller* such a generic challenge for writer and audience. While constantly declaring the past fixed, *Crime Traveller* consistently pursues an ideal of influencing it – in the hope of altering the present, while simultaneously interacting with it. Horowitz has claimed (as if in answer to Dominic May's final critical assessment, above) that further episodes would have had to relax or modify at least some of the admirably conscientious restrictions imposed on those that were made.

The rules were so tough that writing these shows became a little bit like manufacturing a watch with your eyes shut: getting all the pieces together and trying to make everything fit. So, if there were a second series, I think I'd have to start breaking some of the rules of time, for a start – because it became really one step away from impossible to do it (2004).

Slade and Turner might perhaps have contrived access to broader expanses of history, or could have discovered the possibility of more than two perspectives on events. (What happens if you time travel a second time, while *already* on a trip into the past? Or what is the exact logic of an encounter with another traveller, from a 'present' other than your own?) The scene was implicitly set for a quest to rescue Turner's father from the Loop of Infinity (an idea still mined for narrative impetus in later series such as *Supernatural* [2005–] and *Flash Gordon* [2007–08]), particularly after seeing rival traveller Marlowe's enigmatic disappearance in the final episode's dying scenes – an incident also offering story potential comparable to the 'evil Leapers' in *Quantum Leap*'s final season[13]. The fact that supposedly unalterable time exhibits something like a sense of humour in facilitating what it does of the existing escapades invites exploration resonant with the resolutely messianic air of many *Quantum Leap* episodes, particularly the final one ('Mirror Image' 5.22), or Al's seemingly successful prayer for Beckett in another ('Leap of Faith' 3.3).

We are unlikely to discover how a continuing *Crime Traveller* would have developed, but if only from Horowitz's slender speculation we can conjecture that it would have filled out as a more substantially coherent drama than its original reception might suggest. Generically, the series has three complementary supports. As *science-fiction* it strives admirably for an absolutely consistent world, its own innovations kept on a short leash. Its *detective* narratives are constructed in meticulous detail. And its *fantasy* element, the characters' mysterious but dynamic relationship with Time (facilitating their evolving relationship with each other), quietly underpins the entire run.

This last quality is the one thing knitting an otherwise unorganized series into a solidly functioning *serial*, energising the developing partnership that enables individual episodes in the first place, and shaping their succession into a meaningfully continuous sequence in a fashion never attempted in (for example) the original *Star Trek*. The other two generic qualities doubly ensure each episode's internal coherence, and its fair treatment of whatever audience it might attract. Regardless of opinion as to acting, dialogue, clichés or any other element of actual production, buried in *Crime Traveller*'s sole continuous story of two people's emerging relationship is a far more rich and subtle lesson in the application of popular genre than its contemporary reception tends to indicate.

Notes

1. The series was mischievously released on both tape and disc as Part One and Part Two, so the 'Complete Series' DVD Region 2 release still includes two discs labelled *Crime Traveller* and another two labelled *Crime Traveller II*. In truth this was only ever a single series of eight episodes.

2. Mike Ashley (ed.), *The Mammoth Book of Time Travel SF* (London: Robinson, 2013); Ann and Jeff VanderMeer (eds), *The Time Traveller's Almanac* (London: Head of Zeus, 2013).

3. Carr's other relevant novels are *Fire, Burn!* (1957) and (as Carter Dickson) *Fear Is the Same* (1956).

4. The mise en scène declares cultural credibility in other ways, too. In episode four, for example, the murdered artist's landlord has positioned a poster for the Ealing film *The Ladykillers* (1955) behind his desk.

5. Wikipedia points instead to Hawking's article 'Chronology protection conjecture' in the following year's *Physical Review* Vol 46 #2, <http://en.wikipedia.org/wiki/Chronology_protection_conjecture>, accessed 3 December 2013.

6. Paul Levinson, 'The Chronology Protection Case' (*Analog Science Fiction*, September 1995), reprinted in Mike Ashley (ed.), *The Mammoth Book of Time Travel SF* (Robinson, London, 2013), pp. 258–81.

7. Jean Renoir was a filmmaking contemporary of Marcel Carné, director of *Les Enfants du paradis*.

8. W. Heath Robinson was an illustrator famous for depicting elaborate contraptions composed of levers, pulleys and knotted string. Scrutiny of each contrivance would typically reveal a rather unremarkable purpose.

9. Only two of *Star Trek*'s 79 episodes dictate specific chronology: 'I, Mudd' (3 November 1967) is narratively located *after* 'Mudd's Women' (13 October 1966).

10. See Derek Kompare's research, e.g. 'Publishing Flow: DVD Box Sets and the Reconception of Television', *Television & New Media* Vol 7 # 4 (November 2006), pp. 335–60.

11. For this discussion's purposes, 'horror' sublimates into science-fiction if exploiting rational worldly threat, or into fantasy if reliant upon magical/supernatural effects.

12. Producers of TV series *V* and *War of the Worlds*, interviewed by Straczynski and quoted in J Michael Straczynski: 'The Profession of Science Fiction 48: Approaching Babylon', *Foundation* #64 (Summer 1995, pp. 5–19), pp. 6, 7.

13. 'Deliver us From Evil' (10 November 1992); 'Return of the Evil Leaper' (23 February 1993), 'Revenge of the Evil Leaper' (23 February 1993).

9

'Centuries of Evil... Wacky Sidekicks... Yadda, Yadda': Vampire Television, Vampire Time and the Conventions of Flashback

Lorna Jowett

TV, especially serial television drama, has, according to Glen Creeber, 'unparalleled temporal breadth' (2004: 19). Team this with the cultural icon of the ever-youthful, nearly immortal vampire, and time on vampire television becomes endless. Time, for vampires, works differently. Vampires are generally presented as ageing much more slowly than humans, if at all; often they heal faster or regenerate. This is part of their appeal in a contemporary culture dominated by images of youth. The age of the vampire allows for epic scale and travel through time as well as travel across countries and cultures, or what one character from *Angel* (1999–2004) cynically summarises as 'centuries of evil... wacky sidekicks... yadda, yadda' (Lilah Morgan in 'Lullaby' *Angel* 3.9). This vampire version of time as part of serial TV drama necessarily takes existing ways of presenting time and combines them with the conventions of vampire fictions.

Any example of visual storytelling makes demands on its audience in terms of how time is represented. Richard Maltby, discussing Hollywood cinema, notes that 'In the course of the most unremarkable movie, audiences may need to comprehend the significance of acceleration and delay, parallel time-frames, and the mechanisms of temporal continuity and its violation' (2001: 413). I do not wish to argue that vampire TV radically innovates or provides new ways of representing time and/or memory. Flashbacks in vampire TV shows tend to follow some of the basic principles expected of classical Hollywood cinema, for instance. As Allen

Cameron observes, 'where the narration departs from story order, it does so in order to integrate the present, past and future in a coherent way, allowing for the forging of causal connections' (2012: 4). The same pattern is evident in most flashbacks from vampire television, since the 'forging of causal connections' is the main motivation for flashback: we enter the past of a vampire character in order to find meaning in a connection between past and present. Generally, this meaning is constructed as a form of backstory and speaks to character development.

However, it is also worth stating the obvious: that television does not operate in the same ways and with the same narrative structures as film. Character development is one area where television differs from cinema; perhaps not in its nature, but in degree. Maltby suggests that in seeking to construct 'a coherent sequence without the boring bits' (2001: 429), a Hollywood movie adheres to what he calls *mise en temps*. '*Mise en temps*', he argues, is 'another form of Hollywood's textual economy – excising the irrelevant and maximizing our attention to the relevant, showing us all we need to know and getting the most from what we do see' (431). Drama on television need not adhere to textual economy in the same way. Telling a story can take longer when 24 one-hour time slots per year for any given number of years are available over which to unfold the narrative. Moreover, while 'classical narrative', according to Cameron, 'is opposed to *excessively overt* displays of repetition, as it undermines the linear progression and unity of the story' (2012: 10, original emphasis), serialized television drama relies on structures of repetition and familiarity as well as on novelty and ongoing narrative dynamics. Maltby points out that cinema cannot afford its audience to miss vital information and thus signposts it vigorously, while also observing that watching a film more than once allows us to notice things we had not previously paid attention to (2001: 430). Serial drama on TV usually incorporates reminders of previously aired information in 'previously on' segments, and can return to minor details from previous episodes, altering, or at least heightening, their significance by reworking them in relation to the present, ongoing narrative. Thus TV shows encourage detailed attention by audiences, dropping 'clues' for attentive viewers and even relying on repeat viewing of archived episodes.

In this sense, contemporary television drama often operates slightly against the tendency 'in conventional cinema' described by Cameron where 'spectators can be made to "forget" the formal workings of narrative via a process of naturalization, in which temporal structures are simply reflections of the psychological or physical activities of the characters' (2012: 88). Like many other 'quality' TV series from *The Sopranos* (1999–2007) to *Breaking Bad* (2008–2013), most of the examples analysed here offer self-contained episode plots alongside season arcs and ongoing series arcs. Thus television viewers may well enjoy what Jason Mittel dubs the 'operational aesthetic' (in Cameron 2012: 22), or the conscious awareness of how narrative structures unfold in a given drama. Yet at the same time, the flashbacks in vampire

TV *are* naturalized – as part of the conventions of visual storytelling, as part of the structure of their particular narrative, and as routinized 'interruptions' to the forward progression of narrative, necessary televisual digressions that add novelty and spectacle to a familiar premise.

The endless seriality of a soap opera like *Dark Shadows* (1966–1971) continually requires new material and extended flashbacks provide this, adding novelty to the ongoing drama and filling out character backstory. Use of different time frames heightens the sense of Barnabas Collins as not only an immortal vampire but also as a sympathetic character labouring eternally under a curse and forever seeking his lost love. Flashbacks enable character development on a new scale, as well as providing a dynamic sense of change in shows which focus on redemption. The now-common trope of the sympathetic reluctant vampire, dating back to Barnabas Collins, heightens the moral complexity that Milly Williamson argues is inherent in serialized narratives (2005: 48). Vampire TV also uses flashback as memory (point of view), with the ensemble casts of *The Vampire Diaries* (2009–) or *Buffy the Vampire Slayer* (1997–2003) and *Angel* allowing for competing versions of the same story. Vampire TV offers a unique opportunity to analyse how conventions of flashback work in serial drama.

Representation of the vampire, perhaps particularly on television or in serial narrative, tends to oscillate between emphasizing change and highlighting stasis. A vampire character is represented as effectively immortal, experiencing a much longer period of existence than a human. Flashbacks may therefore be used to remind viewers how long a given vampire character has existed: while we may meet this character on a regular basis, and over the course of a season or a series may get to know them, they are not human. 'The vampire,' as Jeffrey Weinstock points out when discussing cinematic versions, 'transcends the limitations of its own body, communicates psychically across distances and defies linear temporality (2012: 12), and thus, he argues, operates as a symbol of our 'desire to transcend the limits of time and space and become something other' (13). Helen Powell takes a rather different view, suggesting that for movie vampires, 'The world around them changes: new inventions, new technologies, new political struggles arise but they do not age', concluding that 'In this context the challenges of immortality are interestingly brought to the fore' (2012: 102). The rise of the sympathetic vampire and the proliferation of stories told from the vampire point of view certainly highlight these 'challenges' (the alienation or loneliness that might result from becoming a vampire). However while its vampires may remain unchanged physically, vampire TV, largely through its flashbacks, insists on change as a form of character development. TV vampires do not remain untouched by passing decades or centuries, rather their attachments, opinions and motivations fluctuate, and flashbacks are used to make connections between different periods of a vampire character's existence.

In *Being Human* (2008–2013), vampire Mitchell's age is emphasized from the start, when we see him turned during World War I. The sense of vampiric stasis contrasting change in the surrounding society identified by Powell is emphasized during a montage showing Mitchell walking down a night-time street, the passing of time denoted by changing fashion rather than by his physical body (1.4). This effect functions as a corollary to the use of 'fast motion photography . . . depicting the speed at which immortals move' (Powell 2012: 98), another convention of vampire film and television. Both have the same effect, emphasizing that vampires experience time differently.

Likewise, *Angel*'s season three develops its title character, the 'vampire with a soul', by unfolding a season arc involving an old adversary. When he was the soulless vampire Angelus, a notorious mass murderer, Angel killed Daniel Holtz's wife and son in 1764, and turned his daughter into a vampire, forcing Holtz to kill her. Thus, when Holtz is magically brought to present day Los Angeles, he is set on vengeance. This is not the first time a character representing Angel's (or Angelus') past has (re)appeared, but the relationship between Holtz, Angel/us and his vampire 'sire' and lover Darla affords rich material for extensive character development, emotional engagement and narrative complexity. When human Lilah Morgan accidentally walks in on a confrontation between Holtz and Angel, and Holtz asks if she knows what Angel is, she says, 'Yeah, I know. Vampire, cursed by Gypsies who restored his soul, destined to atone for centuries of evil . . . wacky sidekicks . . . yadda, yadda' ('Lullaby'). Her comment highlights vampire time: 'centuries of evil' and decades of good are not 'normal' human measurements. In his own series, Stacey Abbott notes that Angel is 'represented as a man who is haunted by his past, which every once in a while emerges into the present to torment him' (2009: 78), with flashbacks emphasizing not only his long years of existence but also his transition from Angelus to Angel, and the consequences of those 'centuries of evil'.

Mary Ann Doane, in a discussion of cinematic time, identifies how film flashbacks can be seen to archive the past, or how they express a desire to do so. Yet she also problematizes this notion: 'What is archived then, would be the experience of presence. But it is the disjunctiveness of a presence relived, of a presence haunted by historicity' (2002: 23). This applies particularly effectively to vampire television, where characters like Angel are regularly 'haunted' by their own history, and where flashbacks can present these characters in identifiable historical moments, yet work simultaneously to create vampire legends (key vampire characters like Angelus or Mitchell often have a reputation for being particularly vicious killers). Vampire time, as Weinstock and others argue, can disrupt linearity. A flashback is experienced as both past and present: it is part of a frame narrative in the present, but events depicted in the past of the flashback inevitably unfold in the present tense. This results in the 'disjunctiveness' Doane identifies. *Dark Shadows*, one of the first examples of complex vampire TV, not only uses flashbacks but also incorporates other time frames. 'The show's heavy reliance on flashbacks, flashforwards, dream sequences, and Parallel Time zones,' states Harry Benshoff, 'complicates and confounds linear narrative structure(s)' (2011: 27).

Just as flashback offers the past as present, Maltby notes, 'The future can be discussed or inferred ... but it cannot be visualized without being translated into the present tense' (2001: 433). Flashforwards, such as those in *Being Human* season four, suggest branching paths to the future and highlight the consequences of present choice and action. This is an extension of the strategy taken in *Buffy the Vampire Slayer*'s 'The Wish' (3.9), where a wish that Buffy had never come to Sunnydale is granted by a vengeance demon, and we see the path not taken: 'Welcome to the future', proclaims the demon, as we move into another time frame. In this timeline, the town is overrun by vampires under the command of the Master, a vampire killed by Buffy in the season one finale, and every regular character but one dies fighting vampires in the showdown. (A similar approach is taken in *Angel*'s 'Time Bomb' (5.19) where Old One Illyria begins to slip through time, moving back and forward, eventually killing all the major characters in one fight scene before her dangerous excess power is siphoned off by Team Angel and the deadly fight is averted.) The future of 'The Wish' is averted by the action of parallel universe Giles, who destroys the demon's power centre, averting the wish and erasing his own timeline, but not before the episode suggests a dystopian ending to the series. Moreover, the present tense of the visualized alternative timeline heightens the impact of this grim alternative: it not only *could* happen, it *is* happening.

Being Human's season four applies the same concept but shows the consequences on a much larger scale. It opens with a flashforward to 'London 2037' and, throughout its episodes, ghost Annie sees a woman from the future who encourages her to take action and save the world from a global vampire apocalypse. During this season, Annie is caring for baby Eve after the deaths of Eve's parents, werewolves George and Nina. The season arc involves a vampire prophecy about a 'war child', initially thought to be the potential destroyer of all vampires, whom we discover to be baby Eve. It is Eve herself, reaching across time as the adult woman she will become, who finally shows Annie vampire Hal's role as the 'poster boy' for vampire world domination. Eve presents scenes from 'my present, your future' and tries to persuade Annie that in order to avert the apocalypse Eve must not survive. In an episode pointedly titled 'Making History' (4.7) the disjunctive temporality of these flashforwards is further enhanced by the way Eve shows Annie a physical location but the future horrors she describes are evoked through sound rather than visuals. The alternative present does not unfold visually, as in 'The Wish'; here Annie, and the audience, *hear* the sounds of the horrors Eve describes but *see* an empty place. While this may be because of budgetary limitations, it offers a jarring sense of the future as a possibility rather than a concrete certainty. The disjunctiveness offered by such alternative timelines, which disrupt the whole premise of a series, requires some form of resolution, and generally such narrative strands return to standard operation, restoring 'normality' in the timeline we are accustomed to[1]. Thus, as with *Buffy* after 'The Wish', *Being Human* averts the vampire apocalypse, though the following and final season also ends in apocalypse, suggesting that once evoked, such threats cannot be entirely dissipated. Analysing *Dark Shadows* as Gothic television, Helen Wheatley comments that unsolvable conflict extends into past as an uncanny narrative structure (2006: 153) and vampire TV applies the same strategy to the future.

True Blood (2008–) takes a slightly different approach, in that its whole premise is a kind of branching path or alternative present. In this world, the development of artificial blood allows vampires to overcome the main reason for centuries of secrecy and admit their presence publically. Now they no longer need to feed on humans to survive, vampires need not behave like monsters themselves, nor be treated as monsters by others. This aspect of the show ties into another aspect of vampire time on TV: an epic scale which allows for moral complexity.

While the majority of vampire TV shows feature at least one reluctant vampire character, it is commonplace to include 'bad' vampires alongside 'good' ones, and to have even the 'good' vampires struggle to control their blood lust. Contemporary narratives often present the vampire's blood lust as an addiction and thus the story of any given reluctant vampire on TV tends to be a series of recoveries, backslidings, interventions and renewed vows to stay clean. In this way, the biological fixity and stasis involved in becoming a vampire is continually contrasted with shifting moral stances as reluctant vampires seek redemption for past (or current) transgressions. In his discussion of the films *Bad Timing* (1980) and *21 Grams* (2003), Cameron points out how the moral failings and/or redemption of characters can be highlighted through narrative structure, especially through different temporal frames (2012: 35). Vampire TV similarly uses structures of narrative and juxtaposition of time frames to point out either transgression or redemption for reluctant vampire characters. The vampire's effective immortality often means vampire TV can play with the notion of the vampire as a fixed point, around which time can fold. Moreover, visiting the past is frequently a means of undermining certainty about morality and identity. The vampire may be a biological fixity in terms of outliving humans, but morally and subjectively vampire TV suggests that vampires are continually changing, or at least attempting to change. In this way, flashbacks in vampire TV stick to the rules for inserting flashbacks, offering visits to the past as secondary narratives subjugated to the primary, present-day narrative which retains its position as *the* ongoing narrative, yet the flashbacks suggest that the scale of that ongoing story is much grander than usual.

One obvious means of addressing morality in vampire TV flashbacks is the origin story. For a vampire, this is the point at which they were 'turned' or 'sired' as a vampire, transitioning from human to 'monster'. Such origin stories are usually inserted into the present-day, forward-moving narrative structure as significant revelations (for other characters and/or for the audience) and continue to have resonance in the present. This notion is extended from individual characters to the vampire 'species' in series such as *The Vampire Diaries*, which features a group of vampires dubbed 'the Originals' and ties their origin story to the evolution of the vampire (revealed in season three), and, to a lesser extent *Being Human*, which features the Old Ones, ancient vampires who are instrumental in trying to bring about the vampire apocalypse averted during season four.

This fascination with origins might suggest that vampire stories are fixated on what makes a vampire, either individually or in the general sense. To an extent this is borne out by their emphasis on the nature of vampires (demons, monsters) and on the attempt to retain humanity by the reluctant vampire characters featured in so many of these shows. In vampire films, because they generally offer closed narratives, relationships between vampires and humans tend to be more black and white. Vampire TV, in contrast, more insistently deconstructs the binary opposition set up between human and monster. Here, the origin of a vampire is not simply the point at which they stopped being human, it is a crisis of identity that is revisited repeatedly throughout the ongoing narrative, either referenced specifically, or by inference each time the reluctant vampire wavers in their determination to continue to 'be human'. The title of *Being Human* promotes this idea as the main aspiration for its triumvirate of vampire, werewolf, and ghost characters; similarly *True Blood*'s title foregrounds the artificial food source that enables vampires to come out of the coffin and 'mainstream' or live among humans. The many difficulties in actually achieving harmonious or non-disruptive vampire-human relationships form the focus of a range of vampire TV series.

'Spike is a work in progress', states Rhonda V. Wilcox (2006: 59), neatly summarizing the changes wrought by several years of narrative on a vampire character initially meant to be a one-dimensional villain briefly introduced into *Buffy the Vampire Slayer*'s second season (see, for example, Marsters in Norton, 2012). As with Barnabas in *Dark Shadows*, the writers and producers were persuaded by Spike's popularity to keep the character and develop his role. Benshoff identifies the moment the *Dark Shadows* team decided they needed 'to soften' Barnabas 'from monster/killer to a more complex ongoing character, the writers began to give him regrets about his monstrous status' (2011: 18) as the birth of the reluctant vampire. Barnabas was seen by audiences as a victim, either of his own condition (as a vampire, he has outlived everyone he knows and feels isolated and lonely), or of its nature (as a vampire, he is forced to be a monster). Thus, while he might behave monstrously to some characters, such as his Renfield-like helper, Willy Loomis, Barnabas demonstrates lingering humanity in other relationships. This pattern is replicated with other characters, such as werewolf Quentin Collins, and Benshoff notes that *Dark Shadows* overturns the standard endings of vampire movies and horror films, where the monster has to be defeated to restore normality. This ongoing story, he argues, 'is more about its gothic characters' struggles with their own desires and identities than any attempt to vanquish him or her in the name of traditional moral order' (2011: 31). A similar structure of struggle and shifting identity over time is seen in subsequent examples of vampire TV.

The apparent opposition between soulless killer Angelus and Angel, 'the vampire with a soul', is an obvious example. In using the notion of the 'soul' as a defining principle in constructing its vampire mythology, *Buffy* and consequently its spin-off *Angel* apparently sets up a clear distinction between vampires and humans: vampires have no soul, they are human shells inhabited by demons, and are therefore evil. Very soon, however, this distinction is complicated and the lines between human and vampire are blurred. A further consequence of this mythology is that Angel's own history has not one but two origin stories. Human Liam became Angelus when sired by Darla in 1753, but another pivotal moment comes nearly a century and a half later in 1898 when Angelus is cursed by gypsies and has his soul returned. Overwhelmed by the horrors he has perpetrated as a vampire, he eventually takes the name Angel and attempts to help humans. This history unfolds slowly over several years and two series, setting the character's oscillations from 'good' reluctant vampire to 'bad' uncaring killer in a fresh context, and deepening the resonances of Angel's struggle to control his vampire desire and retain the identity he has chosen (see Stacey Abbott for more on Angel/us).

The mythology of the shows may describe Angel's problem as relating to his soul, or lack of one (and this is further elaborated when Spike also recovers his soul in seasons six and seven of *Buffy*) but he is also presented to the audience as someone suffering a powerful addiction (see Dale Koontz, for example). Likewise, both reluctant vampires in *Being Human* are also depicted as coping with addiction, though Mitchell and Hal adopt different strategies. Hal engages in repetitive behaviours and, over a period of nearly 60 years, practises how to 'fight small urges' in order to 'resist much bigger ones', alluding to the elements of obsessive-compulsive actions in some versions of vampire lore. 'I like routine', he tells Annie, 'it keeps me – it keeps my mind occupied' ('Being Human 1955' 2.2). Thus we see Hal constructing elaborate domino patterns, building houses from cards, cleaning, and exercising to stave off his 'urges'. As we have seen, season four suggests that Hal might have a leading role in the vampire apocalypse, and the final season of *Being Human* presents him as a kind of split personality, much like Angel/us, with a bad side that eventually comes to the fore however hard Hal tries to repress him.

In her analysis of costume drama films, Julianne Pidduck notes how in certain examples, 'the male protagonist is afforded a depth and complexity that come with ageing and regret, whereas the female object of desire remains frozen in time' (2004: 57). This tendency is a feature of vampire TV, which certainly awards 'depth and complexity' to its male vampire characters, especially as a function of 'ageing and regret', yet here it is the male protagonist who 'remains frozen in time' courtesy of vampire immortality. While *Being Human* is resolutely contemporary and generally eschews extended 'period' flashbacks (in keeping with its social realist aesthetic), this tendency is made highly visible when Mitchell meets a lover from his past, Josie, in the hospital where he works. She has aged physically, while he has not, and she describes him as 'frozen. Like a photograph' ('Where the Wild Things Are' 1.5). Later we discover that Mitchell met Josie in 1969, and she helped him get clean ('The Looking Glass' 2.5).

Here the fixity of the vampire body is an indication of loneliness: in the present, Josie has married and is now widowed and being treated for terminal cancer. Her appearance is thus embedded in mortality, while Mitchell appears unchanged to her. The same effect is achieved in season two, using a slightly different relationship, when vampire Daisy visits an aged woman in hospital ('Cure and Contagion' 2.1). When she is found leaning over the woman with a pair of scissors, Daisy explains that it is her daughter and she wanted to cut 'the last thread' to her human life, felt 'even from the other end of the world'. A similar scene in *True Blood* ('Sparks Fly Out' 1.5) spells out the isolation of vampirism. After Bill is turned into a vampire by Lorena, he returns to his human home and sees his family – but for the last time since, as Lorena asks, 'Do you want to see them grow old? Grow feeble and die, while you remain the same, year after year?' This consequence of vampire fixity sets the stage for vampire alienation and the struggle of reluctant vampires to reconnect with humans. It has also become a characteristic of vampire romance between vampires and humans where it forms an obstacle to the idealized sense of a 'forever' love, as with Angel and Buffy (*Buffy*), Hoyt and Jessica (*True Blood*), and Elena and Stefan (*The Vampire Diaries*).

In the finale to *The Vampire Diaries* season four, Klaus's remark to Caroline, a recently made vampire he unsuccessfully attempts to woo away from her werewolf boyfriend Tyler, is designed to promise exactly this kind of eternal love. He tells her that he has called off a previously issued death threat on Tyler, who may now return home. Klaus follows this up with his exit line: 'Tyler is your first love. I intend to be your last', suggesting that, as two vampires, their love really can last forever ('Graduation' 4.23). In the same episode, however, vampire Lexi tells her friend Stefan that he should not think in terms of 'the one', suggesting that, while vampires may experience 'an epic love' during their long existence, 'contrary to popular belief, there are actually multiple ones – especially for a vampire'. Since even vampire–vampire relationships tend not to last, then, *The Vampire Diaries*, like most narratives in vampire TV are less than optimistic about the longevity of a teenage crush or any kind of 'true love'. The necessities of serial narrative also require that romantic fulfilment is short-lived, since it implies resolution. Obstacles that keep lovers separate are therefore integral structures and vampirism suggests doomed romance from the start. Yet the stasis of vampirism still invokes eternal love, a romance that lasts through the centuries, as promised to Caroline by Klaus.

Again *Dark Shadows* sets the precedent: part of its project in making Barnabas a sympathetic character was to give him a tragic relationship and an eternal quest. Barnabas' 'love for Josette DuPres', states Benshoff, 'permeates the entire series, as Barnabas searches for her (or some reincarnated form of her) throughout time and space' (2011: 58). This successful strategy was revisited in Francis Ford Coppola's film, *Bram Stoker's Dracula* (1992) which, as Powell outlines, 'positions Dracula as a time traveller crossing centuries to be reunited with his reincarnated wife, Mina' (2012: 97). This motif is currently thriving in vampire TV and *The Vampire Diaries* continues to unfold the story of the Salvatore brothers, Stefan and Damon, and their love for the vampire Katherine, who turned them in the 1860s, and subsequently for her 'doppelganger' Elena. This somewhat elaborate but not unfamiliar structure allows double doubling: not only are the two brothers in love with and thus competing for the affections of the same woman but the 'same woman' is actually two different women. Moreover, while the brothers alternate being 'good' and 'bad' vampires (the series starts with Stefan being the typical reluctant and sympathetic vampire and Damon being the conventional bad boy, matching similar contrasts between Angel and Spike in *Buffy* and *Angel*, or Bill and Eric in *True Blood*), Katherine plays 'bad' love object to Elena's 'good girl' (as Lorena does to Sookie and Darla to Buffy). Such elaborate patterning is made possible by vampire time and enables both stasis – the male vampire's desire for his true love remains unchanged over the years – and change – the object of that love may actually change as it is switched from one female to another. In addition, while the love may remain true and be presented as 'epic', the possibility of it being lastingly fulfilled is regularly deferred by other plot points as well as by vampirism. Even when Elena becomes a vampire in season four of *The Vampire Diaries*, both Salvatore brothers strive for possession of an elusive 'cure' so that she may be returned to her humanity rather than taking the opportunity to enjoy existence with her forever.

Vampire romance on television is tinged with melancholy because of the epic scale of vampire existence and the problems this causes relationships. Love is something to be remembered, obsessed over and brooded on, but rarely enjoyed in the present moment. The 'depth and complexity' identified by Pidduck as being assigned to male protagonists of period drama as a function of time passing, appears in vampire TV with the presentness of the past. Pidduck notes that 'the filtering of these events through the memory of its protagonist produces an obsessive structure that returns insistently to moments of encounter and loss' (2004: 52). Because Pidduck is analysing period drama films with one main time frame the 'events' she mentions are the central action of the plot. In vampire TV, however, such events can be from any part of a vampire's long existence, though the 'obsessive' structure means they will often be origin stories, or key relationship moments that signify 'encounter' (as in the origin story) or 'loss' (in the origin story, the loss of humanity, or of family). Since vampire TV uses conventional structures for flashback, these glimpses of the past are generally coded as memories of a particular character. Indeed, this is where the sense of loss derives from – vampire flashbacks are not objective history but personal recollections of the past, subjective memories that engage emotion as well as providing new information.

Cameron points out that 'Within Hollywood cinema, the intensified use of the flashback often coincided with an attempt to represent psychological crisis' (2012: 85), and he cites the use of flashback in *film noir* as an example of aligning flashback with issues of identity and subjectivity. The oscillation between 'good' and 'bad' in vampire characters on television also suggests a form of *ongoing* psychological crisis. I have already mentioned, for instance, how both Angel and Hal are presented as types of split personality, and strive to distance themselves from their evil deeds by projecting them onto another, uncontrolled and monstrous, self.

In some cases, the flashback may, as in *film noir*, not be entirely reliable. If flashback represents memory, is memory always accurate? The added factor of the psychological crisis identified by Cameron as well as contemporary debates about how reliable recovered memories of traumatic events are, further destabilize any notion of accurate memory. *Angel*'s 'Damage' (5.11) tells the story of Dana, a young woman who was abused as a child by a male attacker. As an adult she has mental health problems and has also acquired Slayer strength following the sharing of Slayer power in the series finale of *Buffy*. (In this way the episode demonstrates an unusual form of TV time and memory: it remembers events from its parent show and outlines their consequences). Dana takes vampire Spike captive, drugging him and cutting off his hands, thinking he is her attacker. Flashbacks – over-exposed and bleached out to denote both their status as flashback and Dana's confusion – show Spike as her antagonist. Spike tries to explain that her inherited collective Slayer memories (of him killing a Chinese Slayer in 1900, for example) are becoming confused with her individual human memories. As the identity of the attacker comes into question, he changes visibly in the flashbacks, denoting Dana's psychological crisis and the unreliability of these flashbacks as accurate 'memory'. Moreover, though Spike is finally proved not to be Dana's attacker, a key aspect of the story is that he very well could be, and the viewer is left in doubt until the resolution of the episode, when Spike (hands magically and surgically reattached) himself admits, 'I'm supposed to – what, complain? – because her's wasn't one of the hundreds of families I *did* kill?' Dana's memory may be mistaken in the specific, but not in the general: Spike is a vampire, he was a brutal killer and has committed similar atrocities. His acceptance of this past indicates his remorse and quest for redemption in the present.

Interruption of the forward-moving plot is acceptable in serial drama, of course, and endless deferment is characteristic of soap opera. It is not, therefore, much of a stretch to incorporate frequent flashbacks within a vampire TV show with a contemporary setting, even to the point of embarking on months-long forays into the past or future, as *Dark Shadows* did in the course of its original five year run. 'It is the paradigmatic character relationships that exist across these various story lines which provide the narrative "glue" for ultimately holding the entire series together', Benshoff argues of *Dark Shadows*, noting also, 'This is an ongoing structural effect impossible to achieve in single closed texts such as the gothic novel or the horror film' (2011: 30). Complex stitching together of different time frames and subject positions is commonplace in today's contemporary television drama, and nowhere is this epitomized more than in vampire TV.

In some cases, innovative or experimental episodes play with these complex structures to convey 'the power (as well as the danger) of storytelling', as Wilcox observes (2006: 106). Thus in *Buffy*'s 'Fool for Love' (5.7) we finally see Spike's origins in a tour de force of unreliable narration, as the vampire tells his story to Buffy in the present day, accompanied by a series of flashbacks which often visually contradict his verbal segues. 'What can I say, baby, I've always been bad', he boasts to Buffy, only for us to see him as ineffectual and socially inept human poet William in 1880. This episode increasingly collapses the distinction between past and present until the present-day Spike speaks directly to Buffy (and to the camera and the viewer) from the 1977 flashback, fast crosscutting not quite maintaining clear boundaries between the two time frames. The sense of Spike's past as a subjective, and mediated, story that can be told in different ways is further enhanced by the companion *Angel* episode 'Darla' (2.7), originally broadcast immediately following 'Fool for Love'. 'Darla' covers several of the same flashbacks from Darla's perspective, and includes new action from the same time frame (in the 'China 1900' segments, for example) because of this shift in perspective, making the events part of Darla and Angel's story, rather than Spike's.

Other TV doesn't go quite to the extremes of 'Fool for Love' and 'Darla' but *The Vampire Diaries*' consistent play with doubling does demonstrate that Stefan and Damon have different points of view, and new information from flashbacks might change how we re/read significant events from the past, such as Katherine turning both Salvatore brothers into vampires. Similarly, Klaus' version of the story of the Original vampire family positions him, unsurprisingly, as a hero, while both his sister Rebekah, and brother Elijah offer different perspectives, backed up at times by flashbacks presented as their memories, and supplemented by the stories of their mother Esther and father Mikael.

Such variant perspectives, as well as moral complexity, stories of struggle and redemption, and rocky relationships may all feature in television that doesn't revolve around vampires. Vampire TV does not necessarily break the conventions of how time is represented. It does push them, however, taking advantage of the epic scale of vampire existence to offer a different angle on narrative structure and character development. This epic scale lends itself to the slow and incremental unfolding of story only possible in serialized narrative, as well as to the repetition and return found in much television drama. Ultimately, with 'centuries of evil' to choose from, there will always be a new story to tell, or a new angle to tell that story from in vampire television.

Note

1. *Fringe* (2008–2013) is an obvious exception, though it does not include vampires.

10

Timeless: Memory, Temporality, and Identity in *Once Upon a Time*

Gwyneth Peaty

Once upon a time there was an enchanted forest filled with all the classic characters we know. Or think we know. One day they found themselves trapped in a place where all their happy endings were stolen. Our world. This is how it happened . . .

Fairy tales are often described as 'timeless' classics. Possessed of a magic that never seems to expire, but cycles in fresh waves for each new generation, their contents might appear to inhabit a special atemporal zone. Indeed, some argue this very point. 'Fairy tales are timeless,' states D. L. Ashliman in his *Folk and Fairy Tales: A Handbook*, 'both in their enduring appeal and in their depiction of days and years' (2004: 49). Fairyland is certainly a world very different from our own; a world of magic and impossible happenings. The events that take place in this realm are far removed from contemporary realities, from the devices, schedules, and time-keeping mechanisms that shape the experience of contemporary living. Arguably, for readers in the twenty-first century, 'one of the most arresting qualities of fairy tales is their apparent timelessness,' as their origins are frequently traced back to early folklore and the oral storytelling traditions of ancient cultures (Ziolkowski, 2007: 29). Yet the history of fairy tales is punctuated by revisions and updates, and the 'venerable aura of longevity' acquired by collections such as *Grimms' Fairy Tales* does not account for the fluctuations in such narratives over time (Haase, 2004: 9).

Fairy tales address the issues of their day. These are stories that 'take different forms at different times, and the forms they take reflect the places in which they have settled, and the particular historical moments in which they have been recorded' (Teverson, 2013: 7). In their current form, fairy tales are entwined with the concept of time at a structural level; their essential features exhibiting a keen awareness of its importance. The phrase 'once upon a time' has become synonymous with the fairy tale. Likewise, this opening would be incomplete without its matching conclusion: 'and they all lived happily ever after.' Fairy tales are tied to that which is past *and* that which is still to come – both before and ever after, history and future. Moreover, such narratives typically situate their readers in a temporal continuum that moves in an essentially optimistic direction. Characters may endure many trials, but their efforts are not in vain, and their dreams will come true in the end.

True timelessness would signal the end of the fairy tale. At least, this is the opening premise of *Once Upon A Time* (2011–), a television series that explores the relationship between fairy tales and contemporary reality. As the preface to the pilot episode suggests, this production revises traditional fairy tale narratives by bringing them into direct contact with 'our world.' A whole community of iconic characters – including those from *Snow White and the Seven Dwarfs*, *Beauty and the Beast*, *Peter Pan*, *Little Red Riding Hood*, *Cinderella*, *Pinocchio*, and *Alice in Wonderland* – have been forced through an inter-dimensional portal by an evil curse. Uprooted from fairyland, they have been transplanted into Storybrooke, a fictional town in Maine, USA, where they have lived for the past 28 years. Each individual has been given a new identity: Red Riding Hood has become Ruby, a sultry waitress at the local diner; Jiminy Cricket is Archie Hopper, the town therapist; Snow White is Mary Margaret Blanchard, a primary school teacher. While these new lives are comprehensive, they are also incomplete; made possible only by the forced erasure of memories. Robbed of their magic and true natures by the curse, the townsfolk live as unknowing shadows of their former selves. They are also frozen in time. Without the capacity to remember, the inhabitants of Storybrooke are suspended in a temporal stasis. Trapped in another world, cut off from both past and future, the population does not age or evolve.

In this series, loss of memory breaks the thread leading each person to their happily ever after. It brings the forward motion of every tale to a sudden halt. By suspending time in this way, the series both highlights and jeopardizes a key feature of fairy tales. After all, the notion that the future can be shaped and determined, and that living beings are not entirely helpless, but potential masters of time and space, is key to the allure of these stories. 'Fairy tales,' as Marina Warner has commented, appear 'to offer the possibility of change, far beyond the boundaries of their improbable plots or fantastically illustrated pages' (1995: xii). As Warner points out, fairy tales are about metamorphosis. A poor girl can become a princess; a wooden puppet can become a real child; a human can become an animal, and vice versa. Such shifts in ontological and social status testify to the possibility of 'more of the same, not only in fairy land, but in this world' (1995: xii). Confronted with this 'instability of appearances, these sudden swerves of destiny,' the reader is encouraged to imagine that they too might 'remake the world in the image of desire' (1995: xii). Mary Margaret explicitly offers this reading in *Once Upon A Time*, identifying positive visions of future change as the defining element of fairy tales. As she explains:

> These stories, the classics, there's a reason we all know them. They're a way for us to deal with our world, if it doesn't always make sense. [They provide] the most important thing anyone can have: hope. Believing in even the possibility of a happy ending is a very powerful thing. ('Pilot' 1.1)

This is precisely where *Once Upon a Time* intercepts the fairy tale canon, with its promise of 'no more happy endings.' Shifting backwards and forwards in time, between two very different fictive realms, the series explicates the relationship between memory, temporality, and identity by tracing the emotional contortions of multiple characters. Swapping between the two worlds, between past and present versions of each individual, the series plays on the sometimes painful conflict between fantasy and reality.

It all begins somewhere very familiar. In the opening scenes of the pilot episode, a dashing prince gallops his steed through a forest to find his lady love, only to discover her lying still and pale amidst the trees. 'You're too late,' says one of the seven dwarves clustered sadly around her glass coffin. Of course, as these familiar cues already suggest, nothing could be further from the truth. This is Prince Charming (Josh Dallas) and Snow White (Ginnifer Goodwin): she who bites the poisoned apple and falls into a cursed slumber, and he who must awaken her with a kiss. The script is followed precisely. She opens her eyes, they embrace, and the enchanted forest buzzes with the magic of true love. The scene skips ahead to their lush wedding; a moment of harmonious union that traditionally signals the end of this particular tale. In this case, however, the idyllic dénouement is interrupted by an intruder. The Evil Queen (Lana Parrilla) refuses to give up after the failure of her earlier scheme, and bursts in to menace the couple and their guests. 'Soon,' she vows, 'everything you love, everything *all* of you love, will be taken from you, forever . . . I shall destroy your happiness if it is the last thing I do.' Erasing the possibility of a neat conclusion, this unexpected interruption opens the narrative to further developments, beyond the marriage of its heroes. Disrupted by anxiety about the future, the story cannot end. These events are an early sign that *Once Upon A Time* does not simply reproduce the tropes of classic fairy tales, but reroutes and reimagines them in a new context.

This transformative project becomes more obvious as the series' second world is introduced. The heroine of 'our world' – present-day North America – is Emma Swan, a self-confessed loner who works as a bail bonds agent/bounty hunter and spends her life chasing down liars and cheats. In stark contrast to the medieval fantasy land in which Snow White has her adventures, Emma's urban reality appears to contain no magic whatsoever. The charming man she meets in Boston for a dinner date is not an honourable prince, but a philandering embezzler who has skipped bail. He tips the table over, runs away, and insults her when she follows him. Emma responds by bashing his head in with practiced efficiency, before heading home alone to light a single candle in celebration of her 28th birthday.

The point of intersection between fairyland and the real world is discovered by Henry, the infant Emma gave up for adoption ten years prior. Arriving at her door carrying a large omnibus of stories and demanding attention, the boy articulates the premise of the series for his sceptical biological mother: 'They're not fairy tales, they're true. Every story in this book actually happened' ('Pilot'). The past tense is crucial, because the scenes that unfold in the enchanted forest are all flashbacks; events now decades past that nonetheless provide important context for the present. It is Henry who articulates the links between the two worlds, and identifies the temporal status of his hometown. 'Time is frozen here,' he explains, after Emma drives him back to Storybrooke, where he lives with his adoptive mother, the Mayor (otherwise known as the Evil Queen). And, indeed, the arms of the large town clock have never moved; caught by the same immobilizing curse that affects the townsfolk.

Decoupled from their moorings between the 'once' and the 'ever after', characters are truly timeless. In losing knowledge of the past, they have lost control over the present and future. They cannot grow or change; they certainly cannot shapeshift in any way. The loss of time signals a loss of magic, hope, idealism, and faith in true love. In the same instance, it also signals their presence and participation in the real world – 'our world' – a place with no magic. As a PG-rated programme open to children as well as adult viewers, the series offers a vision of a contemporary society that is defined primarily in terms of cynicism and pessimism. In the present-day setting of *Once Upon A Time*, even the hope of a positive outcome is difficult to maintain. The romance of fairy tales and happy endings seems patently ridiculous. 'This is the *real* world,' Henry is told repeatedly, as he attempts to convince the adults around him of their magical destiny. Fantasy threatens the real world with its promises of joy. 'Not having a happy ending is painful enough,' Emma tells her son, 'but giving someone unrealistic hope is far worse' ('Snow Falls' 1.3). From her perspective, such dreams can be damaging indeed.

Considering the potential meaning of fairy tales, Sheldon Cashdan admits that it could seem 'naive to look for answers to life's problems in tales where evil is eliminated by simply waving a wand, where princes always show up on time, and where everyone lives happily ever after.' Despite this, he suggests that such a reading is valid because 'by addressing human frailties, [fairy tales] use fantasy to illuminate problems that adults repeatedly face in their quest to lead more fulfilling lives' (1999: 252). I would argue that, by revising and remixing such narratives in the context of twenty-first century America, *Once Upon A Time* examines the repercussions of living in a time without happy endings and, by extension, what it means to live a complex and finite human life in the shadow of an uncertain future.

No Time, Like the Present

The stopped clock in the heart of Storybrooke embodies the frozen state of its population. As Heidegger puts it, 'the everyday lives by the clock,' and through this device our 'concern incessantly comes back to the now; it says: from now till then, till the next now' (1992: 17E). Characters in *Once Upon A Time* endure a life without future, for they are perpetually unable to access 'the next now' – the moment that follows the one in which they are trapped. And they must inhabit this moment without the people they love most. Rumpelstiltskin (Robert Carlyle) warns of this suffering in a flashback: 'Your prison, all of our prisons, will be time. Time will stop. And we will be trapped someplace horrible, where everything we love, everything we hold dear will be ripped from us while we suffer for all eternity' ('Pilot'). Everyone in town has lost someone; couples have been separated, parents and children torn apart, close companions made strangers to each other. Although they have no clear remembrance of their lost loved ones, each character feels the absence of something intangible, and exists in a state of unconscious mourning.

When Emma resolves to stay in Storybrooke and spend time with Henry, her decision prompts a singular occurrence: the hands of the stopped clock begin to move again. Her arrival is the catalyst for a series of changes that will ultimately lead to the curse being broken. Yet the steady ticking of clocks is not what creates or powers time – it is merely a measure of its passing. As Christopher Gosden points out, there is a huge difference between measured time and experienced time. 'The time of human experience is not purely successive and defies measurement,' he argues (1994: 2). In our daily experience of time, 'past, present and future meet in complex forms, such that the present is only given meaning through retaining elements of the past and anticipating the future' (1994: 2). Time is socially implicated and culturally informed. It does not simply happen or exist, but is ceaselessly assembled and reassembled in the minds of those who experience it. So it is in *Once Upon A Time* where, while the clock has symbolic potency, it is the characters' complex experiences of time that are the prime focus. For this reason, the reawakening of the clock occurs at the beginning of the series, not the end. It signals the start of a much deeper, slower, and more complicated process than simply jolting a timepiece into action.

As the barriers between the two worlds begin to falter, *Once Upon A Time* interrogates the relationship between identity and memory through interwoven stories that flip backwards and forwards in time. The series explores the extent to which one's identity and personality is dependent upon memories of times past, and how history shapes and delimits the present and future actions of social beings. The episodic nature of the serial television format facilitates an increasingly complex weaving of temporal and narrative fragments – for as events in Storybrooke move forwards toward the breaking of the curse, events in the enchanted forest move forwards, back, and around in time, eventually tracking to the root cause of the Evil Queen's wrath.

While classic fairy tales provide the series' general frame of reference, they are manipulated to highlight certain experiences and challenges that have resonance for a contemporary audience. The clock reacts to Emma's arrival because she is the daughter of Prince Charming and Snow White. Tipped off about the curse by Rumpelstiltskin – who informs them that their unborn child will be the only one who can break the spell – the couple organize a last-minute escape route for their baby via an enchanted tree. Safe from the spell, but alone in the real world, Emma has grown up an orphan with no knowledge of her parents or origins. United again in Storybrooke, the trio remains unaware of their intimate connection. Thanks to the freezing of time, Emma is now the same biological age, or even older, than her parents, who are exactly as they were when she was born. Adding to the confusion, the curse not only erases real memories, but imposes a set of false ones in their place.

Prince Charming, now known as David, epitomizes the themes of memory and identity loss early on, because the curse has a looser grip on his mind. Near death when it began, he has been in a coma since the spell was cast. The traditional positions are reversed as he lies dormant in Storybrooke hospital, until Snow White/Mary Margaret (at Henry's prompting) sits by his bed and reads him the tale of their first meeting in the enchanted forest. Brought back to consciousness by her presence, he staggers from the hospital during the night and has to be rescued. 'Who are you?' asks Mary Margaret, after resuscitating him in the woods. 'I don't know,' he replies ('Snow Falls'). Under the curse, David is meant to remember being married to another woman, Kathryn, and have no feelings for his fairy tale wife whatsoever. As he recovers, however, it becomes clear that a residual amnesia is blocking the full power of the false memories. He resists his new identity, and attempts to form a relationship with Mary Margaret: 'Whoever married Kathryn, it's not me. I didn't choose her' ('The Shepherd' 1.6). Haunted by two alternate visions of the past, David is unable to decide which path to take, and which woman he loves. 'You can't have both,' says Mary Margaret, in hurt exasperation. 'But I do have both,' he responds, 'I know it doesn't make sense. It's like I have these two conflicting lives; memories of feelings for her, and real feelings for you' ('7.15 AM' 1.10). The simple formula of fairy tale romance has given way to a more complex configuration of emotion and allegiance which has no easy resolution. Their unrequited suffering continues until they embark on an affair.

Memory is an awareness of the passage of time; the stringing together of past events into a meaningful thread leading up to, and beyond, the present moment. Luis Buñuel suggests that:

> you have to begin to lose your memory, if only in bits and pieces, to realize that memory is what makes our lives. Life without memory is no life at all ... Our memory is our coherence, our reason, our feeling, even our action. Without it we are nothing. (in Sacks 2007: 25)

Time is the frame on which our memories and identities hang; without it they slip into the abyss. As neurologist Oliver Sacks has explained, memory is crucial, not only for constructing identity, but for understanding relationships between people and objects, and building a practical image of the world around us. He ponders: 'what sort of a life (if any), what sort of a world, what sort of a self, can be preserved in a man who has lost the greater part of his memory, and, with this, his past, and his moorings in time?' (2007: 25). Amnesiacs confront this question when they lose chunks of their lives, and must attempt to piece the remnants back together: 'the fact that one can lose the greater part of a lifetime has peculiar, uncanny horror' (2007: 43). Oscillating between two sets of conflicting memories – one real, one false – David/Prince Charming is bewildered; unable to understand his own mind and the world, or to make reasoned decisions in relation to others.

Marital infidelity is, of course, the antithesis of the happy ending. But the complexities built into the above scenario render moral outrage difficult. Kathryn and David were never actually married; they just believe they were, because they have false memories. Mary Margaret and David *are* married, in another world that they cannot remember. Their affair is thus a return to true love, rather than a betrayal of it. In this context, David's indecision and duplicity is the result of a genuinely divided mind, a man living 'two lives' as the result of his malformed perceptions of times past. The series essentially presents a new kind of fairy tale here; one that addresses divorce and separation, rather than marriage and true love forever. It is a scenario that would appeal to a childlike Henry, whose belief in 'happily ever after' struggles on, despite the failures of the adults around him. Given up by his mother, the notion of Emma's abandonment as a trans-dimensional rescue has a similar charm. That his strict stepmother is an evil witch queen is even more attractive. Henry's book of fairy tales indeed enables him to see magic in the imperfect people around him and, in Warner's words, helps him to 'remake the world in the image of desire' (1995: xii). This is the interpretation of the adult characters in *Once Upon A Time*, who discuss at length how the child uses his 'delusion' as a coping mechanism. Archie is Henry's therapist: 'These stories,' he explains, 'they're his language. He has no idea how to express complex emotions, so he's translating as best he can. This is how he communicates. He's using this book to help deal with his problems' ('The Thing You Love Most' 1.2). While this is a logical 'real world' conclusion to make, viewers know Henry is right – the stories *are* real and the enchanted forest does exist. The series goes out of its way to undercut the analytical scepticism of the adults, fleshing out a fairy tale world that is just as real (or perhaps just as fictive) as our world.

A Little Bit More Gruesome

The erasure of memory coincides with complete relocation in *Once Upon A Time*. Characters quite literally inhabit another realm; a shift not simply spatial, but inter-dimensional – they enter another plane of existence, another time. The world of the enchanted forest is shown to be medieval; people live in small cottages, villages or castles. They ride horses or walk. There are no cars, buses or trains, no telephones or computers. The pace of life is unhurried, much more in tune with the rhythms of nature than a contemporary age of high speed travel and digital technologies. In some ways, the enchanted forest represents an ideal fantasy of a past in which time was plentiful, never rushed but unfolding slowly and naturally. The links between past, present and future make a different kind of sense in this context. Eva Hoffman has suggested that one of the benefits of enjoying a stable life:

> spent in a village, say, or a small locality, [is] that the trajectory of life's stages unfolds with a certain continuous, or at least visible, logic; one can witness the lives of others from the beginning to the end and the development of one's own history can be similarly witnessed and followed. (2009: 179)

So it goes in the land of fairy tales, where life fits a sequential narrative structure: beginning, middle, and end.

Fairy land is a world marked by nostalgia; a dream of 'another time' in which things were different, simpler, and the future was easier to predict. It contrasts starkly with the geographical and social dislocations that characterize much of contemporary life as 'we shuttle among parts of the globe, shedding problems, and sometimes identities, as we go along' (Hoffman 2009: 180). The speed and pressure of contemporary living can be seen to prevent the kind of linear coherence associated with small community living. Instead, 'it is as if we have substituted speed for significance. If we move fast enough, we can fill up time without reflecting on our intentions or purposes' (Hoffman 2009: 182). But while *Once Upon A Time* contrasts the classic model of a fairy tale kingdom with the realities of contemporary life, in some ways the enchanted forest is much closer to the 'real world' than it would first appear. By jumping backwards and forwards in time, juxtaposing past and present events in parallel, the series shows viewers a more complex world than they might have expected. As characters grapple with the absence of happy endings in both realms, the pain of not knowing – of forgetting that which makes us who we are – is contrasted with the pain of knowing; the suffering associated with painful memories that cannot be erased.

As one of the few who retains knowledge of their fairy tale identities, Jefferson (Sebastian Stan) – otherwise known as the Mad Hatter – desperately wants to forget. He longs to lose his memories in an oblivious haze. 'Remembering is the worst curse,' he exclaims to the Evil Queen, 'I want to forget!' ('An Apple Red as Blood' 1.21). Jefferson's position is particularly painful, because his entrapment requires separation from his daughter, who has no memory of him and lives with another family. He watches her from afar, but can never speak or make true contact. Because Emma's arrival restarted the town clock, he assumes that she has magic. Luring her to his house, he forces her to make a hat for him, in the hopes that it will have enough power to take him back to fairy land. When she quizzes him about his motivations, he begins to rage: 'Like everyone else here, what I love has been ripped from me [. . .] Have you any idea what it's like to watch her, day in and day out, happy, with a new family? With a new father?' ('Hat Trick' 1.17). Returning to fairy land is his only hope, because: 'it's the one world where we can be together, where she'll remember who I am.' And yet, as viewers see during pre-curse flashbacks, the same situation arose in the enchanted forest.

At regular intervals the story shifts back in time to fairy world, to show how the Evil Queen tricked Jefferson into leaving his daughter. Living a meagre life with her in a small cottage in the woods, he is persuaded to go and help the Queen on the condition that his daughter will be provided for. Although Grace (Alissa Skovbye) begs him to stay, he decides to leave in the hopes that he can improve her quality of life. The Queen, entirely unsympathetic, then traps him in another dimension, having used his magical hat to find her father. She leaves him with these biting words: 'If you truly cared for your daughter you never would have left her in the first place [. . .] you don't abandon family' ('Hat Trick'). In this way he is denied his happy ending and becomes an absent father in both worlds. Just one of many similarly reimagined fairy tales, the story of the Mad Hatter is both fantastical and entirely applicable to the contemporary experience of broken families.

The second season of *Once Upon A Time* brings home the idea that the Enchanted Forest is not the bastion of timeless simplicity one might expect from fairy tales. After Emma successfully breaks the curse at the end of the first season, magic and memories come flooding back into Storybrooke. Instead of returning to fairy land as anticipated, the characters remain in the real world, albeit with their old identities restored. All except Emma and Snow White, who accidentally fall through the last remaining portal back to the Enchanted Forest ('Broken' 2.1). Here Emma discovers that nothing is as she expected, and her existing knowledge of fairy tales is useless. 'Whatever story you think you know, my dear, is most certainly wrong,' scoffs Captain Hook (Colin O'Donoghue), when she tries to remember the details of Jack and the Beanstalk. Her description 'sounds like a lovely tale,' he comments, 'but the truth's a little bit more gruesome' ('Tallahassee' 2.6). Yet his version of events is later shown to be wrong also – highlighting the complexity that typifies the 'real' Enchanted Forest. Pain and sorrow are just as active here as they are in our world. Emma and Snow White inadvertently cause the death of Sleeping Beauty's prince when they arrive, leaving her broken-hearted. This realm is a true mirror of our own, and, as such, it resists the simplicity of static binaries and one-dimensional character studies.

Memories of times past haunt the living, shaping and reshaping their identities as the series progresses. The Evil Queen was once a sweet girl whose determination to be good was twisted by the manipulative adults around her. The dangerous giant atop Jack's beanstalk is actually a persecuted recluse, whose friends were murdered by greedy humans. Neat lines between good and evil collapse as flashbacks continue to reveal the origin stories of 'bad' characters. Neither is the fairy world free from the pressures of time's inexorable passage. 'In this world, we are slaves to time,' announces Hook, when he tires of waiting for Emma, 'and ours is running out. In other words, tick tock.'

Ever After

As Richard M. Gale points out, time is not a long series of present moments sliding like separate beads along a string, but one single, perpetually liminal moment: 'Time is made continuous by the indivisible, present now-moment, which links the past to the future by serving as the termination of the past and the beginning of the future' (1968: 1). Memories may provide indirect access to past events, but these are shaped by subjectivity and are always incomplete. *Once Upon A Time* uses flashbacks to enable multiple 'now' moments to be observed in parallel, highlighting similarities between events past and present, magical and real. The series twists familiar generic formulas in this context to create revised fairy tales that implicitly, and sometimes explicitly, address the complexities of life in the twenty-first century – a time and space where happy endings simply cannot be guaranteed. But happy endings have never been guaranteed, and the series' focus on undoing the nostalgia and fantasy associated with a mythic past arguably moves, in perhaps a counterintuitive way, to reinstate the idea of a fairy tale destiny. By directly addressing cynicism regarding fairy tales and their application to the real world, refashioning the stories in modern terms, and emphasizing links between past and present, *Once Upon A Time* works to reinstate these stories for contemporary viewers.

This is, of course, not the first time such a project has been undertaken. Haase observes a similar dynamic in his research into much older texts:

> We cannot ignore the irony that the Grimms collected and published their book of tales because they believed the stories were dying out. The times, they thought, were not conducive to the survival of these 'timeless' tales. So it would seem that

the stories were allowed to survive not because they were ageless, but because they were not. (1996: 10)

Fairy tales are kept alive because they are malleable enough to be continually refurbished. Even as *Once Upon A Time* presides over the death of traditional fairy tales, it offers them yet another form of life. Breaking the curse of timelessness, the production reawakens these characters within 'our world,' in new forms that suit the conflicts and complexities of our time.

The series explores the process of finding family in the absence of traditional parental figures (Emma's fairy tale parents are, after all, her own age), accepting that marriage may not bring true love forever, and the difficult emotions involved when families are broken and reformed into new configurations. Issues regarding the construction and maintenance of a coherent identity thread throughout each of these challenges, forming the prime focus of the series overall. In this way the show continues to pursue the prime directive of the fairy tale genre: utilising 'fantasy to illuminate problems that adults repeatedly face in their quest to lead more fulfilling lives' (Cashdan, 1999: 252). As traditional family structures split and change, and both children and adults deal with anxiety about what comes next, *Once Upon A Time* focuses on returning magic to the present and the future. 'You know what the issue is with this world?' rants the Mad Hatter, 'Everyone wants a magical solution to their problems and everyone refuses to believe in magic.' For all its focus on pain and suffering, the series works to dilute cynicism by envisioning new kinds of happy endings in the context of both new and age old problems.

11

'*Bonanza* Was Never Like This...': *Quantum Leap* and Interrogating Nostalgia

David Simmons

Quantum Leap first aired in 1989 and ran for five seasons ending in 1993. Though the show was not initially a commercial success, by its third season it had gained a large enough audience to run for two further 22-episode series. Since its original airing, *Quantum Leap* has remained a favourite in syndication and a cult following has arisen, surrounding the show with rumours persisting to the present of either a feature film spinoff or a televisual reboot[1]. The show's success suggests that something about central character Dr Sam Beckett's adventures chimed with the late twentieth-century US viewing public. Interestingly, critics including Denis McNally and Lynette Porter have attributed this success, in part, to *Quantum Leap*'s evocative repackaging of key moments of twentieth-century US history (the assassination of JFK, Vietnam, Watergate) or use of famous figures (Michael Jackson, Dr Ruth, Marilyn Monroe). This element of *Quantum Leap*, which creator Donald P. Bellisario termed the show's 'kisses with History' (quoted in Blocher), might suggest that the programme relied on the simple recreation or re-staging of recognisable historical markers for its appeal, what Frederic Jameson called the 'complacent play of historical allusion' (1988, 105), symptomatic of 'postmodern nostalgia films' (1991, 18) such as *Rumble Fish* (1983) and *Back to the Future* (1985) or indeed television shows including *Happy Days* (1974–1984). However, this chapter will attempt to argue that, rather than just being an example of the simplistic nostalgia that was considered to be 'holding sway in the 1990s' (Hutcheon), *Quantum Leap* offered a decidedly more complex and surprisingly nuanced critical reading of historicising processes indebted to contemporary post-modern debates.

In particular, I will explore how Sam's ongoing quest to revisit and 'put right what once went wrong' during significant points of crisis in US history embodies a post-modern process of engaging with history that '(while still implicitly invoking) nostalgia undermines... assertions of originality, authenticity, and the burden of the past, even as it acknowledges their continuing (but not paralyzing) validity as aesthetic concerns' (Hutcheon).

Though a much underexplored area of television studies, nostalgia must be understood as an increasingly significant and widespread interpretative strategy, as Brett Mills discusses in relation to the appeal of re-watching old sitcom episodes: 'the massive sales on video and DVD of "classic" series are testament to the fact that viewers are willing to part with money for things they've already seen. In this instance...joy coming from the reiteration of the known' (Mills, 15). Though Mills notes the proclivity amongst audiences to reread shows in a consciously nostalgic fashion, nostalgia can also be embedded into a show on a textual level, informing the structure and content of a series like *Quantum Leap* so that the concept of looking back manifests itself on an initial (rather than subsequent re-) viewing. Indeed, the original meaning of the word nostalgia – 'With its Greek roots, *nostos*, meaning "to return home" and *algos*, meaning "pain"' (Hutcheon) – would appear to form a handy description of the show's central character, as each week he found himself 'trapped in the past...leaping from life to life... and hoping each time, that his next leap will be the leap home.' For the uninitiated, each episode of *Quantum Leap* involved Sam jumping into the body of an individual who required help of some sort; through consultation with Al, a holographic aide from the future, and Al's computer Ziggy, Sam would usually successfully assist those in need and jump away into a new body for the following week's episode. Significantly, episodes would often involve a sense of elation, on the part of the central characters and the audience, when Sam managed to fix what had gone 'wrong' with the historical events he encountered. However, while this recurrent narrative structure might appear to uphold traditional Enlightenment notions of historical progress, implicitly suggesting that someone from mankind's future might be able to improve mankind's past through virtue of his greater knowledge and learning, it is important to note that many episodes foregrounded Sam's exceptionality rather than his position as someone from a more 'advanced' period of time. The plot of the final episode 'Mirror Image' (5.21), in which a mystical bartender reveals to Sam that the leaps are supposedly not being controlled by a higher force, but rather that Sam is making himself leap because he likes helping people, would appear to support such a reading of the character as a 'unique' individual. Furthermore, while both Sam and Al criticize bygone eras ('The fifties were conformist, materialistic, repressive, boring and stupid." 'Rebel Without a Clue' 3.9), in many episodes Sam espouses a longing for the past: be this his own past ('The Leap Home' 3.1) or earlier periods in the twentieth-century history of the USA ('Liberation' 5.12). At times, it is fair to say that the show's valorization of the past verges on fetishization, yet equally its concomitant examination of the inherently problematic nature of our relationship to the past speak to the concerns of postmodern theorists such as Hutcheon concerning the prominence of nostalgia in late twentieth-century art and popular culture.

In her influential essay 'Irony, Nostalgia and the Postmodern' (2000) Hutcheon examines the historicizing processes of the late twentieth century and its popular art-forms. Perplexed by the seemingly dichotomous contemporary treatment of the past and the concept of History, Hutcheon's essay can be read as a sustained attempt to uncover whether:

> This postmodern recalling of the past [is] an example of a conservative – and therefore nostalgic – escape to an idealized, simpler era of 'real' community values? Or did it express, but through its ironic distance, a 'genuine' and legitimate dissatisfaction with modernity and the unquestioned belief in . . . perpetual modernization. .

Taking the proclivity towards nostalgia in the last decades of the twentieth century as her focus, Hutcheon goes on to survey some of the reasons that have been suggested by others for this predilection: 'The explanations offered for this kind of commercialized luxuriating in the culture of the past have ranged from economic cynicism to moral superiority. They usually point to a dissatisfaction with the culture of the present – something that is then either applauded or condemned.' Hutcheon proposes that, central to those who are dissatisfied with the contemporary era, is a belief that a decline in value systems in the West has left us with a deep nostalgia for the imagined moral absolutes of the past.

With its now famous opening sequence in which a disembodied camera transcends the earth to travel over the tops of clouds as the sun rises on a new day, and its indebtedness to overtly Christian televisual narratives such as *Highway to Heaven* (1984–1989), *Quantum Leap* would seem, at first glance, to embody such a recurrent desire for moral certainties. The show frequently couched its narratives with Christian symbolism and contained episodes where Sam variously encountered angels ('It's a Wonderful Leap' 4.18) and met God (as a bartender in 'Mirror Image'). Indeed, the show's tendency towards religiosity is evident in the season three episode 'Leap of Faith' (3.3). In this episode, Sam jumps into the life of priest, Father Francis 'Frank' Giuseppe Pistano, newly appointed to inner city St Dorothy's church. Sam's mission is to stop the death of Father Mack, who has supposedly witnessed a murder and who is now under threat from Tony Pronti, one of two young Italian-American boys who have been lured into a life of crime to survive.

Right from the beginning of 'Leap of Faith' parallels are drawn between Sam's role as a quantum leaper and the life of a priest; in the opening voiceover in an overt display of self-consciousness Sam suggests that 'leaping into other people's lives can be downright spiritual' while Sam later expresses his love of the church with Father Mack, commenting that he'd 'forgotten how beautiful it could be.' The episode proceeds to pick up on the links between Sam and those with a more straightforwardly religious calling, with Sam implicitly acknowledging the ties between his own righteous crusade and that of the priesthood in his words to Mack at the end of the episode: 'All you can do is believe that you'll make a difference in the long run.'

Significantly, the episode initially pits the modern and amoral mafia lifestyle of Tony Pronti against the more conservative and valorized values of Sam's role as priest; Frank initially finds Tony in a seedy bar, all neon lights and shady characters playing pool, where he ends up brawling with and overpowering Tony, whose masculine bravado is revealed to be just that. However, as the episode progresses, the show begins to undermine this portrayal of religion and the church as entirely virtuous. Instead, we are presented with examples of the Church's failings, including Al's loss of faith over the death of his father and Mack's borderline alcoholism and proclivity for violence. Indeed, Sam later finds out that he is in Frank's body not to save his fellow priest, but instead to rescue Tony from a desperate Mack who has lost his way following the death of his parishioner and who ends up holding the teenage Tony at gunpoint on the nearby railway tracks at the culmination of the episode. Sam must save both the priest Mack and his intended victim from an oncoming train that threatens to kill them both.

While 'Leap of Faith' flirts with a critique of organized religion and its inability to actually aid those it should be helping, the episode ultimately seems to revert to a more conservative stance concerning the importance of Christianity in the lives of everyday Americans. When Tony uses the confession box to shoot Mack but ends up shooting Sam instead, Al, in spite of his lost faith, is forced to pray to God in order to try and save Sam's life. Al's prayer: 'God don't do this, he's done too much, he's helped too many people', and Sam's claim at the end of the episode that Al did a great job in praying for him, signal a final desire on the part of the show's creators to re-affirm their religiosity. Indeed, in a somewhat didactic fashion, the episode presents us with a compassionate and forgiving God who is willing to save those that are themselves morally virtuous and deserving. The existence of such a conformist adherence to Christian religiosity in a show that is as reliant upon nostalgia as *Quantum Leap* would seem to point to the popular view that nostalgia is inherently, ideologically conservative, as Hutcheon herself confirms: 'many would argue that, whether used by the right or the left, nostalgia is fundamentally conservative in its praxis'. In her essay, Hutcheon goes on to propose that those who engage in nostalgia want 'to keep things as they were – or, more accurately, as they are imagined to have been.' The implication being that nostalgic texts present us with (often heavily) mediated versions of history as there is often a tendency to imbue historical periods with values believed to have been more widespread than they ever actually were in reality, in the process creating a distorted perception of the past. For Jameson the popular media plays an integral role in this procedure, with examples such as the nostalgia film evoking a sense of the narrative certainties of the past through their appropriation and utilization of cultural myths and stereotypes. Such as the sense of '1950s-ness' (1991, 18) we find in George Lucas' *American Graffiti* (1973) which Jameson believes contributes to the view of the Eisenhower era as a period of lost innocence: 'the 1950s remain the privileged lost object of desire' (1991, 18) Jameson argues that because of this such instances of popular culture offer us a kind of false realism: films about other films, representations of other representations, films 'in which the history of aesthetic styles displaces "real" history' (1991, 18).

The confusion of history with a media filtered version of the past is evident in 'Play it Again Seymour' (1.9). In this incredibly self-conscious first season episode Sam jumps back to 1953 and into the body of a private eye called Nick Allen who shares a striking similarity (in physical appearance and mannerisms) to the star of many Hollywood crime movies, Humphrey Bogart. 'Play it Again Seymour' foregrounds the role that film and TV has to play in constructing a version of the past for its audience. Once Sam has finished spouting quotes from Bogart's more famous roles, and been mistaken for Bogart by an irate old woman (and later in the episode, a young Woody Allen), he sets about trying to solve the case of who killed Nick's partner. The episode uses its Fifties setting to recreate a sense of early private eye movies, replete with recognizable character archetypes (the naive young friend, the femme fatale), lingo ('gumshoe', 'dropper', 'piece'), clothing (fedoras and trench coats) and the use of saxophone music. This desire to evoke a recognizably cinematic, rather than an actual, version of the 1950s continues in the techniques that Sam finds himself using to solve the case; with his young companion, Seymour, offering him pointers drawn from a series of luridly-plotted pulp novels: 'Tommy Trublood's partner was found in the Pacific sucking kelp, Tommy had to take on the cops, the mob, and bad criminal elements, and that's what you're going to do, right Nick?' The episode finishes with one last homage to the noir films of the 1940s and 1950s in the form of an expertly manufactured extended homage to perhaps Bogart's most famous scene in *Casablanca* (1942). Sam saves the day and rescues the dame. Then, as the sultry Alison leaves with tickets for Nick and her to travel together overseas, Al reminds Sam that he can't go with her and that Nick's duties lie with Seymour who has decided to become a crime writer. As the two of them walk across the landing strip with their backs to the camera, seemingly conscious of the filmic nature of their situation, it only remains for Al to suggest that in his opinion 'this is the start of a wonderful friendship'.

While 'Play it Again Seymour' offers a very straightforward, if playful, engagement with the idea of history as mediated by popular art forms such as cinema, 'Goodbye, Norma Jean' (5.18) presents the viewer with a decidedly more multifaceted exploration of the ways in which the media can alter our understanding of history. Sam is accosted at the beginning of the episode by a fan who wants to know what Marilyn is really like: 'the real person', and the episode explores the disparity between Monroe's screen image and the 'reality' of life for the person behind that image, Norma Jean.

At the start of the episode Sam jumps into Dennis, Monroe's bodyguard, and initially feels that his latest leap is like 'I'd died and gone to heaven.' Sam recalls his love of Monroe which is tied up with nostalgic memories of the star on screen: 'at college I used to love sneaking off to the movies so I could get lost in the magic of those big, luscious blue eyes.' As part of his leap, Sam meets Barbara Whitmore, a newly employed, live-in assistant for Jean who suggests that she has repeatedly dealt with the trauma in her life by watching her employer's movies: 'My whole life is Marilyn'. Though 'Goodbye Norma Jean' initially looks as though it is attempting to validate the escapist elements of Monroe's screen roles, through his developing friendship with the real woman behind Monroe, and the sadness that Jean is shown to be experiencing as a result of feeling trapped by her 'creation', Sam comes to realise the potential dangers of the cinematic image. Sam pleads with Barbara that 'You can't base your whole life on an image on the screen ... it isn't real' to which she replies that Marilyn is 'better than real'. In a move that appears to be symbolic of the episode's critical attitude to the more immoral aspects of the Hollywood system, Barbara turns out to be an aspiring actress, Mary Jo Vermullen, who is using Monroe's contacts to advance her own nascent film career without any care for the effects it may have on her employer.

Over the course of 'Goodbye Norma Jean', it is Sam's distance from the situation and his ability to filter out his own nostalgic memories of Marilyn Monroe on screen that allow him to save her. Sam finds himself using his knowledge of Monroe's depression and suicide to help rebuild her self-esteem. After Sam saves Norma Jean from dying of an accidental drug overdose at a Hollywood party, she starts falling in love with him, stating that she is attracted by his capacity to see beyond the Monroe persona: 'I'm not her. She's someone I put on like a cashmere sweater or a mink coat. Somehow I think you're the first man who understands that'. Indeed, in line with the realization that he must retain some critical distance, Sam rebuffs Norma's advances saying that 'I can't let myself get involved with you; it wouldn't be fair to either one of us'. Ironically, Sam's knowledge of what happens to Monroe seems to be based on the many media accounts of Monroe's unhappy last days, including texts such as *Marilyn: The Untold Story* (1980) and *Marilyn: Say Goodbye To The President* (1985), which have effectively contributed to 'the Monroe image' (Dyer, 34). However, while there may be an inherent contradiction in suggesting that 'Goodbye Norma Jean' seeks to destabilize nostalgic perceptions of Monroe by implicitly utilizing documents which are, themselves, often subjective in approach, the episode does noticeably refrain from engaging with any of the more outlandish conspiracies surrounding Monroe's death.

In one sense then, *Quantum Leap* presents us with an explicitly mediatized version of history, yet this is not surprising if we are to believe Hutcheon's reading of nostalgia as intrinsically tied up with a distinctly artificial or constructed interpretation of the past:

Nostalgia, in fact, may depend precisely on the irrecoverable nature of the past for its emotional impact and appeal. It is the very pastness of the past, its inaccessibility, that likely accounts for a large part of nostalgia's power – for both conservatives and radicals alike. This is rarely the past as actually experienced, of course; it is the past as imagined, as idealized through memory and desire. In this sense, however, nostalgia is less about the past than about the present.

Hutcheon's comments here seem particularly interesting in the light of *Quantum Leap*'s recurrent structure, in which Sam's jumps close down the inaccessibility of the past for the character, giving him the ability to 'experience' the lives of others from those previously distant time periods. Though most nostalgic texts might foreground the irrecoverable relationship we have with the past, in *Quantum Leap* Sam gets to re-experience the past 'first-hand' in a manner that facilitates a more critical engagement with it, breaking down the 'Nostalgic distancing [which] sanitizes as it selects, making the past feel complete, stable, coherent, safe' (Hutcheon). In using a central character who is continually historically dislocated from those around him (with the exception of Al) the show creates an exploratory space in which Sam, and we as an audience, are encouraged to ask questions about the construction of history and how our own engagement with these historical narratives might work. These questions are similar to those questions being asked by post-modern thinkers at the time of the show's original airing which often centred on the ethical dimensions of constructing and reconstructing History. Indeed, Scott Bakula (the actor that played Sam) seemed to express a comparable sentiment in a 2012 interview when he suggested that: 'I always think that walking in someone else's shoes – if we all could do that – we'd be less likely to judge others, less likely to put people down, and we'd have more compassion for each other' (Bakula). By depicting Sam's experiences temporarily inhabiting the lives of other people, the show encourages the audience to re-evaluate and reconsider their attitudes to the lived experiences of history.

Though individual episodes of *Quantum Leap* were certainly not averse to presenting a 'rose-tinted' view of problematic points in US history ('The Leap Home: Part 2' for example), at its most interesting, the show moved beyond these kinds of simplistic re-staging to embody post-modernism's ability to interrogate nostalgia, in line with Hutcheon's belief that, while 'our contemporary culture is indeed nostalgic; some parts of it – postmodern parts – are aware of the risks and lures of nostalgia, and seek to expose those.'

In 'Justice' (4.4) Sam leaps into 1965 and the body of Clyde, a newly inducted member of the Ku Klux Klan in Alabama. Unsurprisingly, Sam is upset by the racist views of those around him, yet he is torn by his simultaneous appreciation of these self-same people's compassion for their friends and family: 'In all my leaps I don't think I had ever felt more confused by the people I had leapt into. There was part of me that liked Gene, and Tom and Brady. They were farmers, simple people that cared about their families and each other.' This confusion embodies the show's desire to re-cover those untold stories that are not routinely documented by the official media: 'there's no data on that kind of stuff, no one prints it in the newspapers, it just happens and it gets buried'. While the 1960s are often perceived as a time of advancement for the civil rights movement, 'Justice' explores the entrenched bigoted attitudes to race that remained in the South into the latter part of the twentieth century.

The episode is notable for the way in which it positions Sam as someone from a more progressive future and the white racists as prejudiced because they hold an imagined and nostalgic view of their own Southern past, as Sam's voiceover highlights at the beginning of the episode: 'and yet somehow time had passed them by'. Indeed, Sam repeatedly emphasizes the need for the townsfolk to look forwards – 'every generation has to learn things anew' – in order to solve their problems and explicitly configures their racism as fear and 'a shameful attempt to hold onto the past'. Sam's more enlightened position in relation to the other white characters distances him from them and invokes a critical stance on the part of the audience who are encouraged to align themselves with Sam and oppose the backward looking sentiments espoused by characters such as Tom, the town lawyer, who is scared of what he sees as the insidious influence of African Americans. Though the episode could be accused of advocating African American passivity (Sam talks down any African American attempts to protest that might lead to violence) it nevertheless depicts the dangers of nostalgia in a very real (if extreme) fashion.

Many of the show's more interesting episodes highlight the difficult tension that exists between Sam's assigned mission to assess the situations he jumps into and (alongside Ziggy and Al) critically evaluate the best means forward, and his often emotional connection to those he meets and attempts to help. The show repeatedly suggests that there is an inherent danger in becoming too personally involved, pitting objective professionalism against a more irrational, yet heartfelt response that seems to resonate with post-modern concerns over nostalgia as a 'functionally crippling' (Hutcheon) aesthetic technique which paralyzes us with 'dreams of days when things were better' (Hutcheon). In the season three episode 'The Leap Home' Sam finds himself in an intensely nostalgic situation when he jumps into his 16-year-old self.

The character's strong emotional connection to the situation is established right from the start of the episode. Sam finds himself on his family's farm in Elkridge,

Indiana, in 1969 where he immediately remembers the sights and smells of the cornfield and runs 'home' to be greeted by his mother, all before the opening credits roll. After hugging his mother and telling her how 'glad he is to see' her, Sam, with tears welling in his eyes, gets to meet his father and, wrought with joy, cannot resist from exclaiming 'I love you, dad'. The episode explicitly foregrounds the nostalgic appeal of the situation for Sam, intercutting scenes featuring Sam being 'reunited' with various family members, with exterior shots depicting the archetypal US rural homestead. The presentation of the Beckett homestead, silhouetted against the soft light of the autumn sun as it gently sets over the cornfields, creates an intentionally evocative sense of a homespun pastoral idyll reminiscent of such imaginary family homes as those found in *Little House on the Prairie* (1974–1983) and the Kent family farmhouse in the *Superman* narrative.

In many ways this jump is Sam's ideal situation, as the character himself suggests with some elation: 'I'm 16, I'm home and my dad's alive'. However, this idyllic set-up is quickly ruined when Al turns up and informs Sam that all he needs to do to jump out of his situation is help his high school football team beat their opponents in the Friday playoff against Bentleyville. Unfortunately, Sam's emotional connection to being back home means that Sam has to admit that he doesn't want to jump away from the situation. As he points out to Al, his father dies of a coronary in three years' time, his younger sister elopes with Chuck, an abusive alcoholic, and his older brother Tom is about to come home for Thanksgiving before shipping out to Vietnam where he is killed in action. Sam tells Al that he wants to stay in the body of his 16-year-old self in order to try and save his family even though Al pleads that 'you can't change something that isn't meant to be changed'. Despite Sam's experience of previous jumps where they were unable to change events to benefit Al, he has already lost his critical distance to the emotional pull of the situation, evident in his claim that 'this [jump] is different' and his subsequent dismissal of Ziggy's empiricist scientific calculations: 'I don't give a damn what that hybrid computer says'.

Ironically, Sam's attempts to save his family with the 'superior' knowledge he has as someone from the future are constantly thwarted; he cannot convince his father to change to a healthier diet, his sister Katie unconvincingly humours his advice on being wary of men called Chuck, and his attempts to persuade his brother not to go to Vietnam fall on deaf ears as his brother jokily accuses him of being a dove and a hippy. Indeed, Sam's conversation with Tom makes explicit the complex tensions that exist between Sam's emotional involvement in the situation and the critical distance that he is afforded as part of his unique position. Annoyed with Sam's continued attempts to dissuade him from going to Vietnam, Tom accuses Sam of losing his emotional connection to a series of icons resonant with a nostalgic view of the US: 'What's happened to you, Sam? You used to be for the flag, apple pie and the Fourth of July'. Similarly, when Katie begins to believe that Sam actually is from the future and is upset with the belief that this therefore means that her brother Tom will die in Vietnam as Sam has 'predicted', Sam is initially, in spite of Al's advice, unable to pretend and tell her that he made it all up. It is only when Al exclaims that 'you're not changing their future, Sam, all you're doing is making their present miserable' that Sam relents and in an display of putting others' emotions before his own explains to his family that 'I made it all up, I made up everything because I didn't want Tom to go to Vietnam'. In the crisis that follows this 'admission' Sam declares to Al that he is going to quit jumping because it is 'not fair' that 'he can save strangers but not his own family.' At this point in the episode Sam seems to have become victim to what Tim Reiss describes as the functionally crippling aspects of nostalgia. He is unable to appreciate that, by refusing to do what is required of him (win the game), he cannot move forward and invoke any meaningful change (improving the lives of the rest of the basketball team and their coach).

Interestingly, Al rebuffs Sam's cries for sympathy, stating that: 'I think it's damn fair…I'd give anything to see my father and my sister for a few days, to be able to talk with them again, laugh with them, tell them how much I love them. I'd give anything to have what you have, Sam'. Al's comments here point to a realization that Sam must understand that, while it is inevitable he is likely to feel a nostalgic connection to the situation he is in, he needs to move away from an entirely emotional engagement with the situation and regain a degree of objective, critical distance, appreciating the opportunity that has been given him while following Ziggy's instructions to help people other than himself. In this manner the episode highlights the difficulty of either a solely objective or subjective engagement with history while suggesting that perhaps what is needed is a perspective that combines the two; embodied in someone, like Sam, who is able to look at history with critically distanced eyes, while recognizing the innately personal aspects of it.

In spite of the more critically meritorious interpretation of *Quantum Leap*, as a pop-cultural vehicle for exploring post-modern approaches to historiography, that I have offered here, it is fair to say that the final episode of the show seemed to mark something of a retreat into emotional melodrama. Though driven in part by commercial imperatives (the show makers were unsure whether they would receive a sixth season and so therefore had to provide a sense of closure while also leaving things ambiguous enough to allow for the possibility of further episodes) 'Mirror Image' sees Sam jump into his own body on the day and at the time he was born. In contrast to the standard mechanics of the show that usually see Sam's reflection replaced by that of the host body he has jumped into, when Sam looks in a nearby mirror in 'Mirror Image', Sam sees his own adult body reflected back at him. Seemingly confined to a bar (called Al's Place) in an unnamed mining town in Indiana, various members of the community enter and leave the bar over the course of the episode, conversing with Sam and the bartender who dishes out germane advice to everyone: 'part philosopher, part psychiatrist, part psychic'.

Some of the patrons resemble people Sam has helped through his jumps (Frank Lamotta and Jimmy Lamotta from 'Jimmy' 2.16, Moe Stein from 'Future Boy' 3.13) while others seem to share names and attributes with people in Sam's life (Al the bartender, Gooshie) but they no longer recognize Sam and seem to have no knowledge of their previous manifestations. Faced with an existentialist crisis: 'why am I here . . . what can I do?' one of the miners suggests that Sam 'must be a safety inspector'; and it appears that he must pretend to be a safety inspector in order to help the community to rescue two miners who are trapped with a rapidly expiring supply of oxygen after an explosion in the nearby mine. Yet, after further conversation with the bartender, Sam realises that he must make the ultimate sacrifice, and give up the chance to return home so that he can save Al's marriage. Perhaps to push my reading to breaking point, *Quantum Leap* finally seeks to foreground, in a clear fashion, the inability of any individual to completely, critically distance themselves from the historicizing process. Much as post-modern thinkers such as Patricia Waugh and Hayden White have suggested that history is a subjective process, so Sam realises that he must accept the interconnectedness of his engagement with those he has saved over the years (as the bartender tells him 'the lives you touched, touched others, and those, others') and his inability to remove himself from their ongoing histories. Rather than 'play by the rules' Sam comes to the understanding that he must continue jumping because he has 'a wrong to put right for Al', he then takes his final jump back to save Al's first marriage, telling his wife Beth that Al is alive and that he is coming home to her.

Ultimately the show's approach to history seems to be that the individual, personal experiences are just as important to the construction of history as the supposedly world-shaking events have been judged to be by the official history books. In offering this particular interpretation of the past, *Quantum Leap* structurally undermines any sense of history as monolithic; as a singular narrative in which there is a straightforward battle between the forces of 'good' and 'bad' (see 'Justice' for example). Instead, the show offers a distinctly post-modern sense of the micro-narratives of individual histories, promoting the idea that there are hidden stories within the historical narratives that we think we know; as Marshall suggests, 'Postmodernism is about histories not told . . . Histories forgotten, hidden, invisible, considered unimportant, changed, eradicated.' (4) Characters in the show are often tangentially embroiled in the events that make up world history, but the characters that Sam leaps into are forever motivated by and preoccupied by the minutiae of their individual lives. This is evident in several of the episodes I have looked at here, and is especially prominent in the 'The Leap Home' and 'The Leap Home Part Two: Vietnam' when Sam is directly motivated by the chance to spend time with his family before the death of his brother in the eponymous conflict. It is these individual, often relationship-based, issues which more often than not form the basis for the drama in the show, indicating that *Quantum*

Leap's conceptualization of history is diverse and multi-layered yet always human in its focus.

Note

1. At the 2010 Comic Con *TV Guide* panel star Scott Bakula suggested that Donald P. Bellisario was in the early stages of putting a script for a movie together though Bakula has since retracted these comments, saying that he spoke too early and that the movie is still several years away.

12

Time on TV: Afterword

Lorna Jowett and David Simmons

'All of this has happened before, all of this will happen again'

(Battlestar Galactica)

Through the chapters making up this book, our contributors have demonstrated how important time is to television and to telefantasy in particular. Of course, detailed as many of these analyses have been, the nature of such a collection means that some aspects of time on TV have only been touched upon, and in this brief afterword we wish to draw attention to some significant uses of time in the television landscape that have not yet been directly addressed. In the first section, we examine how reboots and remakes operate in relation to contemporary television, while in the second, we analyse television overflow, or convergence, as other forms of media take on aspects of televisual time.

Reboots and Remakes

Television has often relied on repeating previously shown material to fill its ever-expanding schedules and repetition is also seen to be an integral part of structuring on television. Some of our contributors have taken reboots and remakes as the subject of their scrutiny, and this indicates another area of significance in terms of time, television and repetition. If, as Constantine Verevis notes of film, 'remakes are often thought of as commercial products that repeat successful formulas in order to minimize risk and secure profits in the marketplace' (37) then the same logic can easily be applied to TV. Thus rebooting *Dallas* in 2012 (TNT) presumably seemed like a commercially viable proposition that could potentially draw in the large audiences who watched the show when it first aired (1978–1991). The 'Who shot J.R.?' storyline from the 1980 season of *Dallas* is still a well-known and often cited TV cliffhanger, and this plotline attracted audience numbers that make it one of the most-watched primetime broadcasts in the US. The remake is described on TNT's website:

> *Dallas* centres on the Ewing clan, an enormously wealthy Texas family whose sibling rivalries, romantic betrayals, corruption and even murder are truly legendary. The exciting drama brings back three iconic stars from the original *Dallas*: Patrick Duffy as Bobby Ewing, Linda Gray as Sue Ellen Ewing and Larry Hagman as J.R. Ewing. They are joined by the next generation of Ewings, who take ambition and deception to a new level.

This summary introduces the show to a new audience, unfamiliar with the 1980s version, playing on its primetime soap opera elements, yet it then goes on to advertise the 'three iconic stars' of the classic series, presumably to entice audiences who *did* watch it. The phrase 'joined by the next generation of Ewings' highlights the attempt to segue from one generation of audience to another, but reference to 'the original Dallas' also identifies one of the major problems any remake has to contend with.

Some viewers may be attracted to a remake as an entirely new and unfamiliar product, but those who are already aware of its previous incarnation are always likely to compare it to the 'original'. The very term 'original' suggests that a remake is, by nature, less innovative, being more of a 'copy' that merely seeks to imitate and 'cash-in' on the reputation of the previous product. In addition, a series that reflected or negotiated timely issues in one generation may not have much to say if it is simply reproduced in another era. Certainly the revival of *Dallas* suggests that remaking a successful 1980s primetime soap was not an easy sell, since audience numbers declined rapidly (A newspaper in the UK reports that 'Channel 5's Texas drama went from having 3 million fans tuning in to just 328,000 in a mere three months,' Boyle). Given that the types of telefantasy and cult TV discussed in this book tend to attract a niche audience, even though some are positioned as mainstream television, how a remake of a cult or classic series is positioned, marketed and seeks to address an audience who may have acquired extensive fan knowledge of the previous product is arguably of some importance.

Thus the UK's *Randall and Hopkirk, Deceased* (ITV 1969–1970), remade as *Randall & Hopkirk, Deceased* (BBC One 2000–2001) was not a lasting success despite the involvement of then-popular comedy duo Vic Reeves and Bob Mortimer. However, Syfy acquired rights to the series in 2010, obviously hoping for a different outcome. Remaking a series with the lasting reputation and fandom of *The Prisoner* (ITV 1967–68) might seem doomed to failure. The 1960s series is often lauded as a highly imaginative and countercultural show, regularly ranking high in 'Best Of' cult or science fiction and fantasy TV lists, while its final episode received a Hugo award nomination and finds its way into Top TV Episode lists and countdowns.

Yet *The Prisoner* was relaunched as a miniseries co-production broadcast in 2009 (AMC/ITV) and received, among others, nominations for Emmy and Saturn awards. Its ratings dropped after the first instalment, but since it was constructed as a one-off miniseries, its mixed reviews cannot be compared with continuing success or cancellation.

However, some TV remakes have successfully negotiated remaking a 'classic' series and achieved a sustained run of several seasons and critical success, as *Battlestar Galactica* demonstrates (ABC 1978–79, SciFi 2004–2009). While some fans of the 1970s show criticised the new *BSG* for its dark tone, this grimly realistic portrayal of war, occupation and terrorist infiltrators chimed with the zeitgeist and attracted Emmy nominations and praise from Stephen King (2007) and Joss Whedon (2006), among others. Rather than simply reproducing the original series, *BSG* 'reimagined' key elements for a twenty-first century audience and its themes of humanity/artificial life were echoed in other, albeit less successful, contemporaneous science-fiction television remakes reboots such as *The Bionic Woman* (2007) and *Terminator: The Sarah Connor Chronicles* (2008–2009). Both *Star Trek* and *Doctor Who* demonstrate that science-fiction television can achieve lasting success in television terms, reinventing themselves for new audiences on a regular basis.

The vogue for reimagining classics is still apparent. On Halloween night 2013 NBC premiered its new co-produced series *Dracula* (2013–). Promotional and advertising images featured two taglines – 'A legend is reborn' and 'old legend/new blood' – nodding to its many predecessors. While these materials are clearly aware of having to negotiate the fact that the series is a remake of a well-known and often re/produced story, the use of 'legend' suggests that this version of Dracula might be more of a reimagining, drawing on Dracula as mediated through popular culture and less of a faithful adaptation of Stoker's Victorian novel. The prominence of Jonathan Rhys Meyers' name on advertising materials (the words, 'Jonathan Rhys Meyers/DRACULA,' were sometimes the only words appearing alongside images) – he is both the star playing Dracula and the producer of three episodes – also trades upon the 'new blood' angle by offering the lead actor as a draw for the audience. NBC's website even opens its 'About the show' section with the words: 'Golden Globe winner Jonathan Rhys Meyers (*The Tudors*) stars in this provocative new drama as one of the world's most iconic characters.' In case this is not enough to attract viewers, *Dracula* is also presented as coming with established TV credentials in terms of its production team, aligning it not with other horror television series, or with classic literary adaptations, but with a highly successful period television drama: 'From the producers of the critically acclaimed, Emmy-award-winning hit *Downton Abbey* comes *Dracula*, a twisted, sophisticated and sexy take on Bram Stoker's classic novel, proving that some stories never die'. *Dracula* thus seeks to tap three potential audiences: those who might watch a television 'take' on *Dracula*, those who might watch Rhys Meyers in a new starring TV role, and those who might watch a period drama that promises to be more 'sexy' or 'twisted' than *Downton Abbey*. All appeal to the viewer's television-watching history, a shared past, and a willingness to 'repeat' a previous televisual experience.

As well as playing with and on our perceptions of TV time with remakes, reboots and, reimaginings, television has also started to have some success with prequels. This is not a new concept in television, as Richard Hewett points out. Popular programmes such as the UK's long-running sitcom *Only Fools and Horses* (BBC One 1981–2003) have generated prequels, and *The Carrie Diaries* (CW 2013–) is currently offering a prequel to HBO's hit series *Sex and the City* (1998–2004). Yet Hewett notes that the prequel, while established in movies, holds some problems for television:

> The concept of prequels is not one that, on first consideration, sits easily in the television landscape. Given the serialized nature of so much modern television drama, which essentially hinges on keeping viewers hooked on what will happen next, the idea of showing what happened *before* we met characters with whom we are already familiar – and to whom we therefore know precisely what is going to happen – must, surely, have limited appeal?

TV may thrive on familiarity, but Hewett suggests that the prequel may be just too familiar and too obvious to appeal. The *Star Trek* prequel *Enterprise* sought to get round this problem by offering a prequel to the established history of the Federation, featuring new characters and new situations that would segue into, but not overlap, events already familiar to audiences of other *Trek*s. As Lincoln Geraghty has noted elsewhere, the prequel's 'turn to the past at a time of American uncertainty' (141) shifted the ground somewhat, establishing in its opening title sequence 'an overtly American version of history' (141) that was criticized for contradicting the 'Infinite Diversity in Infinite Combinations' ethos of the ongoing franchise. Thus it often had to retcon (retroactively correct continuity) in its timelines to offer 'a re-visioning of a celebratory past' and presented what some saw as 'a very nationalistic and masculine version of events' (143). Notably, the recent film series (*Star Trek* 2009 and *Star Trek: Into Darkness* 2013) has attempted to avoid this pitfall of reintroducing familiar characters by highlighting that it is a complete reboot, with events taking place in a parallel timeline that does not affect the established continuity of existing series.

2013 brought two serial killer prequels to the small screen, *Hannibal* (NBC 2013–) and *Bates Motel* (A&E 2013–), and both were successful enough to have a second season in 2014. These dramas offer insights into the years before Hannibal Lecter and Norman Bates become the famous (or as *Dracula* would have it, 'legendary') serial killers of *Silence of the Lambs* (and other novels and films such as *Red Dragon* and *Manhunter*) and *Psycho* (film, 1960). In some sense these TV offerings have to be loose reimaginings given that they are based on book/film characters, who may inhabit a series of stories, but nevertheless are generally associated with one main story. Yet, on the other hand, the repetitive and compulsive behaviour of the serial killer lends itself to ongoing TV drama. *Dexter* (2006–2013) certainly proved a success for Showtime, and in taking a serial killer, even a killer in the making, as a focal point both *Bates Motel* and *Hannibal*, as Douglas Howard notes, are tapping into 'the medium's ongoing obsession with the anti-hero,' as seen in series like *The Wire* or *The Shield* (both 2002–2008) and *Breaking Bad* (2008–2013).

Bates Motel has brought the characters into the present and some viewers were slightly scandalized to see Norman texting, yet inevitably, perhaps, it takes Norman's relationship with his mother, Norma as its main focus. Indeed, Vera Farmiga, who plays Norma, received four award nominations for her performance in the first season. *Hannibal* has attracted more critical acclaim, particularly for its visual style, but perhaps also for its reworking of Lecter and his 'manhunter' antagonist FBI agent Will Graham. As Howard points out, *Hannibal*:

> never attempts to offer itself up as a second-rate *Silence of the Lambs* or to mine Anthony Hopkins's Academy Award portrayal for Lecter's character nuances. Rather, it reimagines and reconfigures the characters, the atmosphere, and the storylines so that the familiar no longer feels so familiar and the end result no longer feels so certain.

Throwing off the expected narrative resolution in this way is a key strategy in avoiding the problem identified by Hewett, that is, if we know what is going to happen to these characters, why should we care enough to watch them week after week? Both *Hannibal* and *Bates Motel* seek to offer something new, adding characters and dynamics to offset this familiarity. How long they can successfully maintain this as their respective stories approach the end/start point remains to be seen.

Another way that current television seems to be playing with time is by mashing together different periods. In this volume, Nicola Allen discusses *Life on Mars* and *Ashes to Ashes* as offering new perspectives on the past by introducing characters from the future into it, yet one break-out hit of 2013 *Sleepy Hollow* (Fox) introduces a character from the past into the contemporary era. In what can be perceived as a twist on *Grimm* (NBC 2011–) and *Once Upon a Time*'s relocation of fairy tale characters into the 'real world,' *Sleepy Hollow* reimagines Washington Irving's tale 'The Legend of Sleepy Hollow', originally published in 1820, by awakening its protagonist Ichabod Crane in the twenty-first century. The series can thus be seen as a remake or adaptation, a reboot, *and* a reimagining.

Sleepy Hollow is a contemporary fantasy action series, though it regularly cites US history, often using Crane's out-of-time character to compare the struggles and ideals of the Revolutionary-era United States with present-day US society. Writer, executive producer and co-showrunner Mark Goffman sees this as an attraction for the writers and the audience:

> This show offers a really great opportunity to dig into the world of revolutionary times and recast it [as part of an apocalyptic scenario]. Having Ichabod Crane as this character who can comment on both what we were fighting for back then, and who gets to look at America and look at how our society works today and give us the point of view of our Founding Fathers is really exciting and fun to write (in Ryan).

Both Goffman and actor Tom Mison, who plays Crane, admit to having a fascination with history, which finds its way into the series both through the action plots (Crane worked for General Washington as a kind of secret agent) and the self-aware dialogue and characterization.

One of the engaging aspects of the series is that Crane is rarely shown as unable to cope with the demands or the strangeness of a new society; rather he is positioned frequently as a commentator upon it, who brings his intelligence to bear on new aspects of twenty-first century life, from communications technology to new iterations of capitalism. In this sense he takes on the role of a science-fiction alien, distanced from our world and not part of its assumptions and social training. The show has been praised for tackling issues such as politics and especially race, in both the historical and the contemporary context. Ichabod's partner in saving the world is a black female detective, Abbie Mills, and many key characters are played by actors of colour. As an original inhabitant of a much earlier time, Crane naturally notices changes to the way society operates in the present day and sometimes requires information about these changes. Yet his character's obvious presentation as a man 'out of time' estranges him and his viewpoint sufficiently for the audience to accept direct questioning of, for example, racial history. Goffman remarks, 'I do think there's something innocent about the way that Ichabod Crane can approach it, because he is not from our culture. So he can ask these questions out of a genuine curiosity, and they're not as loaded.'

Gwyneth Peaty argues in this volume that *Once Upon a Time*, despite revising 'timeless' fairy tales and fairy tale characters by bringing them into contact with the present day, still offers the hope of a happy ending. As well as commenting on the historical events that formed our society, *Sleepy Hollow* also engages with a different kind of epic scale: apocalyptic time. In common with other long-running fantasy series like *Buffy the Vampire Slayer*, *Supernatural* (2005–), and *The Walking Dead* (2010–), *Sleepy Hollow* posits an ongoing battle between good and evil forces. Thus the 'timelessness' the show engages with is a timeless, continuing struggle that may end everything, adding weight to its odd couple story of investigation. The current popularity of all kinds of fantasy television suggests that these aspects of time on TV are not likely to disappear soon.

Overflow

While the chapters in this volume have looked at a wide range of examples, both old and new, the pertinence of time as an integral factor to genre TV might now be considered to face a new, transmedia hurdle. It is interesting at this point in the collection to consider what will become of contemporary television's obsession with time in the new (post) TV3 landscape. The continuing success of series such as *Doctor Who* and the plaudits doled out to newly aired shows such as *True Detective* (2014–) (the marketing of which foregrounded its time skipping narrative) appear to testify to time's continuing significance on 'standard' TV. Equally, developments in the field of videogames suggest that time is playing a central part in transmedia ventures. The recent release of the latest videogame consoles appear to have cemented a now long standing desire amongst videogame companies to place greater and greater emphasis on the importance of TV content in what they do. This was demonstrated most clearly in much of the rhetoric used during Microsoft's 2013 reveal of their new console, the Xbox One. Indeed, the 2013 launch conference witnessed a conscious repositioning of the Xbox brand as Xbox One, the name pertaining to the supposed need to only have one box or entertainment hub under your TV, one delivery system for all of your entertainment, be it interactive or not. Yusuf Mehdi, Corporate Vice President of Marketing, Strategy and Business for Microsoft showed off the console's new capabilities, which were focused on TV media as much as they were on 'traditional' videogames. In a move that underscores the increased desire amongst those in the videogame industry to leverage their platforms into the TV-watching arena, Mehdi stressed that the Xbox One 'is the beginning of truly intelligent TV' (TGDaily), emphasising the capabilities of the platform to enable new ways of viewing TV content. One of the ways in which Xbox One enables intelligent TV is through its inbuilt DVR system, a first for a videogames console, which allows for the time shifting capabilities afforded by the Sky+ or TiVo systems.

At the same time as platform holders have been changing their approaches to positioning and marketing their hardware, there has been a concurrent increase in the levels of convergence between videogame software and TV. Such convergence seems to reflect a desire amongst those in the videogames industry to appropriate some of the cultural capital of contemporary 'quality' TV, as then President of Sony Computer Entertainment Phil Harrison's comments suggest: 'I believe games can have the same social currency as a great TV program' (Gamasutra). Given the focus of this collection, perhaps the most interesting of the trends that has emerged from this convergence been the increasing adoption of structural elements relating to the use of time more readily associated with recent (usually 'quality' and genre) TV; as Paul Booth confirms 'in the videogame medium we see similar temporal situations [to those in television]' (204). Games such as *Blinx: The Time Sweeper* (2002), *Timeshift* (2007), *Braid* (2008), and *The Misadventures of P.B. Winterbottom* (2010) all gift the player with the ability to alter or manipulate time in some capacity, confirming the growing emphasis upon 'interactive temporalities' (Booth, 222).

The rise of Telltale games is particularly telling in this regard. The studio, founded in 2004, has developed a distinctive approach to the games they release, involving a number of storytelling conventions drawn from TV that relate to that medium's manipulation of time. Apart from basing several of their games on franchises or intellectual properties that are more readily associated with television (*CSI, Wallace and Gromit, The Walking Dead, Game of Thrones*) Telltale have distinguished themselves in the field by intentionally releasing the majority of their games, be they based on TV properties or not, in an episodic format. As CEO Dan Connors suggested in a 2012 interview, this was a conscious attempt to ape the successes, both commercial and artistic, of episodic contemporary television:

A lot of the best storytelling going on in the past ten years or so has been episodic storytelling, from *The Sopranos* to *Game of Thrones*. We saw the strength in that model as the way to tell a story and it was tied into our digital distribution strategy, which was to break the content up in a way that would engage people over time and have them return to you, instead of just building a one-time experience. [We wanted] to give them smaller, finishable chunks – to change the dynamics of the way people play games. (Gameinformer)

Utilizing the delivery model that still remains for much of contemporary TV drama, completing individual episodes of Telltale's games typically takes a much shorter length of time (1–2 hours) than other comparable videogame releases but each episode is much more cheaply priced as well (Telltale's games are usually less than $5 an episode). Each episode of a Telltale game also ends with a teaser for the next instalment, emulating the techniques of TV series which have long used such a device in order to build anticipation. As a means of further maintaining interest in their games (and in another reflection of their indebtedness to TV storytelling conventions) sequential episodes of a Telltale videogame are usually released on a monthly basis rather than the interval of a year or more that typically accompanies the release of sequels in the videogame industry.

While Telltale's games have adopted the sequential delivery patterns of contemporary TV, much of the pre-release marketing and discussion surrounding Remedy Entertainment's (yet to be released) *Quantum Break* has focused on the centrality of time as a feature in the game; as one online preview suggests:

The concept of time – and the manipulation of it – is at the heart of *Quantum Break*. At the beginning of the game, a failed time travel experiment causes a temporal disaster, causing time to start breaking down. Three people close to that experiment gone [sic] are then gifted time-related powers. (Polygon)

Quantum Break, which will supposedly tell its story through both live action episodes and episodic videogame content, suggests not only the continuing prominence of time within genre TV and videogames but across transmedia properties too. In the game, the player will adopt the persona of (alternately) Jack Joyce, Beth Wilder, and villain Paul Serene. Jack and Beth must attempt to save the world after an experiment gone wrong gifts them (alongside Paul) with the ability to stop time. The idea of super-humans with the ability to manipulate time not only harks back to previously successful shows such as *Heroes* (2006–2010) and characters such as Hiro Nakamura, but also seems to act as an embodiment of the desire we have to control our viewing: choosing when and where, at what speed and in what order, we engage with our favourite television shows from now on.

Both the current vogue for remaking old stories, and the ways that other media forms are adopting elements of televisual time, suggest that notions of time on TV will continue to evolve, and to offer new areas for study. This book, like other recent publications, has attempted to start a conversation about time on television and in telefantasy in particular – we assume it will not finish it, since there is clearly much more to say.

Work Cited

Abbott, Stacey. *Angel* (Detroit, MI: Wayne State University Press, 2009).

——— . 'Walking the Fine Line Between Angel and Angelus.' *Slayage: The Journal of the Whedon Studies Association* 9 (2003) Available: http://slayageonline.com/essays/slayage9/Abbott.htm.

Anders, Lou. 'Introduction: Worlds of If', in Lou Anders (ed) *Sideways in Crime* (Nottingham: Solaris, 2008) pp. 11–14.

Anderson, Steve. 'Loafing in the Garden of Knowledge: History TV and Popular Memory.' *Film & History, Special Focus: Television as Historian, Part 1*, vol. 30, no. 1 (2000) pp. 14–23.

Anonymous. 'Chronology Projection Conjecture'. *Wikipedia*, (2014) Available: http://en.wikipedia.org/wiki/Chronology_protection_conjecture.

Ashley, Mike (ed.). *The Mammoth Book of Time Travel SF* (London: Robinson, 2013).

Ashliman, D.L. *Folk and Fairy Tales: A Handbook* (Westport, CT: Greenwood Press, 2004).

Asimov, Isaac. 'Introduction', in *Asimov's Mysteries* (St Albans: Panther, 1969) pp. 9–11.

——— . 'Time Travel', *Gold* (London: HarperCollins *Publishers*, 1995) pp. 235–38.

Bailey, David. 'Master of Crime', *Cult Times* #19 (April 1997) p. 24.

Bakula, Scott. 'Quantum Cool: An Interview with Scott Bakula', *Chicagoist*, Tony Peregrin, Aug 6 2012. Available: http://chicagoist.com/2012/08/06/quantum_cool_an_interview_with_scot.php.

Banks-Smith, Nancy. 'It's the End of Life on Mars', *Guardian* Online [website] http://www.theguardian.com/media/2007/apr/11/tvandradio.comment.

Barthes, Roland. 'The Nautilus and the Drunken Boat' in *Mythologies* (New York: Noonday, 1972).

Benshoff, Harry M. *Dark Shadows* (Detroit, MI: Wayne State University Press, 2011).

Berkman, Marcus. 'Let's do the time warp again', *Radio Times* (1–7 March 1997) pp. 20–22.

Bignell, Jonathan. *Introduction to Television Studies* (London: Routledge, 2004).

Blocher, Karen Funk. 'Answers to Common Questions About Quantum Leap', *Welcome to the Waiting Room: Project Quantum Leap*, 5 Dec 1997. Available: http://mavarin.com/quantum/cqs5.html.

Boon, T. *Films of Fact: A History of Science in Documentary Films and Television* (London: Wallflower Press, 2008).

Boorstin, Daniel J. *The Discoverers* (Harmondsworth: Penguin Books, 1983).

Booth, Paul. *Time on TV: Temporal Displacement and Mashup Television* (New York: Peter Lang, 2012).

Borges, Jorge Luis. *Fictions*. Trans. Anthony Kerrigan (London: Calder Publications, 1998).

Boswell, R. '*Interview with Pete Boss.*' (15 July 2013).

Boyle, Simon. 'Who shut JR? Dallas remake heading for the axe as viewing figures plummet' *Daily Mirror* online. 18 February 2013. Available: http://www.mirror.co.uk/tv/tv-news/dallas-remake-heading-axe-viewing-1715597#ixzz2uLUNz2J4.

Broadley, Liane. 'Loopy Logic', *TV Zone* #91 (June 1997) p. 38.

Brook, Stephan. 'So Be It: I Shall Stand Alone in Defending Keeley Hawes', *Guardian* Online [website] http://www.theguardian.com/media/organgrinder/2008/feb/15/sobeitishallstandalonei.

Brosnan, John. 'It's Only a Movie', *Starburst* #225 (May 1997, Vol 19 #9) p. 66.

———, Peter Nicholls and Kim Newman. '*Dr Who*', in John Clute and Peter Nicholls (eds.) *The Encyclopedia of Science Fiction* (London: Orbit, 2nd edn 1999) pp. 345–346.

Brown, Anthony. 'Travel Writer', *SFX* #24 (April 1997) pp. 63–65.

Cameron, Allan. *Modular Narratives in Contemporary Cinema* (Houndmills: Palgrave Macmillan, 2012).

Campbell, Joseph. *The Hero with a Thousand Faces* (London: Fontana, 1993).

Cartmell, Deborah, and I.Q. Hunter. 'Introduction: Retrovisions: Historical Makeovers in Film and Literature.' In Deborah Cartmell, I.Q. Hunter, and Imelda Whelehan (eds) *Retrovisions: Reinventing the Past in Film and Fiction* (London: Pluto Press, 2001) pp. 1–7.

Cashdan, Sheldon. *The Witch Must Die: The Hidden Meaning of Fairy Tales* (New York: Basic Books, 1999).

'Christmases Past, Present and Sci-Fi.' *New York Times* (2010) p. 1.

Clark, Stuart. 'Partners in Time', *Starburst* #225 (May 1997, Vol 19 #9) pp. 20–23.

Cook, John R. 'The Age of Aquarius: utopia and anti-utopia in late 1960s' and early 1970s' British Science Fiction' in Cook, John R. and Peter Wright, eds. *British Science Fiction Television: A Hitchhikers Guide* (London: I.B.Tauris, 2006).

——— and Peter Wright. *British Science Fiction Television: A Hitchhikers Guide* (London: I.B.Tauris, 2006).

——— and Mary Irwin. 'Moonage Daydreams: Nostalgia and Cultural Memory Contexts of Life on Mars and Ashes to Ashes' in Lacey, Stephen and McElroy Ruth (eds) (2012), *Life on Mars: From Manchester to New York*, University of Wales Press.

Cox, Greg. *Star Trek: The Eugenics Wars, The Rise and Fall of Khan Noonien Singh – Volume One* (New York, NY: Pocket Books, 2001).

———. *Star Trek: The Eugenics Wars, The Rise and Fall of Khan Noonien Singh – Volume Two* (New York, NY: Pocket Books, 2002).

———. *Star Trek: To Reign in Hell, The Exile of Khan Noonien Singh* (New York, NY: Pocket Books, 2005).

Creeber, Glen. *Serial Television: Big Drama on the Small Screen* (London: BFI Publishing, 2004).

Dallas TNT website. http://www.dallastnt.com/series/dallas/abouttheshow/.

Davies, Russell T. and Benjamin Cook. *Doctor Who: The Writers Tale: The Final Chapter* (London: BBC Publishing, 2013). (Kindle edition)

Doane, Mary Ann. *The Emergence of Cinematic Time* (Harvard University Press, 2002).

Dracula NBC website. http://www.nbc.com/dracula/about.

Dyer, Richard. *Heavenly Bodies: Film Stars and Society* (New York: Routledge, 2004).

Edwards, Malcolm J. and Brian Stableford. 'Time Travel' in John Clute and Peter Nicholls (eds.) *The Encyclopedia of Science Fiction* (London: Orbit, 2nd edn 1999) pp. 1227–1229.

Feuer, Jane. *Seeing Through the Eighties* (London: BFI Publishing, 1996).

Fiske, John. *Television Culture.* 1st ed. (Routledge, 1988).

———, 'The Cultural Economy of Fandom.' In Lisa A. Lewis (ed.) *The Adoring Audience: Fan Culture and Popular Media* (New York, NY: Routledge, 1992) pp. 30–49.

Forster, L. 'Farmers, Feminists, and Dropouts: The Disguises of the Scientist in British Science Fiction Television in the 1970s'. In L. Geraghty (ed.) *Channelling the Future: Essays on Science Fiction and Fantasy Television* (Lanham, MD: The Scarecrow Press, 2009).

Gale, Richard M. '"What, Then, Is Time?": Introduction,' in Richard M. Gale (ed.) *The Philosophy of Time* (MacMillan: London, 1968).

Gale, Simon (2005). 'Stephen Gallagher In His Own Words', *Bugs: the Complete Series.* Revelation Films. Region 2.

Geraghty, Lincoln. *Living With Star Trek: American Culture and the Star Trek Universe* (London: I.B.Tauris, 2007).

Gerrold, David. *The World of Star Trek: The Inside Story of TV's Most Popular Series* (3rd edition) (London: Virgin Books, 1996).

Gosden, Christopher. *Social Being and Time* (Blackwell: Oxford, 1994).

Goulding, Jay. *Empire, Aliens, and Conquest: A Critique of American Ideology in Star Trek and Other Science Fiction Adventures* (Toronto, OT: Sisyphus Press, 1985).

Grant, John. 'Timeslips' in Gary Westfahl (ed.) *The Greenwood Encyclopedia of Science Fiction and Fantasy: Themes, Works, and Wonders Vol 2* (Westport Connecticut: Greenwood Press, 2005) pp. 821–23.

Gray, Jonathan. *Show Sold Separately: Promos, Spoilers, and Other Paratexts* (New York: New York University Press, 2010).

Gregory, Chris. *Star Trek Parallel Narratives* (London: Macmillan Press, 2000)

Haase, Donald. 'Introduction,' in Donald Haase (ed.) *The Reception of Grimms' Fairy Tales: Responses, Reactions, Revisions.* (Detroit, MI: Wayne State University Press, 1996).

Haining, Peter. 'Introduction' in Peter Haining (ed.) *Timescapes: Stories of Time Travel* (London: Souvenir Press, 1997) pp. 7–9.

Hammond, P. J. (2007). 'Interview', *Counting Out Time, Sapphire & Steel.* Network. Region 2.

Hawking, Stephen. 'The Future of the Universe' (January 1991), reprinted in Stephen Hawking, *Black Holes and Baby Universes, and Other Essays* (London: Bantam, 1993) pp. 127–41.

Hawthorn, J. (ed.) *Narrative: From Malory to Motion Pictures* (London: Edward Arnold, 1985).

Hayley, Guy. 'Steeling the Show: Q & A with Peter J Hammond.' 2007 *Haileys Comment* Available: http://guyhaley.wordpress.com/interviews-2/pj-hammond-2007/.

Heidegger, Martin. *The Concept of Time* (Oxford: Blackwell, 1992).

Helgeson, Matt. 'The Masters of Episodic Gaming Speak' *Gameinformer*. 2012. Available: http://www.gameinformer.com/b/features/archive/2012/10/01/interview-kevin-bruner-and-dan-connors-of-telltale-games.aspx.

Hewett, Richard. 'TV Prequels' *CST online* blog. 16 May 2013. Available: http://cst online.tv/tv-prequels.

Hills, Matt. 'Cult TV, Quality and the Role of the Episode/ Programme Guide.' In Michael Hammond and Lucy Mazdon (eds.) *The Contemporary Television Series* (Edinburgh: EUP, 2005) pp. 190–206.

———. 'Mainstream Cult'. In Abbott, Stacey (ed.), *The Cult TV Book* (London and New York: I.B.Tauris, 2010) pp. 67–73.

———. 'The Medium Is The Monster...Or The World: Discourses Of Uncanny "Old Media" And Immersive "New Media" in *Life on Mars*' in Stephen Lacey and Ruth McElroy (eds.) *Life on Mars From Manchester to New York* (Cardiff, University of Wales Press, 2012) pp. 105–115.

Hoffman, Eva. *Time.* (New York: Picador, 2009).

Hogan, Michael. 'An Adventure in Space and Time, BBC Two, review' *Telegraph.* [online]. 21 Nov. 2013. Available: http://www.telegraph.co.uk/culture/tvandradio/tv-and-radio-reviews/10465249/An-Adventure-in-Space-and-Time-BBC-Two-review.html.

Horowitz, Anthony. (2004) 'Interview with Anthony Horowitz', *Crime Traveller.* Revelation Films. Region 2.

———. 'Anthony Horowitz' *Anthony Horowitz.com.* 2007. Available: www.anthony horowitz.com/work/television.html.

Howard, Douglas. 'Good Eats: NBC's Hannibal as Food for Thought' *CST online* blog. 20 June 2013. Available: http://cstonline.tv/good-eats-hannibal-food-for-thought.

Hutcheon, Linda. 'Irony, Nostalgia and the Postmodern', *University of Toronto English Library,* Available: http://www.library.utoronto.ca/utel/criticism/hutchinp.html.

Inglis, F. (1992). *The Cruel Peace: Living Through the Cold War* (London: Aurum., 1992).

Jameson, Fredric. 'The Politics of Theory. Ideological Positions in the Postmodernism Debate' in *The Ideologies of Theory Essays. Volume 2* (London: Routledge, 1988).

———. *Postmodernism, or the Cultural Logic of Late Capitalism* (Durham, N.C: Duke University Press, 1991).

———. *Archaeologies of the Future: The Desire Called Utopia and Other Science Fictions* (London: Verso, 2005).

Jenkins, Henry. *Textual Poachers: Television Fans and Participatory Culture* (New York, NY: Routledge, 1992).

Jindra, Michael. '"It's About Faith in our Future": *Star Trek* Fandom as Cultural Religion.' In Bruce David Forbes and Jeffrey H. Mahan (eds.) *Religion and Popular Culture in America* (Berkeley, CA: University of California Press, 2000) pp. 165–179.

Johnson, Catherine. *Telefantasy* (London: BFI Publishing, 2005).

Johnson, Rian. 'Introduction' in Ann and Jeff VanderMeer (eds.) *The Time Traveller's Almanac* (London: Head of Zeus, 2013) pp. x–xii.

Johnson-Smith, Jan. *American Science Fiction TV – Star Trek, Stargate and Beyond.* (London: I.B.Tauris, 2005).

Jones, Nick. 'Video Review.' *Star Trek Monthly Magazine*, January, 2002a p. 56.

———. 'Retcon Tricks.' *Star Trek Monthly Magazine*, February, 2002b pp. 18–21.

Jowett, Lorna, and Stacey Abbott. *TV Horror: Investigating the Dark Side of the Small Screen* (London: I.B.Tauris, 2013).

Killick, Jane. 'Crime Solving: making the time . . .', *TV Zone* #90 (May 1997) pp. 16–19.

King, Stephen. 'Confessions of TV Slut.' *Entertainment Weekly*. 1 Feb. 2007. Available at: http://www.ew.com/ew/article/0,,1176379,00.html.

Klein, Kerwin Lee. *Frontiers of Historical Imagination: Narrating the European Conquest of Native America, 1890–1990* (Berkeley, CA: University of California Press, 1997).

Kompare, Derek. 'Publishing Flow: DVD Box Sets and the Reconception of Television' *Television & New Media* Vol 7 # 4 (November 2006) pp. 335–60.

Koontz, Dale. 'Twelve Steps Forward, One Step Back: Redemption Through Recovery in the Works of Joss Whedon.' 4th Biennial *Slayage* Conference on the Whedonverses. Flagler College. St. Augustine, FL. 3–6 June 2010. Keynote Address.

Kraft, Jason. 'Episodic Gaming in the Age of Digital Distribution'. *Gamasutra*. 2006. Available: http://www.gamasutra.com/view/feature/3462/blogs/rss/.

Kuhn, Annette. (ed.) *Alien Zone – Cultural Theory and Contemporary Science Fiction Cinema* (London: Verso, 1990).

Lacey, Stephen and McElroy Ruth (eds.) *Life on Mars: From Manchester to New York* (Cardiff: University of Wales Press, 2012).

Landon, Brooks, 'Bet On It: Cyber/video/punk/performance.' In Larry McCaffery (ed.) *Storming the Reality Studio* (Durham, NC: Duke University Press, 1991) pp. 239–244.

———. *The Aesthetics of Ambivalence: Rethinking Science Fiction Film in the Age of Electronic (Re)Production* (Westport: Greenwood Press, 1992).

Lem, Stanislaw, Thomas H. Hoisington, and Darko Suvin. 'The Time Travel Story and Related Matters of SF Structuring', *Science Fiction Studies* 1.3 (1974), pp. 143–154.

Leman, J. Wise Scientists and Female Androids'. In J. Corner (ed), *Popular Television in Britain* (London: BFI, 1991).

Levinson, Paul. 'The Chronology Protection Case' (*Analog Science Fiction*, September 1995), reprinted in Mike Ashley (ed.) *The Mammoth Book of Time Travel SF* (London: Robinson, 2013) pp. 258–81.

'Life on Mars, Series One, Episode Two: Review' *Den of Geek (30 April 2010)*. Available: http://www.denofgeek.com/tv/life-on-mars/9766/life-on-mars-series-1-episode-2-review#ixzz2gxcBu2J5.

Lloyd, Robert. 'Partners in Time Warp' *Los Angeles Times* (9 October 2008). Available: http://articles.latimes.com/2008/oct/09/entertainment/et-lifeonmars9.

May, Dominic. '*Crime Traveller* – Season 1' *TV Zone* #90 (May 1997) pp. 60–61.

———. '*Crime Traveller* – Season 1' *TV Zone* #91 (June 1997) pp. 60–61.

Madsen, Deborah L. *American Exceptionalism* (Edinburgh: Edinburgh University Press, 1998).

Maltby, Richard. *Hollywood Cinema* (Malden, MA/ Oxford: Blackwell, 2001).

Marshall, Brenda. *Teaching the Postmodern: Fiction and Theory* (London: Routledge, 1992).

Martin, Denise. 'Auds Discover "Eureka".' *Daily Variety* 292.12 (2006), p. 1.

McFarlane, Mhairi. 'Ashes to Ashes is Dispiriting' *Guardian* Online (15 February 2008). Available: http://www.theguardian.com/culture/tvandradioblog/2008/feb/15/ashestoashes.

McWerthor, Michael. 'Remedy on how Quantum Break's TV Episodes are affected by gameplay' *Polygon*. 2013. Available: http://www.polygon.com/2013/6/12/4420924/quantum-break-xbox-one-remedy-e3–2013.

Mendlesohn, Farah and Edward James. *A Short History of Fantasy* (London: Middlesex University Press, 2009).

Miller, Steve. 'It's a Crime', *TV Zone* #90 (May 1997) p. 52.

Mills, Bret. *Television Sitcom* (London: BFI, 2005).

Mittell, Jason. 'Narrative Complexity in Contemporary American Television', *The Velvet Light Trap* 58 (2006), pp. 29–40.

Murray, Janet H. *Hamlet on the Holodeck: The Future of Narrative in Cyberspace* (Cambridge, MA: MIT Press, 1997).

Naryan, Lancelot (2006). 'Take a Look at the Lawman: the Making of Life on Mars, Part Two', *Life on Mars*. Contender. Region 2.

Neely, Sarah. 'Cool Intentions: The Literary Classic, the Teenpic and the "Chick Flick".' In Deborah Cartmell, I.Q. Hunter, and Imelda Whelehan (eds.) *Retrovisions: Reinventing the Past in Film and Fiction* (London: Pluto Press, 2001) pp. 74–86.

Nelson, Bryan. 'Magnetic North shifting 40 miles a year, might signal pole reversal' (March 7th, 2011). Available: http://www.mnn.com/earth-matters/climate-weather/stories/magnetic-north-shifting-by-40-miles-a-year-might-signal-pole-r.

Nelson, Robin. '*Life on Mars*: Hybidity and Innovation in A British Television Context' in Stephen Lacey and Ruth McElroy (eds.) *Life on Mars From Manchester to New York* (Cardiff, University of Wales Press, 2012) pp. 19–30.

Newman, Michael Z. 'From Beats to Arcs: Toward a Poetics of Television Narrative', *The Velvet Light Trap* 58 (2006), pp. 16–28.

Niffenegger, Audrey. *The Time Traveler's Wife: a Novel* (Toronto: Vintage Canada, 2004).

Norton, Al. '411mania Interviews: James Marsters (Buffy the Vampire Slayer, Angel)'. 2012. Available http://www.411mania.com/movies/columns/228484/411mania-Interviews:-James-Marsters-(Buffy-the-Vampire-Slayer,-Angel).htm.

Nouveau, Trent. 'Microsoft Touts Next-Gen Xbox One as 360 Successor'. *TGD*. 2013. Available: http://www.tgdaily.com/games-and-entertainment-features/71798-microsoft-touts-next-gen-xbox-one-as-360-successor.

Okuda, Michael and Denise. *Star Trek Chronology: A History of the Future* (New York, NY: Pocket Books, 1993).

———, with Debbie Mirek. *The Star Trek Encyclopedia: A Reference Guide to the Future* (3rd edition) (New York, NY: Pocket Books, 1997).

Pearson, Roberta. 'Lost in Transition'. In Janet McCabe and Kim Akass (eds.) *Quality TV: Contemporary American Television and Beyond* (Londong and New York: I.B.Tauris, 2007) pp. 237–256.

Penley, C. 'Time Travel, The Primal Scene, and the Critical Dystopia (on The Terminator and La Jetee)'. In C. Penley (ed.), *The Future of an Illusion: Film, Feminism, and Psychoanalysis* (London: Routledge, 1989).

Pidduck, Julianne. *Contemporary Costume Film* (London: BFI Publishing, 2004).

Porter, Lynette. 'Quantum Leap' in David Lavery (ed.) *The Essential Cult TV Reader*, (Kentucky: University Press of Kentucky, 2010) pp. 201–207.

Porter, Michael J. *et al.* 'Re(de)fining Narrative Events: Examining Television Narrative Structure', *Journal of Popular Film & Television* 30.1 (2002), p. 23.

Powell, Helen. *Stop the Clocks: Time and Narrative in Cinema* (London: I.B.Tauris, 2012).

Pronzini, Bill. 'Introduction' in John Dickson Carr, *The Devil in Velvet* (1951; cited edn is New York: Carol and Graf, 2nd edn 1994) pp. 1–3.

Roberts, Adam. *Science Fiction*. 2nd ed. (Oxon & New York: Routledge, 2006).

Robins, T. 'Timeslip' *Starburst No 91: Time Travel Special, 8*(7) (March 1986) pp. 8–11.

Robinson Kevin Lee. 'Email interview with Peter J Hammond', October 2013.

Rubiés, Joan-Pau. 'The Logic of Time Travel' *Foundation*, No.69, Spring 1997 pp. 80–84.

Ryan, Maureen. '"Sleepy Hollow" News: Head Honcho On What's Next For Ichabod, Abbie And The Horseman.' *Huffington Post* 12 September 2013. Available: http://www.huffingtonpost.com/2013/12/09/sleepy-hollow-news_n_4415250.html.

Sacks, Oliver. *The Man Who Mistook His Wife For A Hat* (London: Picador, 1986/2007).

Seidman, Robert. '"Eureka" Renewed by Syfy for a 5th Season', *TVbytheNumbers*. Available: http://tvbythenumbers.zap2it.com/2010/08/17/eureka-renewed-by-syfy-for-a-5th-season/60187/.

Shaw, Tony. *British Cinema and the Cold War: The State, Propaganda and Consensus* (London: I.B.Tauris, 2001).

Sidle, Philippa. 'Critical Overview', *Crime Traveller* (2014). Available: www.crimetraveller.co.uk/criticaloverview.asp.

Sobchack, Vivian. *Screening Space: The American Science Fiction Film* (New Brunswick, NJ: Rutgers University Press, 1998).

Stack, Danny. 'Ashley Pharoah Q&A: BBC Writers Series [website] http://dannystack.blogspot.co.uk/2006/03/qa-ashley-pharoah.html, accessed 2 December 2013.

Stewart, B. 'Timeslip Memories Part Two'. Available: http://www.timeslip.org.uk/production/timeslipmemories2.php.

Stewart, Bruce and J. and R. Boswell. *Timeslip* (London, Pan Books Ltd., 1970).

Straczynski, J. Michael. 'The Profession of Science Fiction 48: Approaching Babylon', *Foundation* #64 (Summer 1995) pp. 5–19.

Suvin, D. *Metamorphoses of Science Fiction* (London: Yale University Press, 1979).

Telotte, J.P. 'Science Fiction in Double Focus: Forbidden Planet.' *Film Criticism*, XIII, No.3, Spring 1989, pp. 25–36.

———. *Science Fiction Film* (Cambridge: Cambridge University Press, 2001).

Teverson, Andrew. *Fairy Tale* (New York: Routledge, 2013).

Todorov, Tzvetan. *The Fantastic: A Structural Approach to a Literary Genre* (R. Howard, Trans.) (NY: Cornell University Press, 1975).

Tudor, Andrew. *Monsters and Mad Scientists* (Oxford: Basil Blackwell, 1989).

Tyrrell, William Blake. 'Star Trek as Myth and Television as Mythmaker.' *Journal of Popular Culture*, vol. 10, no. 4, (1997) pp. 711–719.

Unknown, 'Primeval: The Making of (Season One) / 1', Available: http:www.youtube.com/watch?v=lk9WxPKiBzQ.

VanderMeer, Ann and Jeff (eds.) *The Time Traveller's Almanac* (London: Head of Zeus, 2013).

———. 'Preface', Ann and Jeff VanderMeer (eds.) *The Time Traveller's Almanac* (London: Head of Zeus, 2013) pp. vii–xi.

Various (2007–8). Hunts Housewives. Digital Spy Entertainment Zone Forums [web forum], http://www.digitalspy.co.uk/forums/showthread.php?t=765591, accessed 10 June 2013.

Verevis, Constantine. *Film Remakes* (Edinburgh: Edinburgh University Press, 2006).

Warner, Marina. *From the Beast to the Blonde: On Fairy Tales and Their Tellers* (London: Vintage, 1995).

Weinstock, Jeffrey. *The Vampire Film: Undead Cinema* (New York: Wallflower, 2012).

Wheatley, Helen. *Gothic Television* (Manchester: Manchester University Press, 2006).

Whedon, Joss. *Whedonesque* post. 12 June 2006. Available at: http://whedonesque.com/comments/10584#129304.

White, Hayden. *Tropics of Discourse: Essays in Cultural Criticism* (Baltimore, MD: The Johns Hopkins University Press, 1978).

———. *Figural Realism: Studies in the Mimesis Effect* (Baltimore, MD: The Johns Hopkins University Press, 1999).

Wilcox, Rhonda. *Why Buffy Matters: The Art of Buffy the Vampire Slayer* (London: I.B.Tauris, 2005).

Williamson, Milly. *The Lure of the Vampire: Gender, Fiction and Fandom from Bram Stoker to Buffy* (London: Wallflower Press, 2005).

Wright, Peter. 'British Television Science Fiction' in David Seed (ed.) *A Companion to Science Fiction* (Oxford: Blackwell, 2005) pp. 289–305.

———. 'Film and Television: 1960–1980' in Mark Bould, Andrew Butler and Sherryl Vint. (eds.) *The Routledge Companion to Science Fiction* (Oxon and New York, Routledge, 2009) pp. 90–101.

Ziolkowski, Jan M. *Fairy Tales from Before Fairy Tales: The Medieval Latin Past of Wonderful Lies* (University of Michigan Press: Ann Arbor, 2007).

TV and Filmography

TV

24 (Fox, 2001–)
Ace of Wands (ITV, 1970–1972)
Agatha Christie: Poirot (ITV, 1989–2013)
Angel (WB 1999–2004)
An Adventure in Space and Time (BBC Four, 2013)
Ashes to Ashes (BBC One, 2008–2010)
Avengers, The (ABC, 1961–1969)
Babylon 5 (WB, 1993–1998)
Bates Motel (A&E, 2013–)
Battlestar Galactica (ABC, 1978–1979)
Battlestar Galactica (SciFi, 2004–2009)
Being Human (BBC Three, 2008–2013)
Benefits Britain 1949 (Channel 4, 2013)
Bill, The (ITV, 1984–2010)
Bionic Woman, The (NBC, 2007)
Black Easter (BBC, 1995)
Blakes 7 (BBC, 1978–1981)
Blue Peter (BBC One, 1958–2002/CBBC, 2002–)
Boon (ITV, 1986–1995).
Breaking Bad (AMC, 2008–2013)
Buffy the Vampire Slayer (WB, 1997–2001/UPN, 2001–2003)
Bugs (BBC, 1995–1999)
Camberwick Green (BBC, 1966)
Carrie Diaries, The (CW, 2013–)
Champions, The (ITC, 1968–1969)
Chimera (ITV, 1991)
Coronation Street (ITV, 1960–)

Crime Traveller (BBC, 1997)

Dad's Army (BBC, 1968–1977)

Dallas (CBS, 1978–1991/TNT, 2012–)

Dark Shadows (ABC, 1966–1971)

Dempsey and Makepeace (LWT, 1985–1986)

Dexter (Showtime, 2006–2013)

Dixon of Dock Green (BBC, 1955–1976)

Doctor Who (BBC, 1963–1989/2005–)

Doomwatch (BBC, 1970–1972)

Downton Abbey (ITV, 2010–)

Dracula (NBC, 2013–)

EastEnders (BBC, 1985–)

Eldorado (BBC, 1992–1993)

Eleventh Hour (ITV, 2006)

Eureka (Syfy, 2006–2012)

Flash Gordon (Sci Fi Channel, 2007–2008)

Fringe (Fox, 2008–2013)

Goodnight Sweetheart (BBC, 1993–1999)

Grimm (NBC, 2011–)

Hannibal (NBC, 2013–)

Happy Days (ABC, 1974–1984)

Heroes (NBC, 2006–2010)

Highway to Heaven (NBC, 1984–1989)

Home and Away (Seven Network, 1988–)

How (STV, 1966–1981)

Invisible Man, The (NBC, 1975–1976)

Jonathan Creek (BBC, 1997–)

Journeyman (NBC, 2007)

Life on Mars (BBC One, 2006–2007)

Life on Mars (ABC, 2008–2009)

Look and Learn (BBC, 1962–1982)

Lost (ABC, 2004–2010)

Magpie (ITV, 1968–1980)

Midsomer Murders (ITV, 1997–)

Mission: Impossible (CBS, 1966–1973)

Moonbase 3 (BBC, 1973)

Neighbours (Seven Network, 1985/Network Ten, 1986–2010/Eleven, 2011–)

Once Upon a Time (ABC, 2011–)

Only Fools and Horses (BBC, 1981–2003)

Our Friends in the North (BBC Two, 1996)

Primeval (ITV, 2007–2011)

Primeval: New World (Space, 2012)

Prisoner, The (ITV, 1967–1968)

Prisoner, The (AMC/ITV, 2009)

Quantum Leap (NBC, 1989–1993)

Quatermass II (BBC, 1955)

Quatermass and the Pit (BBC, 1958)

Quatermass Experiment, The (BBC, 1953)

Randall and Hopkirk, Deceased (ITV, 1969–1970)

Randall & Hopkirk, Deceased (BBC One, 2000–2001)

Red Dwarf (BBC Two, 1988–1999)

Saint, The (ITV, 1962–1969)

Sapphire & Steel (ITV, 1979–1982)

Sex and the City (HBO, 1998–2004)

Shield, The (FX, 2002–2008)

Sliders (Fox, 1995–2000)

Smallville (WB 2001–2006/CW 2006–2011)

Sopranos, The (HBO, 1999–2007)

Spooks (BBC, 2002–2011)

Sleepy Hollow (Fox, 2013–)

Star Cops (BBC, 1987)

Stargate SG-1 (Showtime 1997–2001/Sfyfy 2002–2007)

Star Trek: Deep Space Nine (Syndicated, 1993–1999)

Star Trek: Enterprise (UPN, 2001–2005)

Star Trek: The Next Generation (Syndicated, 1987–1994)

Star Trek: The Original Series (NBC, 1966–1969)

Star Trek: Voyager (UPN, 1995–2001)

Stark (BBC, ABC, 1993)

Strictly Come Dancing (BBC One, 2004–)

Supernatural (WB 2005–2006/CW, 2006–)

Survivors (BBC, 1975–1977)

Terminator: The Sarah Connor Chronicles (Fox, 2008–2009)

That'll Teach 'em (Channel 4, 2003–2006)

Timeslip (ITV, 1970–1971)

Torchwood (BBC Three 2006–07/BBC Two, 2007–2008)

Torchwood: Children of Earth (BBC One, 2009)

True Blood (HBO, 2008–)

True Detective (HBO, 2014–)

Twilight Zone, The (CBS, 1959–1964, 1985–1989/UPN, 2002–2003)

Vampire Diaries, The (CW, 2009–)

Vanishing Man, The (ITV, 1997–1998)

Walking Dead, The (AMC, 2010–)

Walking with Dinosaurs (BBC, 1999)

Wartime Kitchen and Garden (BBC Two, 2003–)

Wire, The (HBO, 2002–2008)

X-Files, The (Fox, 1993–2002)

Yellowbacks (BBC, 1990)

Z-Cars (BBC, 1962–1978)

Films Cited

21 Grams (Alejandro González Iñárritu, USA, 2003)

Back to the Future (Robert Zemeckis, USA, 1985)

Bad Timing (Nicolas Roeg, UK, 1980)

Bram Stoker's Dracula (Francis Ford Coppola, USA, 1992)

Buffy the Vampire Slayer (Joss Whedon, Twentieth Century Fox, 1997)

Doctor Who (Geoffrey Sax, USA/UK, 1996)

Groundhog Day (Harold Ramis, USA, 1992)

It's a Wonderful Life (Frank Capra, USA, 1947)

Jurassic Park (Steven Spielberg, USA, 1993)

Manhunter (Michael Mann, USA, 1986)

Psycho (Alfred Hitchcock, USA, 1960)

Red Dragon (Brett Ratner, USA, 2002)

Rumble Fish (Francis Ford Coppola, USA, 1983)

Silence of the Lambs (Jonathan Demme, USA, 1991)

Star Trek: First Contact (Jonathan Frakes, USA, 1996)

Star Trek: Into Darkness (J.J. Abrams, USA, 2013)

Time Traveller's Wife, The (Robert Schwentke, USA, 2009)

This Island Earth (Joseph M Newman, USA, 1955)

Index

INVESTIGATING
CULT TV

Series Editor: Stacey Abbott

The **Investigating Cult TV** series is a fresh forum for discussion and debate about the changing nature of cult television. It sets out to reconsider cult television and its intricate networks of fandom by inviting authors to rethink how cult TV is conceived, produced, programmed and consumed. It will also challenge traditional distinctions between cult and quality television.

Offering an accessible path through the intricacies and pleasures of cult TV, the books in this series will interest scholars, students and fans alike. They will include close studies of individual contemporary television shows. They will also reconsider genres at the heart of cult programming, such as science fiction, horror and fantasy, as well as genres like teen TV, animation and reality TV when these have strong claims to cult status. Books will also examine themes or trends that are key to the past, present and future of cult television.

Published and forthcoming titles:

Battlestar Galactica: Investigating Flesh, Spirit and Steel edited by Roz Kaveney and Jennifer Stoy
Being Bionic: The World of TV Cyborgs, by Bronwen Calvert
The Cult TV Book edited by Stacey Abbott
Dancing with the Doctor: Dimensions of Gender in the New Doctor Who Universe by Lorna Jowett
Dexter: Investigating Cutting Edge Television edited by Douglas L. Howard
I'm Buffy and You're History: Buffy the Vampire Slayer and Contemporary Feminism by Patricia J. Pender
Investigating Alias: Secrets and Spies edited by Stacey Abbott and Simon Brown
Investigating Charmed: The Magic Power of TV edited by Karin Beeler and Stan Beeler
Investigating Farscape: Uncharted Territories of Sex and Science Fiction by Jes Battis
Investigating Firefly and Serenity: Science Fiction on the Frontier edited by Rhonda V. Wilcox and Tanya R. Cochran
Love and Monsters: The Doctor Who Experience, 1979 to the Present by Miles Booy
Sounds of Fear and Wonder: Music in Cult TV by Janet K. Halfyard
Torchwood Declassified: Investigating Mainstream Cult Television edited by Rebecca Williams
True Blood: Investigating Vampires and Southern Gothic by Brigid Cherry
TV Horror: Investigating the Dark Side of the Small Screen edited by Lorna Jowett and Stacey Abbott

Ideas and submissions for **Investigating Cult TV** to
s.abbott@roehampton.ac.uk
pbrewster@ibtauris.com

CPSIA information can be obtained
at www.ICGtesting.com
Printed in the USA
LVHW011801071222
734768LV00004B/217